Speaking from the Heart: Gender and the Social Meaning of Emotion

Who gets called "emotional?" And what does it mean when that happens? What tells us that a person is "speaking from the heart?" The prevailing stereotype is that *she* is emotional, while *he* is not. In *Speaking from the Heart* Stephanie Shields draws on examples from everyday life, contemporary culture, and the latest research, to reveal how culturally shared beliefs about emotion shape our identities as women and men. She shows how the discourse of emotion is fundamentally concerned with judgments about authenticity and legitimacy of experience, themes deeply implicated in creating and maintaining gender boundaries. This fascinating exploration of gender and emotion in a clear and engaging style takes up topics as diverse as nineteenth-century ideals of womanhood, weeping politicians, children's play, and the Superbowl. It is a must-read for anyone interested in the way emotion affects our everyday lives.

Stephanie A. Shields is Professor of Psychology and Women's Studies at the Pennsylvania State University.

Second Series

Series editors

Keith Oatley
University of Toronto

Antony Manstead
University of Cambridge

This series is jointly published by the Cambridge University Press and the Editions de la Maison des Sciences de l'Homme, as part of the joint publishing agreement established in 1977 between the Fondation de la Maison des Sciences de l'Homme and the Syndics of the Cambridge University Press.

Cette publication est publiée co-édition par Cambridge University Press et les Editions de la Maison des Sciences de l'Homme. Elle s'intègre dans le programme de co-édition établi en 1977 par la Fondation de la Maison des Sciences de l'Homme et les Syndics de Cambridge University Press.

Titles published in the second series

The Psychology of Facial Expression
0 521 49667 5 hardback and 0 521 58796 4 paperback
Edited by James A. Russell and José Miguel Fernández-Dols

Emotions, the Social Bond, and Human Reality: Part/Whole Analysis
0 521 58491 4 hardback and 0 521 58454 7 paperback
Thomas J. Scheff

Intersubjective Communication and Emotion in Early Ontogeny
0 521 62257 3 hardback and 2 7351 07728 hardback (France only)
Edited by Stein Bråten

Emotion Across Languages and Cultures: Diversity and Universals
0 521 59042 6 hardback and 0 521 59971 7 paperback
Anna Wierzbicka

Communicating Emotion: Social, Moral and Cultural Processes
0 521 55315 6 hardback and 0 521 55741 0 paperback
Sally Planalp

The Social Context of Nonverbal Behavior
0 521 58371 3 hardback and 0 521 58666 6 paperback
Edited by Pierre Philippot, Robert S. Feldman, and Erik J. Coats

Feeling and Thinking: the Role of Affect in Social Cognition
0 521 64223 X hardback
Edited by Joseph P. Forgas

Gender and Emotion: Social Psychological Perspectives
0 521 63015 0 hardback and 0 521 63986 7 paperback
Edited by Agneta H. Fischer

Causes and Consequences of Feelings
0 521 63325 7 hardback and 0 521 63363 X paperback
Leonard Berkowitz

Emotions and Beliefs: How Feelings Influence Thoughts
0 521 77138 2 hardback and 0 521 78734 3 paperback
Edited by Nico H. Frijda, Antony S. R. Manstead, and Sacha Bem

Identity and Emotion: Development Through Self-organization
0 521 66185 4 hardback
Edited by Harke A. Bosma and E. Saskia Kunnen

Speaking from the Heart: Gender and the Social Meaning of Emotion

Stephanie A. Shields

CAMBRIDGE
UNIVERSITY PRESS

#48100250

PUBLISHED BY THE PRESS SYNDICATE OF THE UNIVERSITY OF CAMBRIDGE
The Pitt Building, Trumpington Street, Cambridge, United Kingdom

CAMBRIDGE UNIVERSITY PRESS
The Edinburgh Building, Cambridge CB2 2RU, UK
40 West 20th Street, New York, NY 10011-4211, USA
477 Williamstown Road, Port Melbourne, VIC 3207, Australia
Ruiz de Alarcón 13, 28014 Madrid, Spain
Dock House, The Waterfront, Cape Town 8001, South Africa

http://www.cambridge.org

First published 2002

Printed in the United Kingdom at the University Press, Cambridge

Typeface Palatino 10/12 pt.   *System* LATEX 2$_\varepsilon$ [TB]

A catalogue record for this book is available from the British Library

ISBN 0 521 80297 0 hardback

For Stephanie J. Pavouček Shields and
John F. "Jack" Shields

Contents

Preface   *page* xi

1 That "vivid, unforgettable condition"   1

2 When does gender matter?   21

3 Doing emotion/doing gender: practicing in order
   to "get it right"   43

4 Sentiment, sympathy, and passion in the late
   nineteenth century   69

5 The education of the emotions   89

6 Ideal emotion and the fallacy of the inexpressive male   117

7 Emotional = female; angry = male?   139

8 Speaking from the heart   169

   References   188
   Index   208

Preface

This project aptly enough grew out of emotion. I devised the plan for this book out of frustration that questions relevant to gender and emotion, questions that seemed urgent to students and friends in real life, and that were becoming increasingly central to my own reading of the field, figured as insignificant in mainstream emotions research. Emotions researchers, especially psychologists, at that time paid little attention to gender. When they did consider gender, it was dealt with by enumerating gender similarities and differences, which yielded lots of inconsistent descriptions and not much in the way of explanation. I had no idea where the plan for this project would lead me, but I knew that it needed to be done. Since then, not only has emotions research continued to flourish, but an increasing number of feminist scholars have taken on the question of emotion. The study of gender, too, has continued to grow as an increasingly sophisticated field broadly spanning established social science and humanities disciplines and the interdisciplines of women's studies and gender studies. Nevertheless, these two areas of research (gender and the psychology of emotion) still have had little mutual influence despite the fact that both concern salient social categories interwoven in art and science throughout Western history.

I am especially indebted to the many students in my undergraduate courses on the psychology of emotion and the psychology of gender, both at the University of California, Davis, and at the Pennsylvania State University. Their concerns and questions were the original inspiration for connecting two historically separate fields of research. As the project developed they have continually reminded me about what the really important questions are.

I have enjoyed and learned from wonderful collaborations with graduate students – now colleagues – including especially Angela Simon, Jill Crowley, Karol Maybury, Michael Robinson, Claudia Geer, Mary Mallory, Pamela Steinke, Wendy Smith, and Sonia Worcel. They have each placed their own individual stamp on my thinking, and I hope I have done justice to their influence. My Davis work-in-progress group spent seven important years together. Their intellectual critique and emotional support persuaded me to try to write across disciplines and for an audience beyond academic psychology. I am deeply grateful to these wonderful women: Kari Lokke, Francesca Miller, Anna Kuhn, Carole Joffe, Cynthia Brantley, Alison Berry, Vicki Smith, and Lynn Roller. Of my UC Davis colleagues, I especially thank Karen (Paige) Ericksen with whom I shared writing get-aways and commiserated on the flea bites of life. She gave me friendship and support, and also the courage to pursue cross-disciplinary work and interdisciplinary thinking. Others who have encouraged, inspired, and challenged me and have had more positive influence on me and on this book than they could possibly know include Tom Natsoulas, Kay Deaux, Marianne LaFrance, Agneta Fischer, Rhoda Unger, Jeanne Marecek, Carolyn Saarni, Ben Benjamin, and Tony Manstead. Conversations at Nag's Heart Conferences, the brainchild of Faye Crosby, gave me the space to explore newly-formulated ideas in a supportive and open environment with the help of other feminist psychologists. The Penn State Professional Women's Network of New York has helped me think about how best to ground theory in "real world" emotion, and given me opportunities to practice bringing my academic work on gender and emotion to a wider audience. I am also indebted to my colleagues in the International Society for Research on Emotions for providing an intellectual community that challenges me and friendship that sustains me. Thank you to Joe Campos and Paul Ekman who supported my participation as a charter member of ISRE.

I am indebted to Cambridge editor Sarah Caro for her sage advice on making my writing more effective. It has transformed my relationship to writing. Cathy Guttentag was a terrific graduate assistant and was especially helpful in collecting and interpreting material on children's pretend play. Kris Eyssell kept the lab going while my mind was preoccupied with finishing the manuscript. Many talented undergraduate research assistants have contributed to moving this project forward, and Laura Tach, Jennifer Braun, and Jennifer Kern were especially helpful with innumerable last details.

My work on gender and emotion first began during a year-long NSF Visiting Professorship for Women in Science and Engineering at the University of California, San Francisco. The Rockefeller Foundation funded initial work on the book. That support made it possible for me to think outside the box by giving me that most precious gift of time to ponder contradictions and inconsistencies in emotion bedrock beliefs. Without that grant, I doubt that I would have seen the potential to push past the convention of "she's emotional, he's not" to construct a framework for explaining how beliefs about emotion define and maintain gender boundaries and are implicated in the practice of gender. I was also fortunate to be awarded a fellowship at the University of California, Davis, Humanities Institute and sabbatical support from the University of California at a critical early stage of this project.

I am deeply grateful to the many friends who have kept me healthy and happy and focused on the goal, especially during long and frustrating periods when work on the book was interrupted. Phyllis Berman and Francine Genta have stuck with me through thick and thin over many years. Deborah and Steve Weiner and Eleanor Hamilton gave me encouragement and advice in the early days of the project, and Doris Rogalla and Judy Kroll helped me stay on course when it seemed I would never finish. Mary Shields gave me sisterly advice and encouragement and the benefit of her expertise in publishing. Stephanie Pavouček Shields watched for everyday life examples that could make the story come alive and pondered book titles with me. And I am grateful to Lew Jillings, who took on many assignments to help me meet deadlines, and who, on the side, learned to cook a mean meatloaf. His heart is always in the right place.

Now, some years, 3000 miles, and a number of major life events later, I have at last finished this book. I am gratified that I have taken the project so much farther than I believed possible when I started, but feel lingering frustration that I still tell only the beginning of the story. Yet I am optimistic that this book may encourage others to explore the rich territory of gender and emotion that people find so central to their lives.

CHAPTER 1

That "vivid, unforgettable condition"

The US presidential campaign and election of 2000 will be remembered for years to come. An intensely close race was followed by an unprecedented cliffhanger election that drew to an uneasy conclusion thirty-nine long days after the votes were cast. In this election the ideological lines between the two parties and their candidates (Democrat Al Gore and Republican George W. Bush) were clearly drawn, and for party diehards there was no doubt whom to choose. Indeed, the two candidates were diametrically opposed on every key policy issue. But during the final months of the campaign, polls indicated that the election hinged on a massive swing vote of undecided voters and voters with only a weak preference for one candidate over the other. A rift as big as the Grand Canyon separated the candidates' politics, but public debate continued to drift toward concern about who was the nicer guy. By late in the campaign, discourse was all but disconnected from the issues that anchored each side, and dominated by preoccupation with style and personality. The press and both camps viewed the race as one that depended on which man could better persuade the public that he was a genuine, feeling human, apparently the criterion for fitness to be president. The question of emotional authenticity became critical to winning the election, and it seemed that in the end the voters favored the candidate they thought projected the more authentic and heartfelt persona.

Throughout the campaign and the tense post-election period, the potential for emotion to make or break one of the candidates was a persistent background theme. Vice-President Al Gore, long renowned for emotional stiffness, caused a stir by passionately kissing his wife Tipper before his acceptance speech at the Democratic convention. His impatient sighs during the first televised debate with Bush were blamed by many for a serious fall in the polls. Meanwhile, Texas Governor George W. Bush worked throughout the campaign, on the one hand, to overcome the tendency to smirk and, on the other, to use his relaxed style as the foundation for campaign momentum. The political rhetoric of each camp, too, conveyed an understanding that emotional qualities have to be communicated in just the right way. Bush's self-styled

1

"compassionate conservatism" conveyed an intellectual position made human by emotion. Gore's achievement of persuasively speaking from the heart in his concession speech was widely praised for striking precisely the right balance between dissatisfaction with the injustice of the outcome, and principled support for the victor. *Emotion* was at issue, whether expressed through the candidates' tone of voice, language of feeling, facial expression, or an apparently ineffable emotional "style."[1]

What do we mean by *emotion*? We use "emotional" to refer to what a person is doing in a particular situation – "Stop being so emotional!" – and we also use it to describe an enduring feature of personality – "She's the emotional type." What is it that says *emotion* to us? Something about the situation? Something about the person? At least some of the time the meaning of emotional even depends on who is doing the labeling. We learn early in life that most of the time the label "emotional" is one to be shunned. But at the same time we learn there is a positive side to the image of emotionality, too: A person who "speaks from the heart" is far more credible than someone who merely speaks. When, then, is emotion a valuable quality and when is it a defect?

A clue can be found in the ways in which emotion is gendered. Returning to the 2000 campaign, we can find many instances in which the common sense rules we believe to be true about emotion seemed to be turned on their head. For example, late in the campaign both candidates eagerly accepted invitations to appear on Oprah Winfrey's popular afternoon TV talk show. Appearing a week apart, they each took care to emphasize their concern and emotional authenticity.[2] When Oprah quizzed Gore about his public image as wooden, Gore turned the question into an opportunity to affirm his depth: "They're going to say something, so compared to the alternatives, that's OK . . . I'm a little bit more of a private person than a lot of people in the profession." Bush showed his own emotional *bona fides* by tearing up as he talked about his wife Laura's difficult pregnancy with their now teen-aged twins. Why did Gore go out of his way to portray himself as emotional? Why did Bush allow himself tears – the quintessential sign of feminine emotionality?

The election controversy, however, pales next to the profound and permanent effects of the terror attacks of September 11, 2001. The attacks created an atmosphere in which public expression of intense emotion was an important part of coming to terms with the horror of the events. For men and women alike, raw emotions of anger, grief, determination, and even hope dominated the difficult and confusing aftermath. In the months that have followed, publicly-shared emotion gives us a place in which to work toward collective understanding of how deeply our world has changed. In this changed world, the power of emotion to be constructive or destructive is brought home again and again.

In life-changing and in mundane ways emotion is a fundamental *human* quality. Only in exceptional times does emotion escape a gendered cast.

Everyone knows the prevailing emotion stereotype: She is emotional, he is not. Preschoolers identify sadness and fear with females, and adults of both sexes rate females as the "more emotional" sex. In early work my students and I asked undergraduates to describe "the most emotional person you know," and over 80 per cent of them named a woman first. The stereotype is so powerful that it serves as an overarching organizing principle for other related beliefs. In everyday conversation "stereotype" has a pejorative connotation, but stereotyping is a kind of cognitive short-cut through which a set of features are held to be common to a group. Stereotypes offer a way to think about a group without thinking through the nuance required when one considers the individual members of the group. The problem with stereotyping comes from how inflexibly it is applied, not necessarily from the stereotype's content.[3]

We might be tempted to think of questions of gender as a modern problem, but the linkages between gender and emotion show up long before contemporary American society. No less a philosopher than Plato centuries ago draws a connection between emotion and gender. The *Phaedo* gives a moving account of a collection of friends gathered together to watch Socrates, their intellectual leader, conform to the state's decree and commit suicide by drinking hemlock. Anticipating the heavenly happiness that awaits all just persons (by definition male) in the afterlife, Socrates dispassionately accepts his own imminent death. When the state's messenger arrives with the poison, Socrates takes it from him "quite cheerfully ... without a tremor, without any change of colour or expression." The narrator continues:

> Up till this time most of us had been fairly successful in keeping back our tears; but when we saw that he was drinking, that he had actually drunk it, we could do so no longer; in spite of myself the tears came pouring out, so that I covered my face and wept broken-heartedly – not for him, but for my own calamity in losing such a friend. Crito had given up even before me, and had gone out when he could not restrain his tears. But Apollodorus, who had never stopped crying even before, now broke out into such a storm of passionate weeping that he made everyone in the room break down, except Socrates himself, who said: "Really, my friends, what a way to behave! Why, that was my main reason for sending away the women, to prevent this sort of disturbance; because I am told that one should make one's end in a tranquil frame of mind. Calm yourselves and try to be brave." This made us feel ashamed, and we controlled our tears.[4]

In this brief account we recognize the sense of emotional uncontrollability, the contagion of tears, the rapid transition that can occur between emotions – all qualities familiar to our everyday experience of emotion. Just as clearly, this account also brings into focus the complex intersection of gender and emotion. Socrates' reaction crystallizes the fundamental issues of the gender-emotion relationship: Did Socrates admonish his companions because they were behaving *emotionally*, because they were behaving *like women*, or because they were behaving *emotionally like women*?

What is an emotion?

Before beginning to address questions about gender and emotion, another question takes priority: What is emotion? We are all experts on emotion – we used them to influence others before we could talk, we have been thinking about what they are and what they mean ever since we could reason, and we have all at one time or another wished fervently that we could better understand and manage them. For many years I have taught a university course on the psychology of human emotion and each term I begin by asking class members "What is emotion?" and "How do you know when you've got one?"[5] These deceptively simple questions help to reveal much of the taken for granted assumptions and difficult to articulate practical knowledge shared in contemporary American society. At first students confidently define emotion as a kind of "feeling." When pressed to define feeling, they describe emotion as "mental feelings" and "bodily feelings," as feelings different from feelings of hunger and thirst, as feelings different from senses like touch or hearing, and as feelings different from more enduring attributes of personality or mood. When further pressed, they identify "emotion" as something that is incited by some thing (an idea, an event, an action), observe that emotion reflects a situation that is perceived as having personal significance to the individual, and note that objective reading of the situation by others may not match the subjective reading we, as emotional selves, may give it. They invariably observe that, even with a lot of work, emotion, once it gets going, seems very hard to control. No matter how fully elaborated their definition, each group of students tends to gravitate toward *experience* as the first and central defining feature of emotion. Their focus on emotion-as-feeling reflects the way in which emotion is most often talked about in everyday conversation, that is, in terms of its "felt" quality, the aspect of emotion that is self-consciously experienced. Indeed, psychologist Elizabeth Duffy sixty years ago maintained that the scientific study of emotion was handicapped by the exclusive identification of emotion in everyday life with its "felt" quality, the sense that emotion is a "vivid, unforgettable condition which is different from the ordinary condition" in which one finds oneself.[6]

How do academic experts answer the question?

Emotion is studied from a wide range of disciplinary perspectives, in areas as diverse as psychology, sociology, history, neuroscience, anthropology, linguistics, philosophy, and psychiatry. It is difficult to generalize across such divergent perspectives. Still, it is fair to say that contemporary work tends to focus on the processes that generate emotions, the signs and symptoms of emotion, the intrapersonal and social regulation of emotion, and the consequences of emotion for the individual and for interpersonal relationships.[7]

One of the most striking features of current emotions research is the large degree of overlap between everyday understanding of emotion and the definitions offered by experts in its study. Formal theories tend to diverge most from the everyday conceptualization of emotion in going beyond simply equating all emotion with experience. Classic definitions offered by researchers typically include some notion that emotion is a response to some precipitating event, and often that emotion involves some sort of readiness to act or respond. They frequently, but not always, include some reference to the bodily feelings associated with emotion, such as awareness of heart beat or trembling. Similarly, many note the special cognitive qualities that comprise the experience, such as absorption in what the emotion is about, that is, the object of the emotion. Emotion is also viewed as having an hedonic quality, that is, a quality that elicits approach or withdrawal, pleasure or pain, a sense of well-being or vulnerability. Fifty years ago, in the heyday of behaviorism, emotion was generally construed as a disruptive level of physiological or cognitive arousal that interferes with organized, goal-directed behavior. Today emotions researchers, regardless of their field of study, generally agree that emotion is essentially a short-term adaptive response which, because it is not the result of deliberation and reflection, may not have the most advantageous long-term consequences. In other words, emotion seems to operate more as a tactical response to an immediate situation, rather than as a strategic move toward a long-term goal. Nearly all researchers acknowledge that there is a set of behaviors that are recognizable as a class called "emotion" common to all mammalian species. Beyond these areas of common agreement, however, researchers differ in their positions regarding the operation of emotion, emotion's function, and the extent to which expression and "felt" experience are inevitable components of the occurrence of emotion.

The variety of approaches to emotion is reflected in the difficulty that we have in devising a simple definition of emotion that covers the complexity of the phenomenon. In their textbook on human emotions Keith Oatley and Jenny Jenkins (1996, p. 96) offer a definition that encompasses major themes in contemporary study of emotion. They note that even though emotion is a familiar and everyday concept, it is no simple matter to distill a definition that is sufficiently precise or that would be universally accepted. Oatley and Jenkins offer a three-part definition of emotion:

1. An emotion is usually caused by a person consciously or unconsciously evaluating an event as relevant to a concern (a goal) that is important; the emotion is felt as positive when a concern is advanced and negative when a concern is impeded.
2. The core of an emotion is readiness to act and the prompting of plans, an emotion gives priority for one or a few kinds of action to which it gives a sense of urgency – so it can interrupt, or compete with alternative mental processes or actions. Different types of readiness create different outline relationships with others.
3. An emotion is usually experienced as a distinctive type of mental state, sometimes accompanied or followed by bodily changes, expressions, actions.

I would take this careful and comprehensive definition and sum it up this way: *Emotion is "taking it personally."* Whether the emotion is love for my newborn baby, irritation at myself for procrastinating, fear for my friend who has breast cancer, or pride in my country, each of these situations entails perception of someone or something as having urgent significance for my own well-being or interests. I will have more to say about this in later chapters, here I just want to emphasize the theme that something about the *self* is at stake in emotion.

The difficulty in arriving at a single, simple definition of emotion is reflected in the proliferation of competing theories. In fact, in the third edition of his comprehensive textbook on emotion in the late 1980s, Ken Strongman identified no fewer than twenty-six major psychological and philosophical theories of emotion! The field has continued to grow dramatically since then, and so has the number of competing theoretical accounts.

How to explain emotion

The most influential contemporary theories fall into one of two broad categories: fundamental emotions theories and cognitive-appraisal theories. Fundamental emotions theories assert the existence of a small set of innate basic emotions which may interact with cognitive processes, but which comprise a separate biological system. They tend to look for culturally-universal expressive features of emotion and use those features as the means to investigate what they consider basic emotion processes. Cognitive-appraisal theories think of emotion as a process of evaluation and so emphasize the role of cognitive processing in the generation of emotion. They do not make a sharp distinction between emotion and cognition. Information processing models represent a new generation of cognition-based theories and often borrow from the concepts and approaches of artificial intelligence to map out the dimensions or steps in processing that lead to one affective state or another. Social constructionist models share with cognitive-appraisal theory a focus on the meanings assigned to situations. Social constructionism emphasizes emotions, emotional experience, and display of feeling as cultural artifacts, rejecting the notion of biologically "basic" emotions. The constructionist (also referred to as *constructivist*) point of view has played a significant role in the anthropology and sociology of emotion. American academic psychology, with some important exceptions, has been far less welcoming to this approach.[8] In fact, psychologists' critiques of constructionism often reflect a fundamental misunderstanding of the position, confusing constructionism's emphasis on the process of meaning-making for an indiscriminate rejection of "biological" factors.[9] In this field dominated by theory, there are, of course, other perspectives, but they tend to be held by a minority of researchers. One, which is distantly related to cognitive-appraisal theories, derives from the philosophical standpoint of phenomenology. Phenomenological theories stress the embeddedness of the emotion in the relationship between the individual experiencer and the context in which emotion occurs. This approach has begun to have wider influence through the work of philosophers and European social psychologists.[10] Psychoanalytic theory and therapeutically-based psychologies have so far had more limited impact on current trends.[11]

Neurobiological research, meanwhile, is on the verge of transforming many of the long-held and cherished assumptions about emotion's "built-in" or "hard wired" features. Work on animal models has shown how biological features ranging from neural structures to hormonal state mutually affect and are affected by emotion-linked learning and experience. Research on humans, benefiting from technological advances in brain imaging and the burgeoning field of cognitive neuroscience, has revealed much about the interrelationship among brain structures involved in emotion and emotion-linked processes.[12]

Why I study emotion

As long as I can remember I have been curious about how people make sense of their own experience and try to understand others' experience. Early in my undergraduate days I realized that I was far less interested in the exotic cases described in my abnormal psychology textbook than in what preoccupies ordinary people in everyday life. Garden variety emotion – emotion as people talk about it, think about it, and try to manage it – amazed and continues to amaze me. As a psychology graduate student I wanted to understand how young children think about their own emotions and how they learn to make inferences about what other people are feeling. As my involvement in feminist psychology grew, I realized that many intangibles contribute to these judgments. When children, or grown-ups for that matter, believe a person to be "happy" or "emotional" or neither, they make this complex social assessment on the basis of how the person looks, what the person is doing, and the situation that the person is in. Their own subjective values, expectations, and stereotypes inevitably color what they see and how they think about it in both subtle and obvious ways. These features to me seem as central in importance to an account of human emotion as are the physiological, neural, and cognitive capacities that are built-in dimensions of our emotion equipment. As with any researcher, my own background colors my ideas about what are the best questions for researchers to ask and the best strategies to answer those questions. My training in social and developmental psychology and my years-long work in feminist psychology and women's studies have shaped this book and expanded its scope beyond conventional research psychology. For example, I have found it helpful to look to history, literature, and popular culture as I explore the intriguing connections between gender and emotion. On the other hand, my psychological framework emphasizes "the individual" and I struggle to press beyond the Western, individualized definition of personhood that constrains American psychology's thinking.

Where do I place myself on the continuum of emotion theory? My own position is that humans and other mammals share a built-in capacity for what in human societies is identified as emotion. The meanings assigned to "emotion" vary across cultures and historical periods. At different times and in different places people have thought about what emotion encompasses, who has a right to which emotions, the rules of how to show and feel emotion, understanding about the causes of emotion, how emotion is related to other concepts such as consciousness, mind, intentionality, and so on, in many different ways. I do believe that capacity for and the range of expressions that go with emotion have their roots in our evolutionary heritage. But I also believe that *everything* about emotion changes when the cognitive capacity for symbolic representation, especially language, is introduced. We have the capacity as humans to think about our own feelings and to be conscious of our own consciousness, and so we can conceptualize emotions and use them to create and maintain culture. This is what sets human emotion apart from that of other mammals. Having the capacity for mental representation and language enables us to use language to describe and label emotion, to represent emotion symbolically, to attach moral and aesthetic values to emotion, and to link emotion to other social categories such as gender. The built-in part of emotion does not require language or the capacity for self-conscious reflection for it to work. "Meta-emotion," that is, thinking about one's own and others' emotions, introduces a new and complex set of questions about emotion functioning that is unique to human experience.

Emotion and its social meaning

In conventional psychological research, researchers direct their efforts toward identifying the components, causes, and consequences of emotion in the hope of revealing emotion's true nature. They take as a starting point concepts of "emotion," "emotionality," "facial expression of emotion" without questioning whether these "foundational constructs" should, in fact, be accorded a special status. For example, for some time American psychologists have debated whether the domain of emotion is better represented in terms of discrete emotion types or in terms of its underlying structural dimensions.[13] Within this often lively and sometimes heated debate, however, questions of when, why, and how "emotion" is distinguished from "not emotion" seldom figure. Examining foundational constructs – the unexamined starting point, I believe, leads inevitably to placing emotion in a social context: How is the meaning of emotion negotiated? By whom? And under what circumstances?

Who says it's "emotion"?

What happens when we ask how foundational constructs are given shape and invested with substance by science, popular culture, and interpersonal relationships? The naturalizing of emotion has consequences for how gender and gender relations are construed in the course of daily life. Because concepts of emotion and emotionality are differentially applied to women and men, the gendered emotion scheme inevitably connects to systems of power. Feminist ethnographies reveal the intersection of emotion and gender as a critical locus for revealing how a culture incorporates emotion into its system of social organization. Catherine Lutz (1988), for example, shows that among the Ifaluk of the South Pacific emotion is understood in terms of social relationships, and particular emotions are expected to be connected to one's position to others in terms of age, social rank, and gender. Her analysis challenges the Western presumption that emotion is essentially private and internal and highlights the stereotypic equation drawn between emotion and femaleness which devalues both.[14]

When we problematize foundational constructs, that is, ask questions about assumptions rather than just take them as axiomatic, the focus of the inquiry shifts dramatically. In the case of emotion and gender, the question changes from "Who is more emotional, women or men?" to questions that ask "What does it mean to say someone is 'emotional'?" and "Who decides what is or is not 'emotional' behavior?" Agneta Fischer (1993, p. 303), for example, examined the empirical research on sex-related differences in emotion, and concluded that the stereotype of female emotionality "tells us more about Western sex stereotypes than about women's actual emotions." So I begin with the every-day, taken for granted. What "everyone knows" about emotion can obscure some of the most provocative and interesting questions we might ask. And it is revealing to look for anomalies that violate emotion rules. The behavior that doesn't quite fit often reveals the most about unquestioned assumptions. For example, everyone knows that "real" American men are not emotional, but what about the football field, the basketball court, and anywhere else where competitive sports are played? Emotion is absolutely critical to succeeding in sports, and concern for handling emotion the right way is every bit as important when dealing with defeat. In Chapter 6 I explore the truism of "masculine inexpressivity" to illustrate this point.

Bedrock beliefs

People acquire a rich store of beliefs as they learn to be effectively functioning members of culture. Beliefs about emotion encompass beliefs about what makes good or bad emotion, beliefs about emotion and the body, and beliefs about emotion's relationship to other behaviors such as sex and aggression, to name only a few. This network of beliefs is the basis for expectations we develop about when, where, and how emotion should occur and what the occurrence of emotion signifies. These *bedrock beliefs* are so embedded within the dominant culture that they seem unquestionably to embody the true nature of emotion.

Some of the bedrock beliefs about emotion are explicit and easily named and recognized. In Western cultures, the emotion stereotype that identifies emotion as feminine is an obvious example. Other beliefs, in contrast, are so deeply embedded in the dominant culture that they do not meet the threshold of recognition: one does not realize that one holds the beliefs, nor that one sometimes resists them. These implicit bedrock beliefs are only made apparent by scrutinizing patterns in how emotion is represented in language, social institutions, or social practice. Even when these beliefs are not shared by marginalized or minority cultures, bedrock beliefs of the dominant culture are the standards against which all persons are measured.

Many emotion beliefs have a gendered character in that they express beliefs about emotion that are treated as more typical, natural, or appropriate for one sex or the other. In this book I explore how emotion, especially the network of bedrock beliefs, defines gender and gender differences and how, in turn, beliefs about gender are recruited to further define emotion and value. In other words, I am especially concerned with the social meaning of emotion which is constituted of bedrock beliefs about emotion and its part in negotiating human relationships.[15]

The emotion master stereotype I described above actually rests upon a complex network of culturally-specific, historically shifting, sometimes inconsistent, and often tacitly held bedrock beliefs. They are culturally bound as well as historically bound. Most intriguing are paradoxical beliefs about emotion. They are paradoxical in the sense of expressing equally strong, inherently contradictory assertions about emotion. These paradoxes play out in everyday life in the mixed messages we receive about how best to handle our emotional lives. Consider these truisms: Too much emotion can be destructive; too little emotion can be damaging. Emotion must be controlled, but bottling up emotion just makes things worse. Emotion is irrational, but emotion makes life worth living. Inherently contradictory emotion beliefs often also define gender. To take just one especially powerful example: *emotion* is identified as feminine, but *anger*, a prototypical emotion, is identified as masculine. The account of Socrates' death above vividly illustrates the Western convention that there is inevitable tension between the "rational" aspect of mind or soul and its "passionate," irrational, emotional component. At the same time it is the very force of Socrates' and his companions' passion that signals the authenticity of their convictions.[16]

Where is gender?

Within psychology there has been considerable effort put into disentangling the psychological from the biological embodiment of male–female. Although the distinction is by no means unambiguous, the general practice has been to differentiate between the biologically defined categories of female and male (*sex*) and the psychological features associated with biological states which involve social categories rather than biological categories (*gender*). Thus, sex is used to refer to the physical fact of primary and secondary sex characteristics; gender is used to refer to a psychological and cultural construct, what could be thought of as a loose translation of sex into social terms. Gender is manifested in the public social world, as in culturally-defined standards of sex-appropriate behavior, and within the individual's consciousness, as in one's identification of himself or herself as male or female. *Core gender identity* references one's identification of oneself as a male or female person.[17]

My use of terms has changed over time and reflects the evolving vocabulary of the psychology of gender. Psychology's preoccupation with "sex-roles" in the early 1970s was replaced with an attempt to draw the line between "gender" and "sex" by the late 1970s, which then evolved into an intricate distinction between "sex-related differences" and "gender differences" in the 1980s. In recent years the discussion has moved beyond imagining gender as a fixed, internal, trait-like attribute, to consider gender as always in process. It is a move toward a performative notion of gender and acknowledgment that "sex" is a discursive as well as biological category.

The most influential current psychological gender theories in the US view gender as a multidimensional and multifactorial phenomenon, that is, as more than a single, fixed, unitary trait. Janet Spence (1999, pp. 277–278) points out that "Although male and female groups of a given age may differ significantly [on any given dimension], the specific constellations of gender-related behaviors, attributes, and beliefs that particular individuals display (and fail to display) are highly variable within each gender, have various etiologies, and are sustained by different sets of contemporary influence." Within this general approach there are two major theoretical streams. One construes gender effects as a dimension or result of sex-segregation of social role or sociostructural arrangements. A second takes a process, rather than structural approach, and focuses on gender as a context-sensitive social transaction.[18] A third perspective is more aligned with feminist standpoint theories and emphasizes the ostensibly unique features of female experience that are posited to have an inevitable influence on the person. This position, most often associated with Carol Gilligan (1982) and researchers at the Stone Center, has won a large popular following among educators and community workers concerned with girls' and women's exercise of public voice.[19]

Is there gender in emotion?

I want to turn briefly to the current status of gender in the study of emotion. The study of gender, particularly that undertaken within a feminist theoretical framework, and the psychology of emotion have had almost no influence on one another, despite the fact that both concern social categories that play a central role in social organization and have been interwoven in art and science throughout Western history. The psychology of emotion, which has enjoyed a vigorous revival over the same thirty years that the study of gender has flourished, has paid only passing attention to gender. When gender is figured into the study of emotion, it usually is regarded in terms of sex-related differences. Gender has rarely figured in theoretical developments. Given the power and prevalence of prevailing emotion stereotypes, for example, the territory navigated in this book is surprisingly neglected. There is very little overlap in the kinds of questions that have been asked in these two spheres of inquiry, particularly in psychology. The comprehensive *Handbook of Child Psychology* (1998), to take just one example, includes chapters on both emotional development and on gender development. The emotion chapter briefly considers sex-related differences in empathy; the gender chapter devotes three brief paragraphs of its seventy-plus pages to "emotionality."

Insofar as the psychology of emotion is concerned, gender is downplayed in each of the two major theoretical camps. Given European-American psychology's self-conscious effort to develop a universally-applicable science of emotions, it is not surprising that a multifaceted social variable like gender figures only peripherally in emotions research. Because it is not viewed as intrinsic to developing a full account of the psychology of emotion, study of gender's effects on emotion (much less the effect of emotion on gender) was, until recently, rarely inspired by theory. When gender is included as a variable in empirical research on ordinary emotion, whether that research is concerned with specific emotions such as anger, or global concepts such as emotionality, gender is almost invariably examined only in terms of sex differences. Furthermore, most research reflects an assumption that gender differences should be stable and reflect so-called essential qualities of each sex. The fact is, gender differences do not necessarily behave like stable, essential differences *ought* to behave.

Psychological theories of emotion have failed to incorporate gender into their explanatory structure in part because psychologists, unlike other social scientists, treat emotion's social dimensions as derivative rather than central to the task of emotion theory. Giving priority to the pursuit of "true" emotion and defining essential emotion in terms other than social meaning ensure that gender, race, class, and historical era are set aside as peripheral to the main objectives of theory. This state of things has not been helped by the tendency to view gender effects from the rather theoretically impoverished perspective of empirically identified sex-related differences (and similarities), a situation I will say more about in the next chapter. Psychologists who study emotion, rightly or wrongly, have tended to conclude that gender is not particularly important to explaining emotion.[20]

Is there emotion in feminist theory?

Feminist scholarship has produced the most interesting and innovative research on women and gender. This area continues to grow dramatically in scope and quantity, and includes extensive work on topics that implicate emotion, yet it rarely includes explicit discussion of emotion itself as an object of study.[21] Analyses of everything from eating disorders to motherhood and caregiving acknowledge the significant role played by emotion. Despite the breadth of topics, two features characterize feminist scholarship with reference to emotion. First, when emotion is mentioned, it is often viewed in terms of its problematic or clinical aspects. So, for example, the fact that women are four times more likely than men to be diagnosed as clinically depressed has garnered a good deal of attention and generated much debate and discussion. Second, and more important here, is that "emotion" itself is a taken-for-granted category in feminist scholarship and research. Feminist scholars are keenly aware of emotion's significance and that awareness informs feminist analyses of other social structures and processes. At the same time, however, the special status accorded *emotion* as conceptual scheme is left uninterrogated.

It is not surprising that the topic of emotion has been problematic for feminist scholars. Those who endeavor to reconcile the uneasy relationship between gender and emotion face a precarious situation. The distinctive differentiation made by emotion stereotypes between emotional female/unemotional male is such a prominent theme in Western culture, I believe especially in the US, that it reinforces the notion that the starting point for any gender-based analysis of emotion should be the presumption of gender differences in emotion. Challenging stereotypic visions of emotional women and unemotional men catches the challenger in a no-win situation. To deny differences begs the questions raised by the very fact of the power and prevalence of emotion stereotypes. To accept gender differences leaves two alternatives, either asserting defensively that "Female emotionality is healthy," or adopting a kind of revisionism, "It's really men who are hobbled by emotion because they don't know how to do it right." Neither of these positions explains the frequent devaluation of emotion, especially "female" emotion. The difficulty in developing a credible inversion of the prevailing emotion stereotype is illustrated in Miriam Johnson's pathbreaking *Strong Mothers, Weak Wives*. Laying the theoretical foundation for her argument, Johnson reviews Talcott Parson's distinction between instrumentality and expressivity. Johnson concludes that expressiveness is not "simply being emotional or emotionally labile" (Johnson, 1988, p. 54), but instead should be viewed as emotional skill.

In making this assertion she inadvertently reifies a revisionist gender stereotype:

> Women, in this culture at least, are provided with patterned ways of expressing and negotiating socioemotional subtleties in interaction, whereas men are enjoined to be inexpressive or nonexpressive. Because of this inexpressiveness, men (when the inexpressive mask breaks down) are more likely to express raw emotion, spontaneous unpatterned emotion, than women. Women may resonate with, respond to, cope with, and even define emotion for others, but this is hardly the same as being emotional. (p. 54)

Johnson's analysis accepts the notion of emotion's naturalness and stops short of inquiring how the concept of emotion is linked to that of emotionality and whether the standards for inferring and evaluating the presence of either are in themselves gendered. Johnson reverses the usual story – suggesting that women do emotion correctly, men do it incorrectly. By reifying emotionality she succeeds only in reaffirming the devalued position of emotion. In order to move beyond this "damned if you do, damned if you don't" feminist dilemma, requires acknowledging the significance of belief about emotion (as Johnson does), but then pressing further to question the naturalness of emotion or judgments about emotionality.

A successful feminist analysis must highlight the relations between apparently "natural" emotion and the elaborate beliefs that comprise emotion's social meaning. Important work in the 1980s, including books by sociologists Arlie Hochschild (1983) and Francesca Cancian (1987), and anthropologists Catherine Lutz (1988) and Lila Abu-Loghoud (1986) signalled the advent of an exciting new theoretically-grounded feminist consideration of emotion in which the culturally-shared beliefs about emotion are implicated in the production and reproduction of gender inequalities. Cancian (1987), for example, analyzed feminized definitions of romantic love in contemporary American society, and showed how the gendering of love reinforces conventional gender arrangements that make it women's responsibility to be the caretakers of close relationships.

What is the next step? How are we to understand how beliefs about emotion, including stereotypes, are connected to emotional feelings, language, and behavior in the formation of the gendered self? Assertions regarding the emotionality of females and the repressed emotionality/expressivity of males constitute an especially potent set of widely held, rarely questioned bedrock beliefs. The assessment and labeling of emotion is often an assessment of the value of emotion's experience and expression: Judgments about the presence and meaning of emotion in self and others are made neither casually nor lightly. In this way, emotion beliefs, especially the emotion master stereotype, are recruited in the service of defining, maintaining, and reproducing gender as difference. In other words, ideas about emotion establish gender boundaries: emotion beliefs are used in "telling" the boys the girls. What are the practical, personal and social implications of this proposal? As emotion beliefs create and maintain gender boundaries, they are in the deepest sense implicated in the creation of our identities as women and men. Through doing emotion the "right" way, one lays claim to authenticity as a person. But who defines the right way to do emotion?

Linking gender and emotion

But back to Socrates. Did he admonish his companions because they were behaving *emotionally*, because they were behaving *like women*, or because they were behaving *emotionally like women*? A question that will help us formulate the answer is the focus of the following chapter (Chapter 2). I ask "When does gender matter?" and use it as the framework for examining the current state of (mostly) psychological research on gender and emotion. For the most part, gender matters in very particular conditions. Gender effects are exaggerated, for example, when people are asked to make global, retrospective reports about emotion, but attenuated when people are asked to keep daily emotion diaries. Chapter 3, "Doing Emotion/Doing Gender," goes on to develop a fundamental reformulation of the gender-emotion relationship. In this chapter I propose that beliefs about emotion play an important role in defining and maintaining the beliefs we have about gender differences. Chapter 4, "Sentiment, Sympathy, and Passion in the Late Nineteenth Century," illustrates this point by analyzing notions of natural and ideal masculinity and femininity in the late nineteenth century. Through examination of popular and scientific beliefs about gender difference I explore the way difference was defined by the *kind* of emotion thought to characterize each sex.

Following chapters turn to the linkages between gender and emotion in contemporary life. Chapter 5, "The Education of the Emotions," addresses emotional development and considers how gendered styles of doing emotion are acquired. In this chapter I am concerned with how the experience and display of emotion come to conform to social expectations as well as, more broadly, what it means to experience emotion as one believes it ought to be experienced. Chapter 6, "Ideal Emotion and the Fallacy of the Inexpressive Male," begins by considering contemporary notions of "masculine inexpressivity" and how inexpressivity came to be viewed simultaneously as a handicap and as an essential component of American masculinity. Since the mid-1980s the convention of masculine inexpressivity is often joined by its converse, a celebration of masculine emotion. If inexpressivity is not an ideal, then what is? I also consider the "New Fatherhood" as one important realm where we can see renegotiation of emotion's gender boundaries. This examination of emotion reminds us that one emotion stands out as an anomaly in the emotion repertoire. Chapter 7, "Emotional = Female; Angry = Male?" examines the equation of anger with the male/masculine. Why is it that anger, which is so often portrayed as childish and the essence of the passionate character of emotion, is stereotypically viewed as a hallmark of masculinity? Is anger, in fact, viewed as emotionality when displayed or experienced by adult males? Emotions can be described in terms of what they are about. If anger (and its relatives) is concerned with violations of what one perceives to be one's rights, what makes emotion of violated entitlement special in its stereotypic association with maleness?

In the final chapter, "Speaking from the Heart," I consolidate some of the key themes and apply them to the concerns of everyday life. I especially consider who *owns* the position to speak with emotional authority and the ways in which "speaking from the heart" has been appropriated as an essentially masculine prerogative. I show how the discourse of emotion is fundamentally concerned with judgments of correct/incorrect, healthy/unhealthy, socially appropriate/inappropriate, and, further, how this discourse maintains (and can subvert) gender boundaries. The gendered definition of appropriate emotion colors our views of relationships, evaluations of ourselves, expectations for our children, and our beliefs about the larger society.

Notes

1 It is not clear how much the "undecided" voters drove the press and political rhetoric toward concern with emotional authenticity and how much an emotion and character-focused campaign were created by political strategists and press coverage. David Goldstein, "Who's the Man Behind Clinton?" Knight Ridder Newspapers, June 14, 2000. Ron Littlepage, "Gore's Campaign Pulled Off a Huge Bounce with 'The Kiss'," *The Florida Times-Union*, August 29, 2000. "Bush Says He Feels Gore's Pain," *The Atlanta Journal and Constitution*, December 6, 2000, p. 1A. David Bianculli, "Veep Floors Analysts," *New York Daily News*, December 15, 2000, p. 167. See also articles posted at the conservative site *www.freerepublic.com*. Even the language of opinion-gathering favored emotional reactions. After each appeared, *Oprah.com*, for example, asked viewers to log in to register "how do you feel" about the candidate.
2 *The Oprah Show*, September 11 and September 19, 2000. Through interviewing the candidates, Oprah aimed at discovering each candidate's true self: "To me there's this 'wall' that exists between the people and the authentic part of

the candidate ... My goal is to try to get to know the men behind that wall" (*Oprah.com*, September 11, 2000).

3 See, for example, Pratto and Bargh (1991), and McGarty, Yzerbyt, and Spears (2002).

4 *Phaedo* 117C5 to E3. Translated by Hugh Tredennick (*The Last Days of Socrates*, Penguin Classics, 1969, p. 182). Other translations similarly highlight the significance of weeping and Socrates' admonitions to his friends to be unlike women and to control themselves. Genevieve Lloyd (1984) notes that in the *Phaedo*, Plato envisioned the mind-body relation as a simple dualism and stressed the need for the rational soul to free itself from "error, folly, fear and fierce passions" of the body (p. 6). In his later thought, however, Plato moved toward a more complex view of the soul as a source of inner conflict, with the rational part of the soul struggling to dominate and make subordinate to it other non-rational components of the soul. Plato's re-visioning anticipates the notion of "passion in the service of reason" which characterizes privileged Anglo-American idealized emotion in the nineteenth century and in contemporary society. I am indebted to Garth Kemerling at the Philosophy Pages (*http://www.philosophypages.com*) for helping me locate the publication information for the Tredennick translation.

5 The very questions themselves reflect historicized, culture-specific implied assumptions about the nature of emotion. My intention in using these questions was not to legitimate these assumptions as true, but to help students see for themselves the unquestioned and even unwarranted assumptions about emotion that underlay their emotion expertise.

6 Duffy (1941, p. 284). Critics of Duffy suggest that she wanted to do away with the study of emotion altogether. In fact, she is very much in the vein of today's emotions researchers who view clarity in definition of the phenomena encompassed by "emotion" as necessary to advancing the field.

7 This is but a brief overview of how the study of emotion in the social sciences, especially the psychology of emotion, has developed over the past twenty years. Among those who study emotion there is wide divergence of opinion within the general framework that I describe. For more information, see textbooks by Keith Oatley and Jenny Jenkins (1996) and Randy Cornelius (1996).

8 See Chapter 5 in Cornelius' (1996) textbook on the psychology of emotion for a thoughtful introduction to the social constructionist perspective in psychology.

9 See, for example, Joseph LeDoux (1996, p. 115 ff).

10 See, for example, Robert Solomon (1993), Ronald deSousa (1987), or Nico Frijda (1986).

11 Daniel Stern's (1985) book on infant affective development has been influential beyond psychoanalytic circles. Leslie Greenberg (e.g., Greenberg and Pavio, 1997) has developed an emotion-focused psychotherapy which includes facilitating the client's understanding of how individual emotions can inhibit or further therapy goals.

12 Jaak Panksepp's (1998) model of mammalian emotional response patterns is representative of one direction taken in the research using animal models. See also LeDoux (1996) for a comprehensive, readable account of neural systems of emotion.

13 Those on the side of discrete emotion types propose that there are a small set of distinctively different innate emotions, while those on the other side of the

debate suggest that emotion is better conceptualized as an array of states that can be represented on a two- or three-dimensional space. James Russell (1997) gives a thorough account of the debates among these theoretical camps.

14 See, for example, Rosaldo (1984), Abu Loghoud and Lutz (1990). These feminist analyses make a major contribution to the study of emotion by highlighting the cultural specificity and significance of beliefs about emotion.

15 A variety of different terms have been used to refer to the collected beliefs about emotion within a culture. In their book on the history of American beliefs about anger, for example, Carol and Peter Stearns (1986) coined the term "emotionology" to refer to the conventions and standards by which Americans evaluate emotion and the institutions they develop to reflect and encourage these standards. Another term that captures this sense of emotion's role in defining and maintaining social structures is "emotional culture," which Steve Gordon defines as "a group's set of beliefs, vocabulary, regulative norms, and other ideational resources pertaining to emotion" (1989, p. 322).

16 Philosopher Robert Solomon (1993; first published in 1976) explores the myth of the irrationality of emotion and presents a compelling critique of Western portrayal of emotion as the antithesis of reason.

17 In psychological research, gender (rather than sex) is usually the variable of interest. I try to use *sex-related difference* to refer to the results of studies that report a comparison of subjects by sex and *gender difference* to refer to the inferences drawn from those results. Because I am primarily concerned with the social meaning of emotion as it is deployed in the construction of psychological differences, I tend to rely on the term gender.

18 The social-structural approach has received more thorough treatment among feminist sociologists such as Barbara Risman (1998). The major exponent of this position in psychology is Alice Eagly (1987) in her Social Role Theory. One version of gender-as-process was offered by Kay Deaux and Brenda Major in a much-cited article published in 1987. Their model is compatible with conventional empirical social psychology and has done much to encourage psychologists to think about gender as a feature of the contextualized social interaction. The influence of social constructionism is also growing (e.g., Fine, 1992; Thorne, 1993; Hare-Mustin and Marecek, 1988; Bohan, 1993).

19 Feminist recuperation of Freudian psychoanalytic theories (e.g., Chodorow, 1978; 1995; Kaschak, 1992) has played a much less significant role in experimental social, developmental, and personality psychology.

20 For an engaging and personal view of the development of feminist psychology and its complex relationship to the putative mainstream of American psychology see Unger (1998). In one of my own more cynical moods I compared so-called mainstream psychology's relation to feminist psychology with "blindsight," the unconscious residual capacity for visual localization following damage to the visual cortex (Shields, 1994). The blindsighted individual cannot see a stimulus presented in the affected region of the visual field, but can point with surprising degree of accuracy to the location in which that unseen stimulus was presented. "That object you did not see – point to where it was." Analogously, mainstream (dead center?) experimental psychology has no clue what feminist psychology is, but walk into any professional conference or university department and ask where to find it, and most psychologists can readily point to the one, two, or few colleagues who represent it.

21 Over the past thirty years emotion figures in books by researchers writing on topics as diverse as nonverbal communication (e.g., Mayo and Henley, 1981), power and the state (e.g., Hartsock, 1983), moral reasoning (e.g., Ruddick, 1980; Gilligan, 1982), the family as the locus for reproduction of gender asymmetries (e.g., Chodorow, 1978; Johnson, 1988), and body studies (e.g., Bordo, 1993).

CHAPTER 2

When does gender matter?

The comic strip *Cathy*, drawn by Cathy Guisewite, chronicles the life of a single woman preoccupied with dieting, shopping, and her biological clock. Cathy sometimes goes a bit overboard in examining the minutiae of experience and dissecting meanings in her relationships, whether that relationship is with chocolate, a pair of shoes, her mother, or her once and current boyfriend Irving. In one of my many favorite "emotional Cathy" episodes, Cathy and Irving have just returned home from a party. Irving comments "Nice party," which immediately elicits from Cathy "It was *horrible!*" She goes on to describe one emotional disaster after another that colored the evening. She recounts how Sue felt jealous of Cathy and threw herself at Irving, and how Bill wasn't speaking to Jan, how Bill's old girlfriend showed up with her new husband – a man Cathy used to date, and on and on, concluding "It was one of the most tense, embarrassing, awkward evenings of my life!" To which Irving responds, "Women always have a better time at these things than men do."

We are all experts on emotion and we are all experts on gender. From the day we were born we have been practicing and trying to perfect both. We are continually being reminded of the importance of getting emotion right *and* getting gender right, by friends, family, and the swarms of popular culture images that surround us daily. In everyday life, especially in personal relationships, it occasionally seems as if women and men inhabit different emotional worlds. Just as often, however, our experience tells us that emotions of all sorts and all intensities are common to both sexes. As with so many other human behaviors and qualities, experience also tells us that differences among individuals of the same sex can be as great or greater than any generalized "sex difference." Yet in print, on TV, and at the movies we see women and men portrayed as leading distinctively different emotional lives. Is this one more charade in a media-mediated battle of the sexes? Do women and men actually think of, experience, and display emotions differently? Are the emotions of boys and girls, women and men differently evaluated and valued by the people with whom they come in contact?

This chapter looks at what we currently know about the intersection of gender and the psychology of emotion. For many years questions about emotion and gender tended to be reduced to "who is more emotional – women or men?" This approach focuses research on a search for gender differences (and similarities) and erases the obvious question of *which* women, *which* men? There are three important limitations to this "differences model" beyond its tendency to universalize experience. First, it is built on the assumption that gender operates as a set of fixed, stable, and enduring traits or qualities that differentiate the sexes. As we will see, only rarely does knowledge of a person's gender alone enable us to predict how she or he will act. Gender effects are quite sensitive to the nature of the context and others who are present. Second, *difference* is a relative judgment, and so one category always at least implicitly serves as the standard from which the other is "different" and by implication comparatively deficient.[1] A third limitation is that identifying differences (or similarities) does not, by itself, enable us to explain those differences (or similarities). The differences model, in other words, gives us a description, but not a theory. To get unstuck from simple description, we need to shift the question to "When does gender matter?" The key to explaining gender effects is to focus on the features of the context by examining what drives when and how differences are likely to occur.

A consistent, broad pattern of results emerges from research when the question shifts from "are there differences?" to "what drives the differences?" We find that social context (particularly its interpersonal dimensions) and beliefs about emotion and its social value are significant determinants of when and how gender and emotion are linked. We also find that patterns of gender effects depend on what exactly it is about emotion that is measured: knowledge about emotion, facial expression of emotion, or how people name or talk about their experience. Differences in women's and men's emotions tend to be not in what women and men know about emotion, but in how women and men apply their knowledge and understanding of what emotion is and how it works. There is a built-in inequality in any differences model, whether the differences are based on separate categories – she is this kind, he is that kind, or comparison on the same attribute – she has more of it, he has less. In any differences model, one group is always the standard against which other groups are measured. Especially pernicious are the implicit comparisons in which the standard is an unstated presence. For example, any exchange about whether women are "the emotional sex," suggests two things: first, that some other sex is not to be so labeled, and second, that to be the emotional sex is not a preferred status.

From "differences" to "doing gender"

In the early 1980s, I began to be very interested in the language of emotion and the social rules governing emotional exchanges. At the time, academic psychology focused on debates about facial expression of emotion, cognitive processes and appraisals involved in generating emotion, and effects of mood and emotion on cognition and judgment. My own interest was the social meaning of emotion, that is, culturally prevalent implicit and explicit beliefs about emotion. These beliefs vary across culture and historical era, and many beliefs are shared within Western cultures, such as the opinion that emotion is passively experienced, that emotion is difficult to control, that the "right" kind and quantity of emotion is good and healthy, while the "wrong" kind or amount is not. The further I delved into the topic, the clearer it became to me that the answers were often inextricably linked with questions of gender. So my work on emotion began more closely to focus on the intersection of gender and emotion. For psychology and for women's studies this was (and still is) largely unexplored territory.

At that time, the revival of interest in emotion in the behavioral and social sciences was just beginning to gain momentum, and meetings of the newly founded International Society for Research on Emotions were major forums for the discussion of new lines of research and theory within an international and interdisciplinary context. At the ISRE meetings, when I would mention my new program of research, psychologist colleagues would react with puzzlement. Not that they had any particularly negative feelings about studying sex or gender, but rather, because they thought it a research dead-end. Everyone knows, so they said, that experimental research on the psychology of emotion doesn't reveal interesting differences between women and men, or girls and boys. They pointed out that, with the exception of accuracy in producing and reading facial expressions of emotion and some self-report about emotional experience, sex-related differences tended to be quite modest, apparently unpredictable, and therefore theoretically uninteresting. In everyday life, however, the story was quite different. When I talked with students, watched movies, or discussed my work with neighbors or people at parties, the reaction to my interest in gender and emotion was quick and enthusiastic. Everyone knows, they would say, that there are *vast* differences between the sexes in emotion – and it's about time that someone explained these differences and why they are so important.

So there was clearly a huge discrepancy between the way emotions researchers and ordinary people viewed the intersection of gender and emotion. To me, that discrepancy seemed to be precisely where to begin my study. I needed to take a closer look at the research literature to see what may have been overlooked, because those missing pieces can reveal important patterns in emotion beliefs. I also needed to take a closer look at what "everyone knows" to see what it might be obscuring, because what we *think* we know can conceal important features of emotion beliefs. And before too long I also realized that any thorough study of gendered emotion would also have to incorporate the dimensions of social class, racial ethnicity, and historical period.

This project began with the question of emotion labeling – Who is called "emotional"? When does it happen? What does it mean when it happens? – and has since evolved into an inquiry into the links between beliefs about emotion and beliefs about being a gendered person in the contemporary US. Early on, it became clear to me that gender plays a significant role in questions concerned with emotion's social value and meaning. I originally believed that I would find a fairly straightforward relationship between gender and emotion. I expected to find that women are likely to be identified as emotional given the same circumstances in which men are not so identified, that women's emotion is negatively evaluated compared to men's, and that labeling someone as emotional is a strategy for discounting that person's rationality. In short, I expected that emotion would invariably be less valued than rationality and that women's emotion, in particular, would be undervalued. What I found, however, was far more complex and far more interesting than that. The intersection between gender and emotion instead reveals the central role that beliefs about emotion play in defining and maintaining gender boundaries.

Whose stereotype is it?

One of the first hurdles I faced was the approach that American psychology tends to take toward studying how culture, including historical era, creates a distinctive context for who people are and how they behave. Social class, racial ethnicity, and culture (not to be mistaken with national identity) tend to be excluded from study on the grounds that they are sociological and not psychological. Psychology's lack of attention to the intersections of race, class, and ethnicity is typically explained away by invoking psychology's endeavor to explain universal psychological phenomena. Turning to the psychology of emotion, we find that most research involves North American and Western European countries. While this can give us some clues regarding cross-national trends, generalizing across historical period, culture, or racial or ethnic groups within a dominant culture requires something more. A notable deficiency in academic psychology's questions about gender and emotion is the tendency to totalize, that is, the tendency to treat the typical research participant pool as if it were incontestably representative of all people. Research psychologists often rely on college students (mostly white and mostly aged 20 or younger), which becomes problematic when conclusions drawn from this research are unselfconsciously represented as descriptive of adults in general. Conversely, the psychologist who draws research participants from "special" populations – such as lesbians, working adults, or Asian Americans – is urged to be extra cautious in applying the results of research beyond that group.[2]

In this book I limit my discussion to the contemporary US, a Westernized post-industrial society. There are important limitations on how I can represent "contemporary Westernized post-industrial society." In nearly all of the research I draw on here, neither racial ethnicity nor class is considered. When they are, it is not usually because they are believed to be part of the explanation; usually they are looked at just to ensure that they are *not* important. In other words, only rarely are these important features of peoples' social selves accorded a role in the theory that drives the research question. Focusing on gender while bracketing social class, racial ethnicity, and other within-gender differences, what Mary Parlee (1995) calls "gender-with-brackets-on," acknowledges the issues raised, but sets them outside the "normal" course of inquiry.[3] I will try to resist that impulse and to make special note of those areas or topics in which there already is or could be sophisticated (i.e., beyond the merely additive) inclusion of race, class, or ethnicity in the theory framing the work. My goal is to move the discussion about gender and emotion beyond the discussion of differences, not only to advance theory on gender and emotion, but also to set the stage for a more sophisticated discussion of the intersections of gender and emotion with racial ethnicity, historical period, culture, and social class. That said, I can be only partially successful; real progress would require placing these variables at the center, not the periphery, of the inquiry. Without greater attentiveness to the ways in which social identity other than gender (or in addition to gender) may play a role in the individual's experience of emotion and representations of that experience, we risk mistaking effects that are representative of one segment of society for effects representative of all women and men. Further, we may mistakenly conclude that a gender difference exists when what we have observed is attributable to variables other than gender (Unger, 1996).

Most research on gender differences in garden-variety, everyday life emotion has been concerned with one of three general question areas: what people know about what emotion is and how it works, what people can describe about their own emotional experience, and how people show emotion, especially through facial expression. The following sections give an overview of the research in each of these areas in order to tease out what we know so far about when and how gender matters in emotion.[4] This is not meant to be an exhaustive survey, but one that gives the general lay of the land. A literature review is rarely in itself fascinating, so what I concentrate on – and what I would like you, the reader, to think about – is how we might use these sometimes disparate sets of research conclusions to craft a larger pattern of theory. It is a starting point for transforming the question of "Are there differences?" to "When does gender matter?"

What do people know about emotion? Understanding and explaining emotion as a concept

How do people understand emotion? What can they express concerning their knowledge of the antecedents, constituents, and consequences of emotions or about their knowledge of emotion-relevant stereotypes? The pattern of gender-relevant results depends on whether we are comparing the women and men who participate in the research, or what those participants say about female and male stimulus persons or "targets." Here I should explain how research psychologists would study this question in the laboratory. When the investigator is interested in learning about the factors that influence judgments of others' behavior, she or he asks participants to assess particular emotions and the situations that evoke them, or asks about hypothetical or real male and female targets in emotion-evoking situations. The investigator can also examine how women and men who are the research participants themselves differ, by virtue of sex, in their pattern of responses. If we consider the research in psychology that is concerned with people's beliefs about emotion and how it works, it turns out that there is a distinct difference between what we see when we compare the performance of women and men research *participants*, and when we compare beliefs about women and men *targets*. In this regard, the study of emotion is much like research on gender in other areas of psychology.[5]

When women and men research participants (or girls and boys) are compared in terms of what they know about emotion, the general pattern of findings suggests very few or no gender differences. That is, when adults are asked to make judgments about emotion labels, for example, or participate in experiments on mood and memory, or make judgments about emotion stereotypes, or engage in other tasks that tap culturally-shared beliefs about emotion, gender differences among participants rarely occur (e.g., Zammuner, 2000). The same is also true in research with children (e.g., Smith and Walden, 1998). The comparability of girls' and boys' understanding of emotion is somewhat surprising given that girls tend to be more socially mature than boys of the same age, and so it might be expected that girls would consistently outperform boys.

The importance of social context

Gender similarities are the rule. That said, the more that *social context* is embedded in the research question, the more likely we will find gender differences. Whether asked to provide descriptions of emotion episodes or outline the circumstances in which particular types of emotion, such as sadness, occur, girls and women are more likely than boys and men to give accounts that include some reference to interpersonal causes and consequences of emotion. This is not a particularly dramatic finding, but it is one that crops up often enough that it is worth looking more closely at what it might reveal. In one often-cited study, Muriel Egerton (1988) examined adults' accounts of anger and weeping episodes while they imagined themselves in the emotion-evoking scenario. Most notable of the gender differences obtained for the two types of emotion scenario was women's greater reported conflict about the anger episode (describing anger as effective, but upsetting and costly to relationships) and men's more frequent use of "passion schemas" that disembed emotion from its social framework (representing anger as externally caused and uncontrollable). In other words, women tended to anchor their evaluations of anger in perceptions of costs and benefits to relationships, whereas men appeared to be more inclined to consider anger a "thing" on its own, separate from the relationships that define its causes and consequences. The greater likelihood for girls to take into account the interpersonal nature of emotion is evident even before middle childhood. It is not that boys and men do not recognize emotion as an interpersonal event, it seems more likely that the interpersonal quality is just not a feature of emotion that is among those most consistently salient to them. When adults are specifically asked about the interpersonal aspects of emotion, women's and men's accounts may differ in detail, but men can describe significant interpersonal dimensions as readily as women (e.g., Buss, 1991). Thus, the finding that boys and men are less likely to insert reference to the connection between emotion and social roles or relationships in their accounts of emotion appears to be a discrepancy between knowledge and performance, not a gender difference in knowledge about emotion.[6]

Women and men alike rely on emotion stereotypes, more so when they have very sketchy or limited information about that other person.

This tendency is put to use in research that aims to identify "typical" or prevailing beliefs about females and males, or about emotion. The contours of gendered emotion stereotypes become emphasized in research studies that involve participants in making judgments of "targets" about whom they have little or no individuating information. The typical method in this research is to present a picture or sketch of an individual, or a brief scenario about an emotion incident, and then to ask questions about the target's emotional expression or experience. In a now-classic series of studies psychologist Dana Birnbaum and her colleagues showed that beliefs about gendered emotion are learned by early childhood and persist in adulthood even when they conflict with other gender-related values. In one study, preschoolers as well as college students associated anger with males and happiness, sadness, and fear with females (Birnbaum, Nosanchuk, and Croll, 1980). In another study by the same team, preschool children similarly associated angry statements with boys and happy statements with girls (Birnbaum and Chemelski, 1984). Sad statements were not consistently associated with either sex, showing that even in these studies of emotion stereotypes the results are not always uniform. Among working-class parents and college students, males were associated with anger and females with sadness and fear (Birnbaum and Croll, 1984). More recent work has begun to consider both the context of judgment and kind of judgment in more detail. Kelly and Hutson-Comeaux (1999), for example, reported that gender-emotion stereotypes are influenced by context such that emotional "over-reaction" is believed to be more characteristic of men's anger in achievement contexts, but more characteristic of women's happiness and sadness in interpersonal contexts. I will have more to say about gendered stereotypes of emotionality in the following chapter.

In summary, if we take a look at what people know about emotion, that is, their understanding of emotion as a concept, what they know about different emotions, the causes and consequences of emotion, and emotion stereotypes – all evidence points to great similarities between women and men and girls and boys. One of the most striking areas of similarity is in knowledge of gendered emotion stereotypes. People are very knowledgeable about the stereotypes, and this stereotype knowledge is evident even at a very young age. Gendered emotion stereotypes are more than abstract ideas unconnected to real behavior. They play an important role in both learning and practicing gender, "practicing" both in the sense of the everyday practice or performance of gendered behavior, and in the sense that I will explore in greater detail in the following chapter, namely, an ongoing striving to get gender "right."

What do people say about their own emotions? Self-reports about experience and expressiveness

One of the main research strategies that psychologists use to study the occurrence of emotion in peoples' lives is to ask them direct questions about those experiences. Sometimes questions take the form of a general or summary assessment of what one views as typical of oneself for a particular emotion, such as anger, or for emotions or emotional expression more generally. The form of questioning may also be directed more to one's understanding of a particular emotion episode or period of time, for example through keeping a diary of anger-provoking situations or rating the intensity with which a set of emotions was experienced over the course of a laboratory experiment designed to induce some specific emotions. Self-report may be an open-ended narrative or it may be a set of responses to specific questions where the response is in the form of a numerical scale. The range of ways that self-report is collected by research psychologists has a very direct connection to the pattern of gender differences and similarities that they observe. Self-reports about emotions follow a very distinct pattern, but that pattern depends on how the question is asked.

What do women say? What do men say?

The typical finding is that self-reports yield gender differences that correspond to stereotypes, but there are some important caveats to that general conclusion. Emotion seems to be particularly sensitive to different methods of obtaining self-report, and this may be because "emotion" is so heavily larded with stereotypes and tacit beliefs. The patterns of self-report do not in themselves point to an explanation about why similarities or differences are found. Take, for example, an early study of people's beliefs about the relation between feeling and showing emotion. Malatesta (now Magai) and Kalnok (1984) surveyed nonstudent adults in three age groups and found that men were more likely to agree with the belief that men should conceal their feelings, but when reporting on their own behavior, it was women rather than men who reported actually trying to inhibit emotional expression. What are we to make of this? Do women try to inhibit expression more out of necessity because they have more feelings to contain? Do men report less attempt to control because they – rightly or wrongly – believe they are already not very expressive? Are women over-reporting expressive control? Or are men underreporting expressive control? This study also reminds us that identifying a gender difference – or even a pattern of difference – by itself is descriptive and does not tell us what causes the difference or keeps it in place.

When differences are obtained, they typically take the form of women reporting greater frequency or intensity of the emotion in question, but there is one very interesting exception to this pattern.[7] For anger, an emotion that is prototypically masculine, the gender difference in report usually disappears or occasionally shows greater reported frequency by men. A number of different investigators using a variety of techniques have observed this pattern, and two classic research studies show how important it is to look at the circumstances in which people tell us about their emotion. James Averill (1983), for example, obtained college students' self-reports concerning anger episodes. He found no sex-related differences in reported frequency or causes of anger, but did find that women rated their anger as more intense and out of proportion to the precipitating event than did men. Laboratory manipulations of anger also tend to be equally effective for research participants of both sexes. In a much-cited early study, Ann Frodi (1978) observed how women and men verbalized their reactions to and feelings toward a person who had provoked their anger. The provocateur was actually a confederate of the researcher. After the incident, half the participants were asked to write down their thoughts about their experience. Women tended to downplay anger and aggression in their writing, whereas men "tended to preoccupy themselves with thoughts of anger or 'stirring themselves up'" (p. 347). Then all participants were given an opportunity to select the intensity of annoying sound that ostensibly would be heard by their anger-provoking partner. The men, but not the women, who had been instructed to ruminate on the event delivered more intense sounds than did men who had not.

The fact that gender differences in self-report are less likely to occur the closer to the actual occurrence of the emotion suggests that self-report conforms to gender stereotypes (i.e., women are emotional; men are not) the more distant in time from actual emotion that the judgment is made and the more general the self-assessment. This raises a very provocative question: When the whole notion of "stereotype" is so negative, and people (Americans) so highly value individual uniqueness, what would make people's self-descriptions repeat gender stereotypes? The tendency to rely on generalized beliefs may be especially likely when it is difficult to retrieve specific accurate recollection of one's own experience. Research on mood and the menstrual cycle offers a particularly striking example. The early research was largely based on retrospective checklists. It usually involved asking women to check off or rate a list of moods and emotions that they typically experience at specific points during the menstrual cycle. Not surprisingly, these global retrospective reports, which are heavily influenced by beliefs about what ought to occur or beliefs about what is typical, tended to show the classic pattern of mood variation over the cycle. More recent work, which employs concurrent diaries or daily mood checklists, shows no such cycle-related pattern.[8] Instead, these diaries show that women's recall and report is more related to the level of everyday hassles they are experiencing than their menstrual cycle.[9]

What happens when children are studied? Different research strategies tend to be used to tap children's and adults' beliefs about their own emotional experience, making it difficult to compare age-related differences in reports about emotional experience. With adults and adolescents, investigators tend to rely on standardized scales and ask the participant to imagine an experience or set of experiences from her or his own past. The finding of gender difference in this case is more or less directly related to the general nature of the emotion and the time frame, with the more general more likely to yield gender differences. Children are usually presented with a hypothetical situation, asked to think about how they might feel in that situation, and then choose or rate the intensity of the emotion that would be likely to occur. Occasionally the child's self-ratings are obtained after mild emotion is induced. When these methods are used, investigators generally find gender similarities rather than differences up till adolescence (e.g., Harris, 1989; Wintre, Polivy, and Murray, 1990). Sometimes, though, girls and boys interpret emotion-eliciting vignettes as likely to bring about different specific emotions, such as sadness versus anger (e.g., Strayer, 1989).

What does self-report really tell us?

Self-report is an index of what people believe to be true about themselves (Steinke and Shields, 1992). It would be a mistake to consider self-report a literal record of emotion occurrences. Psychologists have shown that memory, even personal memory, is very malleable, and that we almost invariably forget, add, and reconstruct the details or even the shape of a recalled event. The tendency to inaccuracy in memory may be especially true for the stream of experience – like emotion – in which there are few persistent external or tangible reminders of the ordinary range of experiences once they have passed. With the exception of the occasional sentimental card, broken dish, or other physical reminder, the most vivid record of the emotion is the story we tell in our own memory.

Because self-report measures beliefs about one's own behavior and experience, it is fundamentally a reconstruction of experience, an account that interweaves memory, immediate bodily sensation, expectancies, and heuristics (problem-solving short-cuts). The self-report is not the literal description of a discrete event or attitude, but an amalgam, sharpened or leveled, of the many factors that might bear upon the individual's interpretation of "experience." How many and what sort of influences can play upon people's reconstructions of their experience depends on many factors. Self-report can be based on research participants' notions of what ought to be true or what is typically true, as well as what actually occurred. And reliance on "ought" and "typical" seems especially heavy when people are asked to make aggregate, retrospective self-assessments. The research participant's report may be better able to reflect beliefs about ongoing experience when the report is concurrent with the experience or when very specific questions are asked. In the case of emotion, timing may not be everything, but it is very important. The form of the questions is also quite important. Like other kinds of events for which the individual may have a great deal of accumulated knowledge but little tangible or specific data, the occurrence of gender differences depends on how the question is asked.

Another reason to interpret self-report as an indicator of beliefs and values is that self-report does not invariably correlate with behavioral measures of the same or related events. When behavior and reports are discrepant, the fact of discrepancy itself may be important data. People are able to generate socially plausible theories, even when they have no direct knowledge on which to form a judgment, and they do so in a systematic, nonrandom fashion. The dissociation between reports and behavior is an index of the importance that the individual assigns to a value or belief. For example, if we find that men report that it is very important for fathers to spend time at home with their children, but observe that fathers do this, on average, less than an hour a day, we have an indicator of how much fathers value their role in childrearing (in terms of their beliefs about what fathers ought to do). This is the case even if the indicator alone does not allow us to specify why actual time spent is small, that is, whether personal disposition, work pressures, commuting, other personal responsibilities, and so on, intervene between the value held and its behavioral expression.

The significance of self-report as a belief, rather than as a fact subject to validation, makes it a valuable tool in interpreting the reports that people provide about their own emotions. The concept of emotion is very sensitive to the format in which self-report is obtained. As noted above, gender differences are more likely to occur when people make aggregate, retrospective self-assessments, than when people report about specific emotional occurrences, and particularly when their report is obtained very close to the time of the event. Taken as a whole, the research suggests that when people have little immediate information to go on, they may fall back on using emotion stereotypes as a kind of heuristic device to generate a satisfying, plausible response. What makes these gendered standards more or less salient in the person's self-evaluation? People are much more inclined to believe that these stereotypes are descriptive of a hypothetical other or someone they know little about rather than themselves. People may even use gendered emotion stereotypes to describe their *own* behavior in quite specific circumstances. In the next chapter I will take a closer look at when and why people rely on the stereotypes for making self-judgments.[10]

How do people show emotion? Producing and reading expression of emotion

Across the areas of emotions research, the production and judgment of emotional expression shows the most consistent performance differences between women and men. In adults, a small but consistent gender difference is found in producing and recognizing specific emotions. That said, the questions *"who* shows 'readable' emotion *when?"* and *"who* is an accurate judge of expression in which *contexts?"* show subtle and not so subtle patterns of results. These patterns bear a marked resemblance to the patterns noted for self-report about emotion and understanding of emotion concepts.

Emotion is expressed in many channels – through the voice, through gesture, through the pace and tempo of movement – but the bulk of research has focused on specific facial signals. Typically this involves assessing the accuracy with which people can produce (encode) discernible expressions, and the accuracy with which people can identify others' discernible expression (decode). In general, this line of research finds that women tend to be better at identifying the emotion expressed in others' facial expressions, whether those expressions are posed, that is, deliberately made or selected by the researcher to represent a specific emotion, or not deliberately posed ("spontaneous"). Women also are better at having their own spontaneous facial expressions recognized accurately by others. There is one emotion in which men occasionally are found to have more readable expressions and to read more accurately: anger. When greater accuracy is observed in men, it is for the expression of anger. Of course, many aspects of the situation can influence how much and how unambiguously one shows emotion in facial expression, and the recognition that context is extremely important tends to be carefully considered by researchers who work in this area. One of the research techniques that has come to be used very successfully in teasing apart when and how context makes a difference is *meta-analysis*, which is a statistical method for quantifying the size of effect across a set of studies. Several of the most informative studies on gender and facial expression have used this technique.

Compared to the extensive work on facial expressions of specific emotions, there is relatively little work that contrasts women's and men's production or judgment of vocal, gestural, or other expressive channels. Similarly, few investigators have studied how producing and understanding facial expressions or other emotionally expressive behavior may be moderated by racial ethnicity within a culture. The greater emphasis placed on facial expression compared to other forms of expression has more to do with the way this field of research originated than the actual range of emotional signs and signals that people pay attention to.

A number of factors influence when and how women and men express emotion in their faces, voices, and gesture. Various researchers have noted that these differences are embedded in a larger pattern of gendered nonverbal communication style, such as the tendency for female faces to be more expressive, smile more, and use body movements and positions that are more expressive and more self-conscious, but less expansive. Hall (1987), in fact, pointed out an important mitigating factor in interpreting these data: the contexts in which expressive behavior is measured tend to be settings in which there are demand characteristics for gender-appropriate behavior. She observes, for example, that most of these studies employ college student research participants and take place in waiting periods for experiments ostensibly on other topics or during "get acquainted" sessions. These situations are immediately recognizable as social situations with strong implicit demands to be nice. As in self-report about experience, the social context of measurement has a discernible influence on the pattern of results an investigator is likely to find. Marianne LaFrance and her students show how subtle communication processes reflect and maintain gender and power differences. Her Expressivity Demand Theory begins with the premise that power and gender do not merely modify the display of nonverbal behavior, rather, they constitute the context for expressive display. Some situational demands apply equally to women and men, while other contexts may involve greater demands (to be more expressive or to modulate expressive behavior) for one sex or the other. LaFrance and Hecht's (2000) comprehensive meta-analysis of research on gender and smiling revealed that the presence of others is important in moderating who smiles when. When engaging with others socially, men's rate of smiling, for example, is actually less than women's.

Insofar as children's ability to recognize and label facial expressions of emotion is concerned, the pattern is similar to other areas of emotion knowledge: Gender differences are essentially absent, and older children out-perform younger children. Nor do there appear to be gender differences in children's knowledge about expressions or children's expressive competence. Similarly, studies of facial expression production, both spontaneous and posed expressions, reveal no gender differences in accuracy of producing expressions of specific emotions. Manstead (1992) and Brody (1985) each summarized the research literature on children's judgment and production of facial expression of emotion. They drew their conclusions from somewhat different sets of studies, but both concluded that there is no evidence of gender differences in readability of spontaneous expressiveness in infants or children, although individual studies may report a gender difference in the frequency with which specific emotional expressions occur. For the most part these differences are consistent with emotion stereotypes. As these studies typically involve gross behavioral assessments in which the rater knows the child's sex, it is not possible to unconfound observer expectancies from the behavior that is observed. By early adolescence the gender differences in reading and producing facial expression that are fairly consistently seen in adults become evident.

Facial expression of emotion is not an infallible index of emotional experience. Some emotions researchers hypothesize a deep connection between expression and the motivational and cognitive state that comprises the "true" emotion. Yet, even they emphasize that, given the controllability of expressive behavior, that strong connection may represent only a brief portion, even just seconds, of a full-blown emotion episode.[11] Expressiveness is a modality for signaling things about emotion, but it is not justifiable to infer that expression, particularly expression in the well-socialized adult, is an uncontaminated index of emotion. Even though paradigmatic expressions may signal specific emotions – an angry face does not look like a happy face – personal life as well as research tell us that any given emotional state can be communicated by a range in kind and intensity of expression. In later chapters I will return to the question of how expressive style identifies "appropriate" and "inappropriate" emotion. One of the most important themes to keep in mind is that when we read others' emotional expressions, we not only make inferences about which emotion they are feeling, but also how intensely they feel and what action on their part the feeling is likely to lead to.

What does expression tell us?

Emotional expression of course involves far more than identifiable facial expressions of specific emotions. Voice quality, gesture, intonation, all convey information about emotional state. Some of these "channels" are more readily controlled by the individual than others, some are more unambiguous in what they convey, and none are necessarily highly correlated with what is expressed in another channel if the individual is in any way self-conscious about or making some effort to manage the communication of emotion. For example, the give and take of getting along with others requires us to pay attention to how we express emotion around others and what their expressive communication tells us. The back-and-forth of communication has a huge amount of it devoted to being attentive to, carefully watching, and continually evaluating our own and others' emotional expressivity. To be sure, it is equally human to make deliberate efforts to control one's expression to deceive an observer about one's true feelings. Even though, for example, the capacity to smile while conveying negative messages can be about disguising one's own "true" feelings, it need not simply be a deceptive device, but can be used as a strategy for maintaining the positive affective side of the relationship while negotiating conflicting goals. While most emotions researchers have focused on how the emotion content of expression is understood, it is equally important to look at the factors involved in the interplay of expressive exchange. In the course of everyday life successful negotiation of interpersonal relationships depends in large part on correctly "reading" the emotions of those with whom we interact. Reading is not limited to inferences about which emotions are present or how strongly or intensely those emotions are being experienced. The police officer on the street, the counselor of troubled children, and the wife of an abusive husband all need to judge accurately not only which emotion or emotions are being expressed, but also the intensity of the underlying felt emotion. When we infer the felt intensity of others' emotion, we have a basis for predicting that person's next actions, for assessing his or her capacity for self-control, and appraising the consequences of that person's state for our own well-being. This side of expressivity will be taken up further in later chapters that consider "appropriate emotion."

There are stable individual differences in expressive style, but the tendency to be expressive can be moderated, depending on situational demands and constraints (Gallaher, 1992). The social facets of the situation may be especially important in moderating expressivity. It has been proposed, for example, that expression is the complex product of social context, relationship between the audience and the expressor, and emotional intensity (Hess, Banse, and Kappas, 1995). Fernández-Dols and Ruiz-Belda (1995) hypothesize that spontaneous expressive behavior, as it occurs in ordinary situations, becomes prototypical, that is expressive of specific emotions, only when the individual is engaged in social interaction. They videotaped the reactions of people in situations guaranteed to elicit particular emotions: Olympic gold medalists at the awards ceremony and soccer fans watching televised matches. In each case the "purer" expressions of happy emotion and, in the case of the soccer fans, unhappy reactions to negative events, were more tightly linked to social sharing – whether there was someone interacting with the person – than the emotion-evoking situation *per se*.

People distinguish between showing and feeling emotion, both in describing themselves and others (Johnson and Schulman, 1988). Kring, Smith, and Neale (1994) developed a self-report measure of the extent to which people believe that they outwardly display their emotions, and found that self-reported expressivity was unrelated or modestly related to self-report measures of emotional experience. Another line of research also suggests that when people evaluate the intensity of their own experience they do not include magnitude of expression as an index for determining the strength of their emotional feeling (Sonnemans and Frijda, 1994). Barr and Kleck (1995) report that, when there is no audience present or the individual is given no direction on how expressive she or he should be, people believe their own facial behavior to be significantly more expressive than judges' ratings indicate it had been. When participants are asked to communicate their feelings, however, their self-assessment is more in line with that of judges. This work suggests that people may not be particularly accurate in assessing the magnitude of their own spontaneous expressive behavior and in any event do not consider the degree to which they show emotion to be an unambiguous indicator of what they feel. In addition, there is some evidence to suggest that research participants are more likely to attribute causality for a female target's emotion to personality and a male target's emotion to the situation (Shields and Crowley, 1996).

What makes expression "emotional"?

Some dimensions of expressivity show consistent gender-typical differences. Gallaher (1992) reports that in the US women tend to be more expressive than men in three important ways: (1) modulating, changing facial expression, (2) gesturing, and (3) rate and inflection of speech. This gender difference does not appear until adolescence (Manstead, 1992), and individual differences in expressiveness are fairly consistent, although, of course, they vary with situational demands and constraints. Frequency of expressive change may also contribute to findings of gender differences in the production of readable expressions and how observers interpret expressive behavior (Buck, Baron, Goodman, and Shapiro, 1980). Riggio and Friedman (1986), for example, have suggested that women and men may be held to different standards of "appropriate" expressivity within the same interpersonal contexts. They found that social impressions of men and women are in part based on how successfully gender-coded expressive styles are used: men who used gesture and movement directed toward the people they were speaking to were more favorably evaluated than men less nonverbally skilled. For women, on the other hand, it was facial expressiveness that most contributed to making a more positive initial impression. The hearty handshaking style we associate with the successful politician works well for men, while for women the face says it all. Women may be more pressured to smile in social situations, but, as we found true for descriptions of emotional experience, social *context* sets the parameters for whether gender matters.

In summary, research suggests that people readily distinguish between what they feel and what they show when they think about themselves. When evaluating others, however, people are more inclined to read expression as an indicator of quality and intensity of experience.[12] Their judgments are also influenced by that other person's gender, even when the facial expression or its description is identical for both sexes. In everyday life expressive styles do tend to differ by gender, which sets the stage for women's and men's expressive behavior to be "read" differently by observers. We would expect that other socially significant attributes, such as perceived racial ethnicity, status, and age, would also affect the framework within which expressive behavior is evaluated, including even whether and how much that expressive behavior is perceived to encompass emotionality.

What these laboratory results might mean for everyday life is that what women do and what men do are evaluated differently *because* they are women or men. It appears that what counts for men is a kind of "other orientation" – engaging verbally with others. For women, on the other hand, appearance may make the most difference. Does she smile? Is she expressive? Is she emotionally engaged and expressive of that engagement? It may well be that women and men are, in fact, understood differently even when they show the same expressive behavior.[13]

The complexity of expressive messages

A variety of vocal cues such as pitch, intonation, and rate of speech, can augment or can contradict the words one utters, as can face or gesture. More than one affective message can be communicated simultaneously, sometimes inadvertently, but also quite deliberately. Paul Ekman (1993), for example, describes three distinctive patterns of smiling. "Felt smiles" tend to occur spontaneously and to reflect genuine positive affect, while "false smiles" are those that are intentional and which may conceal neutrality or something other than genuine positive affect. Signal multiplexing is most evident in the third type of smile, "miserable smiles," characterized by a worried brow in combination with the deliberate smile. This miserable smile simultaneously expresses the individual's dissatisfaction with a situation at the same time as it communicates his or her willingness to bear up under the conditions. Deliberate mixing of contradictory facial expressions enables a person to maintain the positive affective side of the relationship while dealing with threats to the relationship arising from conflicting goals. In other words, delivering an aggressive, insulting, or otherwise negative message with words and voice, but with a positive face, can give a person a sort of "plausible deniability" for the message. In a classic study, Daphne Bugental (Bugental, Love, and Gianetto, 1971) researched the ways in which parents communicate emotion to their young children. She found that mothers and fathers used different communicative styles such that smiling was correlated with fathers' approval, but not with mothers'. Even when middle-class mothers were delivering a message of nonapproval, they tended to smile. While these results could be interpreted as reflecting a kind of inconsistency in maternal communication, an alternate explanation is that mothers were concerned with simultaneously showing *both* their disapproval and their unconditional affection. Mothers' expressive style may be intentionally double coded. I will return to this idea later in the book, but here I just want to draw attention to the multiple meanings that facial expressions can have and the richness and complexity of emotional messages that can be conveyed. Developing skill with emotional communication enables one to understand – as both a sender and a receiver of information – that multiple messages can be contained within the emotional envelope of voice, face, language, and gesture.

Putting the pieces together: Linking gender and emotion

In 1910, one of the first generation of American women psychologists, Helen Thompson Woolley surveyed the then-growing study of psychological sex differences for one of the most prestigious professional periodicals in psychology.[14] After carefully listing and summarizing the research studies that were then available, she determined that the study of sex differences as then practiced was a sorry mess. Her disappointment and frustration with the poor quality of the research was so strong that she concluded that, as far as the psychology of sex differences was concerned,

> There is perhaps no field aspiring to be scientific where flagrant personal bias, logic martyred in the cause of supporting a prejudice, unfounded assertions, and even sentimental rot and drivel have run riot to such an extent as here. (1910, p. 340)

The study of gender has come a long way since the turn of the last century, and serious work on the links between gender and emotion has grown considerably more sophisticated as well. Nevertheless, the current state of affairs still has its share of unfounded assertions and, even occasionally, martyred logic. The greater problem in current research, however, stems from the continued reliance on the sex differences model, and from the fact that most of that work rarely moves beyond the descriptive level.

Are there gender differences in emotion? Of course there are. What is interesting about these differences, however, is that they are far more context-dependent than the prevailing emotion stereotype leads us to expect. To answer questions about gender and emotion we first need to recognize that simply enumerating differences and similarities is not particularly informative: Finding a gender difference (or similarity) neither explains how the difference got there nor what maintains it. Without a grounding in theory, the fact of difference (or similarity) on any dimension increases the tendency to interpret the meaning of difference/similarity in terms of folk belief. So when women report greater intensity of felt emotion than men do, for example, much of the research has become stalled on the question of whether this difference means that women are more emotional than men or that men have less ability than women to acknowledge their own emotion. Meanwhile, other potentially more urgent or productive questions are overlooked. Among the vexing questions that can remain untapped are: What exactly about emotion does self-report represent? What difference does it make – to the individual or to others with whom the person interacts – whether and how emotion is explicitly labeled? What are the consequences of explicitly identifying someone's behavior as "emotional"?

In this chapter I have tried to give a sense of the insights that psychological research so far offers for gender and emotion. What each sex knows about emotion differs far less than what each sex is likely to do with that knowledge. This generalization holds whether children or adults are studied. When gender differences are identified in research, the differences by and large conform to emotion stereotypes, but differences are context dependent (e.g., self-reported emotion experience), or of less magnitude than stereotypes would predict (e.g., adult encoding and decoding of facial expression), or altogether absent (e.g., most understanding and application of emotion knowledge). Looking at context can help us think about what pushes gender effects, what exaggerates them and what attenuates them.

In the following chapters I will explore further the central role that emotion beliefs play in telling the boys from the girls. I propose that beliefs about emotion play an important role in defining and maintaining the beliefs we have about gender differences. I develop an account of the role that beliefs about emotion play in the acquisition and practice of gender-coded behavior. By *gender-coded* I mean behavior or experience that is expected to be more typical, natural, or appropriate for one sex than the other. My account accords a central role to emotion beliefs in proposing that they define cultural representations of masculinity/femininity, and, in that role, are the framework for the individual's acquisition and maintenance of a gendered identity. At the conceptual level, beliefs about emotion are used to "tell" the boys from the girls and, at the practical level, are used as a way of understanding ourselves as gendered individuals. Examining shared beliefs about emotion reveals what gender means, how gender operates, and how gender is negotiated in our relationships with others.

Notes

1 See Bacchi (1990) and Glenn (1999). Carol Tavris (1992) analyzes the practical and important consequences of the differences approach. She shows, for example, how the sometimes implicit and often explicit male standard has had harmful effects on our understanding of women's health issues.

2 Saarni (1998) critiques the Western cultural model that dominates investigation of emotional development across cultures.

3 See also Yoder and Kahn (1993) and Wyche (1998).

4 Extensive reviews of the literature can be found in Brody (1985), Brody and Hall (1993), LaFrance and Banaji (1992), Manstead (1992), and Shields (1991; 1995). Ideally I would describe development from childhood to maturity, but few studies go beyond simple age-based comparisons. Furthermore, adults and children are rarely included in the same study, and so apparent age-related differences are difficult to uncouple from methodological differences among studies.

5 The preponderance of this research employs college students as research participants and identifies targets by gender, and only rarely by age, racial ethnicity, or class. Targets are rarely specified beyond male/female; in the following chapter I consider some of my research with Jill Crowley that begins to address the complexity of interaction among gender, ethnicity, and status.

6 Women and men are equally responsive to the display rule differences between communal and exchange relationships (Clark and Taraban, 1991), even though they anticipate different rewards and costs of expressing emotion within social situations (Stoppard, 1993; LaFrance, 1998).

7 Some research has found these gender differences in self-report to be attenuated or reversed in Asian and Asian American samples. Brody (1999, p. 32) suggests that the explanation lies in the difference between individualistic and collectivistic cultures. I believe that the explanation lies in an American preoccupation with differentiating the genders in a cultural environment in which there are few other clear, stable markers of gender boundaries. I develop this argument in the following chapters.

8 McFarlane and Williams (1990; 1994), for example, have demonstrated the discrepancy between prospective and retrospective reports of menstrual symptoms, and shown that mood cycles in women and men exist but are fairly specific to the individual in their duration and timing.

9 Research participants' reports about their own experience and expressive behavior reflect their understanding of cultural and personal values and their
   beliefs about their own behavior, and it is usually not possible to discern the
   extent to which norms and self-observation each contribute to that report.
   Angela Simon and I (in preparation), for example, wanted to see if we could
   sort out the relation between the person's understanding of her or his own
   experience and the person's understanding of cultural norms regarding that
   experience. Romantic love offers a nearly ideal context for comparison of
   concurrent and retrospective reports of emotion symptoms. Furthermore,
   romantic love is an emotion with which a university student cohort has
   wide experience – so, for once, our sample of convenience was precisely the
   best group to study. To narrow the scope of romantic love to the experience
   at its most intense, we defined the emotion for our research participants as
   "the experience of love as it is in infatuation or the early exciting part of a new
   relationship." Those who said they were currently in love then rated how
   descriptive a set of romantic love symptoms was of their current in-love experience, while those not in love were asked to focus on their typical experience
   of romantic love as they answered the questions. We wanted to determine
   how much, if any, of the notions of a racing heart, loss of appetite, and so on,
   were actually noticed by people in love and how much these same symptoms show up in descriptions of past love experiences or imagined love experiences. Individuals providing retrospective accounts and imagined love
   experiences actually reported that bodily reactions were *more* descriptive
   of the romantic love state than people who were currently in love. It appears that as verbal reports become removed from the actual emotional state,
   individuals' reliance on common beliefs and cultural stereotypes concerning
   the state becomes greater.
10 I will argue that gendered stereotypes have a major role in the creation and
   maintenance of a gendered sense of self.
11 See Ekman (1993).
12 The actor-observer discrepancy takes an interesting form in evaluations of
   emotion. Johnson and Shulman (1988) were the first, I believe, to show that
   people believe that their own experience of emotion is stronger than what
   they show. Friends' emotions are believed to be somewhat less intense and
   strangers' even less.
13 Kleck, Hess, Adams, and Walbott (2000).
14 Woolley (1910, p. 340). Woolley earned her PhD in psychology at the
   University of Chicago in 1903. For biographies of her and other American
   women psychologists in that era, see Scarborough and Furumoto (1987).

CHAPTER 3

Doing emotion/doing gender: practicing in order to "get it right"

The first time I heard of the notion of "doing gender," I found it confusing. Even though this was some years ago, I vividly remember being stumped: How could gender be a *verb*? Yet, in a highly influential paper, West and Zimmerman (1987) made exactly that case. They proposed that gender can be understood by examining the interactional work that goes along with being a gendered person. In other words, gender is not something one "has," but is something that one "does." The point is that, even if in our heart of hearts we believe with certainty that we are either female or male, the trappings of womanhood and manhood that assure us (and others) of that identity are always being contested, disputed, negotiated. In a sense, we are always practicing gender, even when totally comfortable within our own skin. With practice we come to own the role in much the same way that a TV actor seems "naturally" the character that she or he plays. But unlike the TV actor, we move in and out of situations that may make gender "performance" more salient or that require us to improvise ways to meet the challenges of the situation while continuing to believe in the consistency and truth of our own gendered character. We are our own toughest audience.

Textile artist Mary Yaeger has done an interesting series of "woman badges." Using small industrial patches as a base, she applies hand embroidery to create pictures on the patches that are reminiscent of scouting merit badges. There is the eyebrow tweezing badge, the bathroom scale badge, the tampon badge, and, of course, the Girl Scout cookie badge, to name but a few. With the badges, Yaeger reminds us not only of the important rites of passage that mark our development from childhood to adult womanhood, but the sheer quantity and concentration of practice that goes into making the countless actions, ideas, and details of woman/feminine/female seem totally natural.[1] Drag queens know how to convincingly assemble a set of these details for the sake of performance, but it is a self-conscious performance and, though convincing, it is not genuine. The hugely popular 1994 Australian film *Priscilla, Queen of the Desert* makes a clear distinction between gender performance-as-parody and gender-as-performance. The film chronicles the adventures of three drag queens who plan to take their cabaret act to the Australian outback. The character of Felicia (Guy Pearce) is a flamboyant queen whose gender performance is a caricature of excess. His is a self-conscious performance that rarely pretends to be otherwise. In contrast, the male-to-female transsexual Bernadette (Terence Stamp) shows in an almost painful way the challenge of making the outside "look" of femininity match her inside identity as female. The details of Bernadette's gender performance are more subtle and more careful and aiming toward creating a natural expression of a genuine feminine self. Her on-stage performance of gender is theatrical; her off-stage performance is aimed at revealing identity rather than its parody.

Like other stereotypes, emotion stereotypes can be powerful filters of information that the individual takes in about the world. Emotion stereotypes are but one component of the larger network of implicit and explicit beliefs that each of us holds regarding emotion. Some beliefs may reflect idiosyncrasies of personal experience, while others are threads in the fabric of a shared culture. In this chapter I focus on those shared beliefs about emotion and the role they play in defining and maintaining the beliefs we have about gender difference. I also propose that our beliefs about emotion play a central role in defining the differences between male/masculine and female/feminine, and through their cultural representation these beliefs provide the framework for the individual's acquisition and practice of a gendered identity.

As previously discussed, research on ordinary emotion, whether that research is concerned with specific emotions such as anger, or global concepts such as emotionality, has framed the question simply as "Do women and men (or girls and boys) differ or are they similar when some specific behavior or trait is measured?" This approach is flawed in that it is little more than a descriptive exercise and cannot tell us what causes, moderates, or maintains that difference. The key to answering questions about gender is to try to understand the contexts in which gender effects show up. This means we must shift from merely describing what women and men, boys and girls do and believe, to examining those beliefs and behaviors as they operate in the ongoing social relationships within which those beliefs and behaviors have meaning. In theorizing context, the growing empirical research on gender differences in emotion reveals a pattern showing that gender's greatest effect lies less in what each sex knows about emotion than in what each sex is likely to do with that knowledge. If we take a look at existing gender differences research within the framework of social *contexts*, the story of the gender-emotion relationship is transformed. The new perspective enables us to move beyond enumerating differences to explaining when, why, and how they might occur. As important, it helps to train our focus on the malleable and multidimensional nature of gender.

Beliefs about emotion are gender coded

Many of our bedrock beliefs about emotion can easily and readily be articulated by children as well as adults. We could call these the "everyone knows" category of beliefs about emotion, as in "everyone knows that . . . " expressing too much emotion is immature, or holding emotion in is bad for your health, or emotion is irrational. These emotion truisms also frequently have a gendered character in the way that they are connected to beliefs about what is more typical, natural, or appropriate for one sex or the other. Probably the most easily recognized gender-coded belief is the emotion master stereotype that equates emotionality and femaleness. Emotion-specific gender stereotypes are also common. Preschoolers and adults, for example, believe that males experience more anger but less sadness than females.[2]

Other emotion beliefs, however, are not so easily articulated. We could call these the "I know it when I see it" category of beliefs. In some respects these beliefs constitute what we don't know we "know." What do we look for when we judge whether someone is being emotionally honest, speaking from the heart? What do we use to tell us whether our own feelings are genuine, strong enough, or under control? We may not be able to put our knowledge into words, but we conduct our emotional lives guided by it. These tacitly held beliefs ground our understanding of emotion and in ordinary discourse may seem simply to be a manifestation of emotion's "natural" character. Further, what we don't know that we "know" can be as gendered as what "everyone knows."

Karen and Brian "get emotional"

To see if people evaluate the "emotional" responses of men and women differently, Jill Crowley and I developed a questionnaire which contained scenarios that portrayed both stereotypic and counter-stereotypic gendered emotion. Each questionnaire contained one scenario depicting a male (Brian) or female (Karen) actor responding to an emotionally provoking situation. Each scenario described the actor responding to one of four emotionally provoking situations. Their responses were either described as "emotional" or "sad," "angry," "happy," or "enthusiastic" depending on the situation. In selecting the scenarios, we attempted to provide respondents with situations that were close enough to their own daily experiences to be personally meaningful.

The questionnaire consisted of both closed-ended and open-ended questions. The closed-ended questions assessed respondents' attitudes about the person in the scenario on several dimensions. These included judgments about the appropriateness, control, and intensity of the response, and the degree to which the response was caused by personality or situational factors. The last question was open-ended. The question asked whether the respondent had created a picture of the scenario in her or his imagination, and if so, to describe the picture.

"Emotional Brian" and "emotional Karen" were both seen as feeling more intensely and having less control than the angry Karen or Brian. Responses to the question about perceived control and appropriateness showed that people felt that "emotional" responses were less controlled and less appropriate than responses described by specific emotion terms. Yet the emotional label does not carry all meaning. This corroborated what I had found concerning people's assessments of "emotional" behavior in an earlier project in which I had asked people to "think of the most emotional person you know." In that work I had found that my respondents viewed "emotionality" as a tendency to respond too quickly or too much to an emotion-precipitating event. It was also clear that the criteria for "too much" and "too quickly" were in the eye of the beholder – as in "this is not how *I* would respond" or "this is not what *I* think is appropriate" (Shields, 1987). Emotional Brian is understood to have a very good reason for his anger: he was described in terms that convey a much greater degree of focus, self-control, and time-limited response than the emotional Karen. And when the label contradicted the evaluators' ideas of when and how it can be applied to a male, they changed the target to conform to the rules. The combination of closed-ended and open-ended responses enabled us to pin down the gender specificity of emotionality. In one scenario, Karen or Brian had just discovered that her or his car had been stolen ("Brian was emotional when he found out that his car had been stolen"). When both Karen and Brian were described as emotional in this scenario, people not only made inferences about them, but made judgments about what it meant to be "emotional" in this context: being "emotional" meant something different for each. When both Brian and Karen were described as "emotional," people attributed Karen's reaction more to her personality. In other words, he *acts* emotional (if provoked); she *is* emotional (whenever).[3] The open-ended responses corroborated this interpretation.

- [I imagined] Karen at a parking lot crying h[y]sterically because her car had been stolen. She lacked control and was too emotional for that particular situation.
- [I imagined] a woman (Karen) standing in the parking lot crying, looking around for her car, clutching the keys in her hand.
- Karen's car got ripped off and she flipped!! Started screaming and crying[;] no one could calm her down.

Responses to Brain's emotional behavior were markedly different. When writing about their impressions of the scenario, people seemed to make excuses for Brian's emotional behavior and attribute his reaction to the situation. Respondents tended to put themselves into the situation more often and downplay or rationalize Brian's emotional response. Following are some of the statements that people made about emotional Brian:

- I just imagined any average reaction (i.e., my own) if I found out that my car was stolen. I just imagined that he probably worked pretty hard for his car, and that he had taken care of it, so of course it would be upsetting.
- I assume Brian's initial response was shock but then weigh[ing] out the consequences he realized life goes on. There is probably disappointment but he can live with it.
- I thought about how upset I would be if someone stole my car. I imagined Brian as being shocked and upset and confused about what to do next.

Our respondents interpreted the meaning of "emotional" differently when applied to Brian rather than Karen. The stereotypical feminine "emotional" characteristics did not come to mind when evaluating Brian. It appears that beliefs about emotion, at least in part, depend on gender knowledge. Carol Martin and her colleagues have also observed this interplay of gender knowledge and emotion knowledge in young children. In one study, they found that preschoolers recall counter-gender-stereotypic emotional displays in still cartoons as if they were gender "correct."[4]

The plasticity of emotion language

Open-ended responses to other scenarios indicated that people not only understood the meaning of emotion terms to fit their beliefs about gender, but understood gender in terms of stereotypic beliefs about emotion. For example, when Brian was described as "sad" in one scenario ("Brian was sad when he found out that his dog had died"), people seemed to adjust Brian's age to reconcile their conception of maleness with the emotion. More often than not, when asked to describe their impressions of Brian in this scenario, respondents referred to him as a boy. We interpreted this as an important expression of beliefs about gendered emotionality. The implication here seems clear: Brian is not exhibiting "manly" emotion, so he must not be a man. In other words, when people were confronted with counter-stereotypical emotion reactions, they either redefined that emotion to fit stereotypical beliefs about gender or redefined gender to fit stereotypical beliefs about emotion. The semantic flexibility of emotion labels is not lost on people who use the rhetoric of emotion for political ends. Listen carefully to politicians, political commentators, and "spin doctors" and you will hear very artful use of emotion descriptors. In one of our earliest studies on beliefs about appropriate emotion, Kathleen MacDowell and I found that political affiliation predicted how emotional behavior was described (Shields and MacDowell, 1987). We examined commentary that immediately followed the nationally-televised debate between 1984 vice-presidential candidates George Bush (R) and Geraldine Ferraro (D). Ferraro, you may recall, was the first woman to run on the presidential ticket of a major party, and she had to be mindful of the thin line that separates the expression of enthusiasm from the appearance of emotionalism. Her performance in the nationally-televised vice-presidential candidates' debate was especially impressive. With women so often and so easily portrayed as overly emotional, Ferraro's professional demeanor dented the stereotype. How did the audience see her and her opponent, George Bush? What the audience saw in the debate was in no small way influenced by political allegiances. Asked for comments after the debate, Maureen Reagan, activist Republican and daughter of Ronald Reagan, who was then President, said "I think the vice-president did an excellent job. I felt very comfortable with his positions and with the way he expressed himself. And I like a little emotion in my vice-presidential debates. I get real bored real easy with people who just sort of lounge along . . . " When queried as to whether Representative Ferraro was lounging, Reagan replied, "Well, if the shoe fits . . . " Contrast this account of events with liberal feminist Gloria Steinem's reasons for concluding that Ferraro had won the debate: "Because she was calm and presidential and in command of the facts, and Bush was shrill and hysterical." Both Steinem and Reagan were well aware of the potential impact of her words and chose those words carefully. In each case the presence or absence of appropriate emotion was the factor selected to justify an opinion. The careful selection of words to describe emotion can make all the difference to political "spin"!

Who is Karen?

In working to sort out the way in which emotionality is gendered, we were confronted with the problem that besets much of the research on stereotyping research, that is, *whose* stereotype is it anyway? Research of the past twenty years has shown that gender stereotypes are constituted of separate components – physical appearance, traits, behaviors, and occupational status – that are relatively independent (Deaux and

Lewis, 1984). Furthermore, there are distinctive within-gender stereotypes as well. This suggests that study of emotion stereotypes ought to factor in racial ethnicity and social class as they define stereotypes. When participants are left to their own imagination, they imagine a white target. And when they do, gender emotion stereotypes are *very* easy to find and *very* noticeable. Next to no information comes from studies of gender emotion stereotypes because they routinely leave out the important variable of racial ethnicity. On the other hand, studies of racial stereotypes rarely specify the gender of the target. In one of the few studies to try to understand how stereotypes of women vary by race and class, Hope Landrine (1985) asked undergraduates to identify stereotypes associated with "white woman," "middle-class woman," "black woman," and "lower-class woman." The role that emotion-related descriptors played in each stereotype is quite revealing. White women were rated significantly higher than black women on the terms "dependent," "emotional," and "passive" – all of which are part of the classic stereotype of female emotionality. Some of the written comments in our Karen and Brian study suggested to us that just as our research participants changed Brian from boy to man to suit the stereotypes consonant with individual emotion scenarios, so too, they presumed that Karen and Brian were white.[5] If emotions researchers continue to be concerned with when and how stereotypes matter in evaluation of others, we must do so within a framework that includes attention to the interaction of variables like gender, status, and racial ethnicity – not separately, but as they mutually affect observers' judgments.

Beliefs about emotion code gender

If we examine the features that define the difference between concepts of masculine and feminine, we find that beliefs about emotion are at the core. The history of how the scientific constructs of psychological masculinity and femininity ("M" and "F" respectively) codified gender stereotypes usefully illustrates this point (Shields, 1991b). One of the most striking features of M/F measures is that they are heavily loaded with emotion-relevant items. The central role played by emotion-related concepts in differentiating genders is dramatically illustrated in scientific psychology's efforts to measure and quantify femininity and masculinity as psychological attributes. The systematic search for stable enduring traits that unambiguously distinguish one sex psychologically from the other was an enterprise begun in earnest in the 1920s by Lewis Terman, today better known for his contributions to the study of intellectually gifted children. His research on personality traits, like his work on intelligence, was grounded in a presupposition of the preeminence of biological factors in determining the capacities of the individual. Terman's work and the work of those who follow show that beliefs about emotion and emotionality have been a major criterion for differentiating between psychological femininity and masculinity.[6]

Femininity, masculinity, and sexual "inverts"

The first M/F scale, developed by Terman and his former PhD student Catherine Cox Miles, was a questionnaire comprised of over 450 multiple-choice and yes/no items in each of its two forms. The development and applications of the scale, dubbed the Attitude-Interest Analysis Test to disguise its purpose, are discussed in Terman and Miles' 1936 book, *Sex and Personality*.[7] The scale proved impossible to validate against external criteria. It had low reliability, it was uncorrelated with behavioral measures predicted to be related to it, and peak scores were not obtained by adults, but by boys and girls – at different ages. Nevertheless, Terman and Miles concluded that because the masculine and feminine items were empirically identified, that is, distinguished on the basis of different patterns of response to them by boys and girls, the test was "automatically validated" (p. 89).[8]

The rationale that Terman gives for pursuing the development of an instrument for measurement of masculinity and femininity is quite revealing. Acknowledging the changing facts of social life, specifically the "growing tendency to concede equality or near equality [between the sexes] with respect to general intelligence and the majority of special talents" (pp. 1–2), Terman goes on to point out the persistence of beliefs in the inherent, fundamental differences between women and men. Terman asserts that even though "observers do not agree in regard to the multitudinous attributes which are supposed to differentiate" women and men, "the composite pictures yielded by majority opinion stand out with considerable clearness." As Terman summarizes them, attributes of masculinity and femininity are almost exclusively affective or expressive in character. It is worth reproducing an extended quote in which Terman summarizes the putative differences, because it so clearly illustrates the prevailing gender-emotion stereotype and the subtle changes in that profile that have occurred in the decades since his book's publication. Terman masterfully captures the prevailing beliefs about the ways in which women differ from men – and does so by expressing how the female deviates from the male standard.

> In modern Occidental cultures, at least, the typical woman is believed to differ from the typical man in the greater richness and variety of her emotional life and in the extent to which her everyday behavior is emotionally determined. In particular, she is believed to experience

in greater degree than the average man the tender emotions, including sympathy, pity, and parental love; to be more given to cherishing and protective behavior of all kinds. Compared with man she is more timid and more readily overcome by fear. She is more religious and at the same time more prone to jealousy, suspicion, and injured feelings. Sexually she is by nature less promiscuous than man, so coy rather than aggressive, and her sexual feelings are less specifically localized in her body [!]. Submissiveness, docility, inferior steadfastness of purpose, and a general lack of aggressiveness reflect her weaker conative tendencies. Her moral life is shaped less by principles than by personal relationships, but thanks to her lack of adventurousness she is much less subject than man to most types of criminal behavior. Her sentiments are more complex than man's and dispose her personality to refinement, gentility, and preoccupations with the artistic and cultural. (p. 2)

Note that the attributes of the typical feminine character are, with the exception of some aspects of sexual behavior and morality, defined in terms of emotion. It is also telling that Terman provides no corresponding description of the typical man: he is the standard and she is what he is not.[9]

From stereotype to scientific construct

If the distinctive character of women was so widely agreed upon, why did Terman need a test to measure it? Terman asserted that his aim was to "enable the clinician or other investigator to obtain a more exact and meaningful, as well as a more objective, rating of those aspects of personality in which the sexes tend to differ" (p. 6). Terman's protestations of objectivity notwithstanding, the only application he discusses at length is the diagnosis of "sexual inversion." In Terman's view homosexual men were psychologically feminine; lesbians were psychologically masculine, and there was some urgency to their detection.[10] Although their inventory is no longer used by psychologists, Terman and Miles' M/F scale was the first of many paper and pencil tests to measure psychological "masculinity" and "femininity." The many tests that followed include items or indices of "emotionality" like the original Attitude-Interest Analysis Test. Items usually refer to expressiveness (emotional or otherwise) and/or items indicating awareness of mood or emotion.[11]

By the early 1970s the assumption that masculinity and femininity represented opposite anchors on a unidimensional, bipolar continuum of "sex role identity" was beginning to be challenged.[12] The alternative view that rapidly became popular is that Masculinity and Femininity should be construed as independent dimensions of gender-as-trait, and that each of these dimensions can be expressed on its own bipolar continuum: high M to low M; high F to low F. Thus, an individual could be located on both M and F continua. The original aim of M/F tests – to identify gender "inverts" – was eclipsed by concerns with a new kind of psychological health. The search for an ideal way to measure the psychological aspect of sex as a stable, enduring personality trait continued, but with the new assumption that masculinity and femininity, as independent dimensions of personality unrelated to biological sex and sexuality, would *both* be expressed to some degree in any individual. This "new and improved" conceptualization of masculinity and femininity as combinatory underlay Sandra Bem's proposal that the psychologically healthy individual is one who is androgynous, that is, a person who exhibits a balance of high-scoring M and high-scoring F components.[13] Even with the shift of emphasis from the bipolar model of masculinity and femininity to the inclusive model of androgyny, however, emotion-related traits continued to figure prominently in measuring and defining psychological gender.[14] The modern conceptualization of androgyny assumes that the traits that identify the well-adjusted individual are not sex-specific, but that high quantities of both stereotypically masculine and feminine characteristics are necessary: Androgyny thus becomes the new standard of mental health for both sexes.[15] Within the construct of androgyny, emotion and emotion-relevant attributes are not refigured as neutral human capacities; instead, emotion retains its place as a category which contains specific feminine and masculine attributes whose sum defines the whole (i.e., androgynous) person. The content of masculine and feminine categories within the androgyny model is no different from that which defines the older bipolar M/F model; only valorization of those categories has changed. Whereas in the older, unidimensional model, emotion-related traits *discriminated* the M pole from the F pole, androgyny scales employed emotion-related traits to *define* the separate dimensions of M and F. Over the years the tests themselves have not changed much in content, but the interpretation of the results has.[16]

Controlling emotion/controlled by emotion

The prevailing emotion stereotype plays a conspicuous role in discriminating and defining the concepts of masculine and feminine. Beliefs about the gendered nature of inexpressivity and emotionality form the keystone of the masculinity and femininity profile. Despite (or perhaps because of) the patently sex-stereotypical content of these M/F inventories, psychologists embraced at one time the view that the extent to which an individual describes himself or herself in terms of stereotypes is a legitimate indicator of healthy psychological gender. This in spite of the fact that M/F scales are not good predictors of either gendered behavior or other "traits" hypothesized to be related to psychological masculinity and femininity.[17] The list of "masculine" traits included on M/F inventories bears a strong resemblance to the attributes that define masculine stereotypes. In both cases there are many items that clearly designate felt emotion or include some emotional component (e.g., sexual interest, aggressiveness, competitiveness, anger) or that specifically refer to the *active* suppression or management of felt emotion or emotional expressiveness.[18] Checklists or rating scales are more often used than open-ended response formats in the study of gender stereotypes, and because items for new checklists are typically drawn from previously developed checklists and scales, sociohistorical shifts in stereotype content are slow to be reflected in research. In fact, Richard Ashmore and Frances Del Boca (1986) observe that, as a result, the major dimensions or themes identified in research on gender stereotypes in the US are typically some variant of the instrumental-expressive dimensions identified decades ago by Talcott Parsons. People who rate themselves as possessing a high degree of masculine characteristics on M/F scales also endorse emotion beliefs/values that are stereotypically masculine, whereas subjects high on femininity endorse the feminine.[19] The relation between M/F scores and emotion-related attributes may be explained by the fact that both measure the same attribute: the extent to which the individual believes she or he conforms to gender-coded emotion stereotypes. Janet Spence (1993), for example, has shown that self-ratings on the single items "masculine" and "feminine" are each significantly correlated expressive items for women (positive correlation with "feminine," negative correlation with "masculine") and instrumental items for men (negative correlation with "feminine," positive correlation with "masculine") on the two most widely used M/F self-report scales. Spence concludes, therefore, that scores on these M/F scales are probably related to gender-linked characteristics and behaviors only "as they happen to be influenced by instrumentality and expressiveness *per se*" (p. 624).

Ashmore and Del Boca's work suggests that the thematic glue that holds the "unemotional male" stereotype together is a notion of self-control, including tendencies to control expression of emotion and tendencies to lead and control others. The contrasting theme for the female stereotype is one of being controlled by some force, whether one's own emotions, the situation (e.g., "excitable in a crisis"), or other people. Stereotype structure suggests that the gender-emotion link entails more than a simple association between gender and the presence or absence of emotion or particular type of emotion. Gender and emotion, at least in the US today, seem especially linked through ideas about women's and men's capacities for *management* of their emotion.

Doing gender through doing emotion

In everyday conversation "gender" calls to mind a single unified feature of personality. Gender does not actually operate in that way. Janet Spence (1984; 1993) has shown that gender is a multidimensional phenomenon which is only partially represented by the expressivity-instrumentality components of conventional M/F scales. By multidimensional she means that "the various categories of attributes, attitudes, preferences, and behaviors that empirically distinguish between men and women in a given culture do not contribute to a single underlying property but instead to a number of more or less independent factors," (Spence, 1993, p. 625). These independent factors include personality traits in the conventional psychological sense; political and social values, such as attitudes toward women; sex role behavior; sexual orientation; and core gender identity.[20]

Gender also seems to function as actively created, negotiated, and performed and shaped through social interaction.[21] Theories that construe gender as performance are very different from earlier generations of theory that try to pin down the constituent traits of masculinity, femininity, and androgyny. It is in the practice – sometimes self-conscious, but most often not – of the behaviors, beliefs, and "style" of being a boy/man or girl/woman that the multidimensionality of gender characteristics becomes a coherent, unique gendered self. Like a play or piece of music, the whole comes together through performance, and audience is crucial to performance. Deaux and Major (1987) describe how three aspects of the context (expectations of perceivers, self-systems of the actor, and situational cues) together mediate gender performance. In this view, interpersonal context (perceivers' expectations and the nature of the situation) is construed as *integral* to gender performance; context is not simply the medium within which gendered behavior occurs.[22]

Why perform gender? What is at stake that makes people so attentive to doing gender the right way that seems natural to you, to me, and to anybody who happens to be watching? The gender-as-performance approach focuses on doing gender as a way to create and maintain identity. Deaux and Major, for example, proposed that the performance of gender, as a socially-embedded negotiation of identity, is directed toward self-confirmation and self-presentation. Gender performance as verification of the authenticity of the self is, I propose, the key link between gender and emotion.[23] If gender is not an achieved state, but something that actively is created through ongoing practice, it has a certain flexibility that enables us to adjust our performance to meet the variation in demands across relationships and social contexts. At the same time, gender would never truly be a finished product. We remain vulnerable as gender performers, and questions of whether one is a "real man" or "womanly enough" lurk at the borders of a secure sense of self.

What's so special about emotion?

As a social identity, gender is multi-faceted and is expressed through appearance and behavior. The *what* of gender can be learned from physical appearance and from the tangible artifacts of social organization. Barbie® models womanhood for girls as surely as toys of pretend destruction signal manly activity to boys. In a holiday catalog, web e-tailer *Amazon.com* even offers gender-specific guidelines for a range of gifts that are not themselves explicitly gender-coded. (Apparently gender neutral gifts do not sell on their own and customers must be able to comfortably distinguish between "girl gifts" for girls and "boy gifts" for boys.) For boys ages 2 to 4 Amazon suggests *Big Silver Space Shuttle*, an interactive book to "blast off at bedtime"; for girls, the choice is the picture book *And If the Moon Could Talk*, so she can "head straight to dreamland." He *goes* to the moon, she *listens* to it! But gender is more than what we do, it is also *how* we do it. The accoutrements of gender, by themselves, are not sufficient to create a fully successful enactment of "masculine," "feminine," or a self-conscious alternative to either. Successful performance of gender as social identity must pass the judgments of others, and more important, it must be experienced as an authentic expression of the self. Neither older children nor adults believe that to "dress like a girl" or "throw like a girl" actually makes one a girl. Appearance must have presence. Gender is expressed through the style and tone of behavior – *how* the dress is worn, *how* throwing meshes with other actions and the intent behind them.

Emotion plays a role in doing gender in two pivotal ways. First, beliefs about emotion reveal the distinctive "how" of being a gendered person; doing emotion – expressing emotional feelings and emotion values – signals one's genuineness as female or male, feminine or masculine.[24] For example, because emotionally expressive behavior is gender coded, an important component of the child's gender practice (i.e., enacting a gendered identity) involves practicing emotion – its expression, values, interests – as befits gender. Doing gender through doing emotion encompasses not only emotional display, of course, but also emotion values (e.g., real girls value emotional self-disclosure) and beliefs about emotional experience (e.g., anger is appropriate only when one's rights are violated). Second, the actual occurrence of emotion itself is part of doing gender, mirroring the operation of the individual's self-conceptualization. Deaux (1993) has proposed that the individual's formulation and reformulation of identity is fashioned as a response to the events and circumstances of one's life. As a dimension of gender, emotion beliefs and values, and their instantiation in emotion episodes, may provide continuity through formation and change in the individual's social identities.

Can "acting" be the real thing?

I want to emphasize again that neither "doing" emotion nor "doing" gender is a deliberate or even self-conscious act. Certainly one *can* deliberately make the effort to conform to or reject conventional gender rules and one can play at exaggerating, flouting, or subverting gender conventions. The sense in which I am using "doing" gender and "doing" emotion, however, differentiates between superficial management of behavior and expression and behavior that expresses beliefs, values, and goals vital to creating a sense of personal identity. Sometimes my students have difficulty with the notion that *genuine* emotion or *genuine* gender could have any discernible "acting" component – after all, they argue, if it's "just acting," it cannot be genuine. It is important, I stress, not to oversimplify and equate the creation of a gendered identity with the deliberate manipulation of one's "social face." Postponing an appointment with the excuse "I have to visit a sick friend," or meeting a rude customer with a friendly smile might be socially necessary, but it is "just acting." I think it is the implied dishonesty and inauthenticity of this type of deliberate emotion acting that makes it difficult to imagine genuine emotion, emotion subjectively experienced as consistent with one's true self, as anything other than totally spontaneous.[25]

Carolyn Saarni's extensive research on children's acquisition and use of emotion display rules offers a striking illustration of the near interchangeability of doing gender and doing emotion. *Display rules* are the often tacit social rules directing when, how much, and which emotions should be expressed to others. Although Saarni finds no gender differences in children's *knowledge* about affective display rules and the conditions for dissembling, gender differences in *performance* occur, particularly in older children. Rather than view them as contradictory or disingenuous positions, we may regard these statements as expressions of values which constitute a gendered identity. In one study, for example, she interviewed children regarding their beliefs about emotional dissembling (Saarni, 1988). She found very few gender differences, and these were primarily due to reports of the oldest girls (ages 13 to 14) included in the study. These girls were highly sophisticated about emotion in the sense of being keenly attuned to emotion's social functions. Thus they were quite knowledgeable about the strategic functions of emotional communication in relationships, including some of the apparent contradictions in how emotion expertise is best deployed. They reported, for example, that they value honest expression of emotion to peers, yet they also reported that expressive dissembling is very effective. In other words, by early adolescence these girls had learned that certain positive social values connected to emotion are simultaneously connected to one's identity as a girl. Although they probably had not expressly articulated this relationship to themselves, they had learned that one way to be a genuine girl is to value emotion and know how to use it. One eighth grade girl, for example, described her decision to show emotion as reflecting a kind of balancing act: "It depends on the situation and if my feelings are real strong; also how other people act with me and what I thought of them would make a difference. Also if it was a group and not just one person, I would probably not show my feelings as much" (p. 290).[26] So, when Saarni's research participants endorse the importance of occasionally altering one's emotional expression, and then themselves use smiles to hide disappointment, they are also prodding their own felt emotion into line with what they believe it ought to be for that occasion.[27]

Emotion beliefs give one a position from which to assess one's own emotional life, and thereby, one's genuineness or authenticity as a person. The emotional sharing that especially characterizes girls' friendships (Maccoby, 1990) is part of learning how to "do girl" at a certain moment in development, and over the longer term, this earlier experience with emotional sharing defines the parameters for when and how to engage in some kinds of emotional self-regulation. In this way, emotion beliefs can color the individual's expectations for the near term regarding the consequences of expressing or withholding felt emotion. In the larger scheme of things, emotion beliefs are recruited in creating and refining the definition of mature, appropriate behavior, both prescriptively (e.g., a "real man" responds appropriately with anger when he is deprived of what he is entitled to) and proscriptively (e.g., a "real man" does not cry like a girl). Children have ample opportunity to learn and practice gender-coded emotion.[28] Chapter 5 covers the developmental course of learning and practicing gendered emotion, so here I will give just one example. The peer group is an especially potent medium for rehearsal of practicing and coming to understand emotion (von Salisch, 1997). Amy Sheldon (1992; 1993) found that white middle-class preschool girls employ a conflict-management style within same-sex groups that is simultaneously self-assertive and conciliatory, whereas boys tend to engage in a larger proportion of coercive talk. She compared two same-sex trios' progression of conflict over possession of a plastic toy pickle. The three boys' dispute consisted mostly of rounds of opposition-insistence-more opposition. The girls, too, used physical coercion and threats, but made more attempts at jointly negotiating a resolution to end the pickle fight. Sheldon is cautious about extrapolating from these instances to girls' groups and boys' groups more generally, but she points out that the main difference between the groups was not in the expression of conflict per se, but in the girls' attention to coming to some solution to the problem even in the course of trying to get one's way.

One way to think about how "doing emotion" may simultaneously be "doing gender" is to think about the ways in which beliefs about emotion can function as a type of gender schema.[29] Beliefs about who should show emotion and how that emotion should be displayed can exert a dramatic effect on how people think about information that is in any way linked to gender. Research psychologists who study cognition, social behavior, and development use the term "schema" to describe "abstract expectations about how the world generally operates, built up from past experience with specific examples" (Fiske and Taylor, 1991, p. 554). Schemas tend to guide people to information that appears to have relevance to prior knowledge. Simplifying somewhat, we can say that schemas – to a certain degree – tend to direct us to pay attention to what we already know, and to give us a kind of script for dealing with uncertain or ambiguous situations. If emotion beliefs operate as gender schemas, they should also, like gender schemas, provide a basis for making inferences about ambiguous or partial information. In fact, they can affect how events or images are remembered. Psychologists Richard Fabes and Carol Martin and their collaborators revealed how influential emotion stereotypes can be in organizing children's recall of information about gender. They showed preschool children pictures of people expressing emotions that were stereotypic (e.g., boy angry) and counter-stereotypic (e.g., boy crying), then measured what children later recalled and where they made errors in the content of what they recalled.[30] Children were three times more likely to recall incorrectly the sex of the person expressing an emotion when the emotion was counter-stereotypic – for example, they reported having seen a *girl* rather than a boy cry. In other words, the children's understanding of emotion defined their expectations concerning gender. Boys were more likely to distort than were girls and there was more distortion for images of boys than of girls. Furthermore, children were more likely to recall sex-consistent emotions as being more intense than sex-inconsistent emotions, even though pictures did not objectively differ in intensity of expression. If preschoolers' recall of pictures can be affected by how well those images conform to emotion stereotypes, what about other kinds of information? And what about older children and adults who ought to have developed sufficient sophistication to be resistant to the tricks that stereotypes can play on memory?

Gender categories are used to make sense of gender-ambiguous behavior, as can be seen in caregivers' gender-coded contingent responses to infants. The late Beverly Fagot and her colleagues (Fagot and Hagan, 1991; Fagot and Leinbach, 1993) hypothesized that caregivers are particularly susceptible to using gender stereotypes to guide their reactions to infants and toddlers, because gender-ambiguous behavior lends itself to being read in gender stereotypic ways. And most relevant to doing-emotion-as-doing-gender, the variety and intensity of infants' and toddlers' expressive behavior especially lends itself to contingent responding. For example, in one study (Fagot, Hagan, Leinbach, and Kronsberg, 1985) Fagot first observed adult caregivers with a playgroup of infants who were about one year old. These infants were observed again nearly a year later, again in small play groups and with daycare teachers minding each group. The investigators were particularly interested in whether gender would influence how adults responded to the children's assertive behavior and attempts to communicate with the adults. They chose these two areas of behavior because of their associations with gender stereotypes. If gender stereotypes influence how adults respond, then we would expect to see the adults act differently toward infants of each sex even if there was no difference in the girls' and the boys' behavior. Indeed, in the infant group the researchers found that, even though boys and girls showed the same amount and intensity of assertive and communicative behavior, adults responded to the infants in a sex stereotypic way: they paid more attention to boys' assertive acts and intense communications and more to girls' mild communications. That is, girls were noticed when they were quiet "good girls," and boys when they were noisy and "acting like boys." By the time the toddlers were observed, however, the girls and boys had learned their gender lessons well – the toddlers' behavior had become more defined by gender and the adults responded accordingly. So the adults' gender schemas, that is, their expectations of how boys and girls are likely to act, guided them to see girls' and boys' expressive behavior differently and respond to each sex differently. That differential treatment, Fagot and her colleagues theorize, sets the stage for toddlers to acquire more gender-defined repertoires which, in turn, influence how adults will respond to them. The actor, the perceiver, and the context – to use Deaux and Major's (1987) terminology – are mutually implicated in producing and reproducing gender through practice.

Gender, emotion, and identity

I believe some of the most powerful evidence that to do emotion is to do gender comes from a line of research that shows how gender-coded stereotypes of emotion can actually cue people's self-assessment. Gender-coded emotion beliefs tend to come into play especially when we retrospectively think about our own emotion experience in very general terms. For example, it is difficult to produce an accurate count of one's own emotion episodes. How many times were you angry last week? How frequently were you irritable over the past month? On average, how many times do you experience a positive emotion over the course of a day? The experiential dimension of emotion usually does not provide sufficient hard data to allow a person to make a reliable quantitative self-assessment without keeping a diary or noting the emotion episodes when they occur. Most of us, however, do not do this on a day to day basis. We may have strong or specific recollections of individual occurrences because of their meaning to us or because something about the situation or others' response to us made us pay attention, but not as verifiable a record as meals eaten, days missed from work, fights with spouse, altercations with kids over their messy rooms or being late to school. Moskowitz (1986) proposed that self-reports are most effective in assessing characteristics that have stability, coherence, and generality across situations. Gender-coded emotion beliefs have all of these features, whereas recall of felt emotion does not. When research participants do not have much immediate information about experience, features of the research context may trigger the use of gender stereotypes as a heuristic device. We know that research participants are clearly aware of gender-coded emotion standards, and that this knowledge can influence what people say about themselves in research settings. To be sure, gender differences in the occurrent report of emotional experience are sometimes found (e.g., Grossman and Wood, 1993). More typical, though, is the finding reported by Banaji and LaFrance (cited in LaFrance, 1993) that self-reports of emotionality obtained in a public setting tend to conform to gender stereotypes, while self-reports that are made anonymously and privately are less likely to.

Stereotypes as a cognitive short-cut

Gender-coded emotion beliefs can actually shape individuals' interpretation of their own emotional experience under certain conditions. My colleagues Michael Robinson and Joel Johnson and I explored the conditions under which people use gender stereotypes about emotion to make judgments about the emotions of themselves and others (Robinson,

Johnson, and Shields, 1998). We hypothesized that when people lack concrete information about emotion experience and behavior, they rely on stereotypes as a kind of heuristic device to make inferences about what happened. In a first study participants either played or watched a competitive word game (actual game conditions) or imagined themselves playing or watching the game (hypothetical condition). Participants in the actual game conditions made judgments about emotion either immediately after they played the game or after a delay of one day (observers) or one week (players). With the passage of time, both self-reports of emotional experience and perceptions of the emotional displays of others showed an influence of gender stereotypes. Self-reports as well as the perceptions of observers more closely matched stereotypes the more distant in time from the event. In a second study we compared self-ratings with ratings of hypothetical others and found that participants who rated others were more likely to use gender stereotypes of emotion than were participants who rated themselves. Lisa Feldman Barrett and her colleagues have also found that global, retrospective self-reports tend to match gender stereotypes, but that on-line momentary self-descriptions do not. These empirical results converge with conclusions drawn in research reviews that show how stereotypes may serve as a heuristic device when distinctive details of experience have faded from memory or when people are quizzed about fuzzy concepts like emotionality.[31]

But why apply stereotypes to the *self*? Why rely on gender stereotypes, stereotypes that under other circumstances people are loath to apply to themselves, stereotypes that people (at least our college student research participants) reject as insufficiently representative of their own individuality. Why do emotion stereotypes sometimes fill in the gaps of memory or inform one's answer to a vague and general question? Perhaps the answers lie in the narratives that we construct to understand ourselves as human beings. As the evidence above suggests, self-evaluation is not a deliberate or self-conscious act, but is implicit in the question "What do *I* feel? What do *I* express?" where that *I* is gendered.

Emotion narratives as identity narratives

Crawford, Kippax, Onyx, Gault, and Benton (1992) explored this question using the technique of "memory-work" to examine the ways in which women construct their emotions. Through collective discussions of group members' individual memories of emotions on a specific theme, they searched for common elements and meanings, and then further distilled these commonalities into a sense of what their individual reflections meant for a more general understanding of women's

emotional lives. They found emotional interaction to have strong over-
tones of "gendered-ness." For anger episodes, for example, they concluded that women are condemned as neurotic if they show uncontrolled anger, but they are also censured for suppressing anger and are
then labeled depressed. Crawford *et al.*'s work offers a convincing illustration of the inseparability of gender and emotion as aspects of the
social self.

Emotion beliefs as gender schemas may also help to explain a somewhat puzzling difference between children's reports about their emotional experience and the reports of adults. In the previous chapter I
summarized how age is related to findings of gender difference and
similarity in several different emotion domains. In general, it is quite
unusual to find gender differences in emotion concepts or understanding at any age. In the area of emotional expression and control of that
expression, girls are much more savvy than boys by middle childhood,
and in reports about one's own experience, gender differences do not
regularly occur until adolescence. As with adults, differences between
adolescent girls' and boys' accounts of emotional experience seem to be
limited to the specific areas of connecting emotion to relationships and
interpersonal situations, as well as a greater interest in talking about
emotion.

Gender differences in children's reports about emotional experience
begin to appear at about the same age at which they acquire the cognitive
flexibility that enables them to understand and apply multiple classification dimensions to gender. That is, just as they begin to show an
understanding that moms can work *and* be moms, their descriptions of
their own emotional experience begins more closely to resemble gender
stereotypes. This is curious. Why would stereotypic differences in self-
report emerge at the very time that cognitive capacities are advanced
enough to comprehend the complexities of gender? It may be that gender stereotypes provide a basis for making inferences about ambiguous
information. If so, as the individual develops an understanding of the
multidimensionality of gender, gender as *difference* becomes a kind of
heuristic device to bring some order or pattern to ambiguity. This may
be more than simple conjecture. Monica Biernat (1991) found the negative correlation between judgments about masculinity and femininity
increases with age (kindergarten to college students). That is, adults
judge gender in more oppositional terms than do children. Biernat interprets this trend as a shift from viewing masculinity and femininity as
separate categories to viewing gender as a unidimensional construct. In
other words, adults are more cognitively capable of making judgments
about people based on their individuating characteristics than on their

sex, yet adults are also more likely to view gender in oppositional terms: to be more masculine on a trait means being less feminine on that trait. Gender-coded emotion beliefs, like a unidimensional conceptualization of gender, tend to dichotomize male/female, masculine/feminine as distinct, nonoverlapping categories: feminine is emotional; masculine is not. Emotion beliefs could thus reassert gender *difference* in the face of gender-ambiguous or contradictory information. For example, told that "the man cried," the hearer makes gender inferences.[32] If emotion beliefs operate as gender schemas, the hearer would be likely to infer gender-consistent causes of the emotion, assuming, for example, that the man experienced a grave loss. The hearer would also infer gender-consistent consequences or outcomes of the emotion's occurrence. In other words, that when he cried, he did it in a "manly" restrained way. This is, in fact, what we found in our "Karen and Brian" research. When research participants responded to the scenario "Brian got emotional when his dog died," they often described Brian as a boy rather than a man, reconciling the emotion stereotype with the gender stereotype. Responding to "Brian got emotional when his car was stolen," their descriptions brought Brian's behavior into line with their expectations: Of course he was emotional, and he had a darn good reason to be!

The claim that I outline here is that beliefs about emotion are *central* to understanding the social construction and maintenance of gender-as-difference. Ideas about emotion pervade gender performance, both "doing" gender in gender's conventional sense of masculine and feminine, and, as I will discuss in later chapters, deliberate confrontation/subversion of those notions. To take just one example, emotional extravagance and emotion that is palpably signalled as "feminine" are central to the creation of gender parody by the drag queen trio in *Priscilla*. Without appropriation of a certain style of emotion, their act would not be much more than outrageous outfits and music by AƎBA.

Beliefs about gendered emotion can reveal what gender means, how gender operates, and how gender is negotiated in our relationships with others. In the following chapters I develop the theme that beliefs about emotion are routinely appropriated within popular culture to define and maintain beliefs about gender differences. Within the broad cultural context, beliefs about emotion serve to define the difference between masculine and feminine, male and female. Whether explicitly represented in statements of beliefs about emotion or more subtly transmitted via judgments about the appropriateness of others' emotions and emotional display, gender limits are clearly delineated by emotional standards. In our lived experience, beliefs about emotion are among the more powerful guides by which we understand ourselves as women and men.

Notes

1 Yaeger's work can be found at *http://www.artscomm.org/yaeger-emblems/*

2 See, for example, Fabes and Martin (1991), Karbon, Fabes, Carlo, and Martin (1992), and Plant, Hyde, Keltner and Devine (2000). I do need to add a *caveat* here that these and other stereotyping studies do not specify racial ethnicity of the target, and that there is evidence that gender emotion stereotypes are not equally pronounced or uniform across racial ethnic groups in the US.

3 This study is reported in Shields and Crowley (1996). This pattern parallels what we have found in advice literature directed to parents (Shields and Koster, 1989; Shields, Steinke, and Koster, 1995). In that work my students and I found that no matter what the date of publication, the childrearing philosophy, the prominence of emotion in the discussion, the sex of the author, the particular emotion under discussion, or any other variable we looked at, maternal emotion was portrayed as a barely-controllable tendency to "overreact" emotionally, and as inevitably damaging to the child's development. Father's emotion was also portrayed as having potentially harmful effects on the child's development, but when he is cautioned about emotional display, the caution is restricted to negative emotions elicited by *external* emotional hazards. The source of the problem is portrayed not as within the father, but as instigated by his wife, his job, or the children themselves.

4 Martin, Fabes, Eisenbud, Karbon, and Rose (1990). Templeton (1999) has reported that gender labels triggered gender-schematic processing of ambiguous situations (e.g., child character encountering a snake on the path).

5 Whom and what do the stereotypes reflect? It could be the projected self-image of the rater or an imagined universal. In any event, it seems that our respondents, in the absence of other individuating information, imagine the target as white, perhaps because of presumptions regarding who psychologists study. My students and I call this the "Barbie and Ken problem" because it seems that our research participants tend to imagine some idealized young and pretty white archetype unless we provide information to the contrary.

6 Accounts of the history of these measurement efforts are discussed extensively by Miriam Lewin (1984a, 1984b) and by Jill Morawski (1987).

7 This description of the M/F scale is drawn from Lewin (1984a). Quotations are taken from Terman and Lewis (1936). Terman's M/F scale contained seven subtests which had been normed on elementary and junior high school age students. One subtest, Emotional and Ethical Attitudes, Terman believed to be one of the two strongest and most reliable (the other was "Interests," in which he was so confident that it was weighted twice in computing the M/F score). The Emotional and Ethical Attitudes subtest was comprised of about 100 phrases that refer to people, things, or situations that may evoke specific emotions (anger, fear, pity, and disgust were the emotions tested) or that are "acts of various degrees of wickedness or badness" (p. 497).

8 By reliability psychologists mean that the scale or inventory measures consistently; by validity they mean that it measures what it is designed to measure. Indicators of reliability include, for example, consistency across the items included on the scale, consistency in results from one time of measurement to the next, and consistency across different forms of the same scale. Two

types of validity are generally used. First, does the test show predictable relationships with other hypothesized related or unrelated measures? Thus, a
measure of M/F should be positively correlated with other paper-and-pencil
measures of M/F related traits and behaviors that are presumed to reflect
M/F. Assumptions about erotic attachments and about conformity to gender
role behaviors led to the belief that these should be useful indicators of the
validity of M/F scales.

 9 Note that Terman states that his description pertains to Western culture,
perhaps implying that here there is a greater differentiation between male
and female personality. Also note that he begins the passage by saying that
"the typical woman *is believed* to differ from the typical man," but by the
end of the passage his language has shifted to describing what the typical
woman *is*.

10 Terman had intended to use this scale to show that gifted boys were not more
effeminate than boys of average intelligence. When the M/F scale failed to
differentiate intellectually gifted children from a control group of boys who
were not selected on the basis of intelligence, the project would have gone no
further, but for the "spectacular evidence" (p.14) of one high-feminine scor-
ing boy's interest in cross-dressing. Terman, like other psychologists of the
time, equated transvestitism and homosexuality, and pathologized homosexuality, particularly and almost exclusively male homosexuality. Terman's
preoccupation with what he and other psychologists termed "sexual
inversion" is reflected in the three chapters of *Sex and Personality* devoted
to male homosexuals. See Joseph Pleck's (1984) discussion of the early years
in psychological testing.

11 Most scales incorporate novel items as well as items from earlier scales.
The California Psychological Inventory (CPI), developed by Harrison Gough
(1952) specifically for use with normal, nonclinical populations, is today one
of the most widely used personality tests. The original fifty-nine-item femininity (Fem) scale (as well as a thirty-eight-item 1957 revision) includes
many emotion-related items, such as statements describing feelings of sensitivity, compassion, and fear (e.g., "I am somewhat afraid of the dark.") J.
P. Guilford's personality scale measured Masculinity via six subtests, four
of which are indices of self-reported emotional expressiveness or felt emotion of a particular type: Disgustfulness, Fearfulness, and Sympathy (high
scores indicate femininity) and Inhibition of Emotional Expression (high
scores indicate masculinity) (Guilford and Zimmerman, 1956). The M/F
scale of the original version of the Minnesota Multiphasic Personality Inventory (MMPI), published in 1943, is also rich with emotion-relevant items.
About one-third of the sixty-item M/F scale (Scale 5) pertains to altruism
and personal and emotional sensitivity; of these, ten items explicitly mention emotional experience or expression, for example, "I think I feel more
intensely than most people"; "Some of my family have habits that bother
and annoy me very much"; "I have been disappointed in love" (Dahlstrom,
Welsh, and Dahlstrom,1972; pp. 202–203). The MMPI is an empirically con-
structed scale, that is, items are not selected on the basis of theory, but because
they are responded to differently by a criterion group (who are presumed to
be high on the trait) compared to other groups or nonselected individuals.
So, for example, an MMPI scale that indicates hypochondriacal tendencies is
comprised of items that known hypochondriacs respond differently to than
do people with other psychological diagnoses. Lewin (1984b) reports that

the MMPI Scale 5 (the M/F scale) was validated first on a criterion group of thirteen gay men.

12 See, for example, Constantinople (1973). The earlier literature conflates facets of gender (satisfaction with sex assignment, conformity to sex-coded social role, etc.), erotic orientation, and core gender identity. Constantinople questioned what precisely these concepts of masculinity and femininity represent – Behavior? Preferences? Something else? Her observations foreshadowed themes in Unger (1979), Sherif (1982), and others who challenged the entire notion of M/F and androgyny as a unidimensional bundle of trait-like variables.

13 A balance between M and F in which both scores are low results in classification as "undifferentiated," which again illustrates the tendency in psychological research to valorize gender coding. Bem herself, however, challenges the necessity and social value of gender coding in *The Lenses of Gender* (Bem, 1993).

14 The concept of androgyny as a personality type has its modern source in the movement to measure gender as a psychological attribute. Since the 1970s it has become increasingly clear that M/F is not a rigid trait that reliably predicts an individual's behavior across time and situations. Self-report M/F inventories are now generally agreed to be measures of gender role self-concept rather than classic personality traits. In other words, it is more accurate to interpret responses on M/F questionnaires as representations of the respondent's self-image as it matches gender stereotypes than as a quantitative expression of a deeper psychological gender.

15 Morawski (1987) describes the link between the development of androgyny as a scientific concept and extra-scientific political reality. Jill Morawski (1987) tells the story of American psychology's search for ways to measure the apparently elusive quality of psychological "masculinity" and "femininity." She shows how a certain set of core assumptions have guided this enterprise from the beginning – even when it would seem at the surface level that androgyny was an absolutely revolutionary construct compared to the older M/F formulation. Despite the reformulation of sex role identity as ideally androgynous, she says, certain core assumptions of the older bipolar model of M/F were retained. For example, the notion that "masculine is direct, instrumental, and independent whereas feminine is indirect, expressive, and dependent" persisted (Morawski, 1987, p. 50).

16 The two most widely used tests of androgyny in psychological research today are the Bem Sex Role Inventory (BSRI) developed by Sandra Bem, and the Personal Attributes Questionnaire (PAQ) developed by Janet Spence and Robert Helmreich. The BSRI asks the subject to rate how frequently each of a list of adjectives are descriptive of him or her. Of the sixty items on the BSRI, forty are used in formulating the individual's M, F, and androgyny scores. Items reflecting emotion or concern with emotion comprise about half of the twenty items indicative of femininity, including affectionate, eager to soothe hurt feelings, warm, cheerful, tender, and shy. The M scale contains only two clearly emotion-related items (assertive; aggressive). The PAQ, which asks the subject to rate how descriptive a series of statements are about himself or herself, contains twenty-four items, six of which pertain directly to emotion: very emotional (F); not at all excitable in a major crisis (M); feelings not easily hurt (M-F); very aware of feelings of others (F); never cries (M-F); very warm in relations with others (F). Many other items may include an

emotional component, whether they refer to behavior (very aggressive) or a personality trait (feels very superior).

17 See Matlin (2000) for a discussion of what is and is not predicted by self-report measures of masculinity, femininity, and androgyny. Harris (1994) showed that twenty-plus years after its development, the BSRI still reflects American cultural definitions of dominant culture notions of masculinity and femininity, but less so for Latinos or African Americans. Miriam Lewin (1984b) ironically notes that Talcott Parsons, whose name has become irrevocably identified with the equation of instrumentality with males and expressivity with females, originally emphasized the causal role of sex discrimination and limited opportunities for college-educated women in promoting rigid gender roles. In his early work Parsons (1942) hypothesized that tensions in marriage resulted from a wife's need for marriage as a source of status as well as companionship, and that the husband's specialized occupational role brought about further strain on the marriage. This early acknowledgment of contextual tensions in women's roles gave way to Parsons' later, and better known expressivity-instrumentality formulation. By 1955 he had come to view gender roles as universal, inevitable, and functional, with the husband-father as the family's instrumental leader and the wife-mother as the expressive leader (Lewin, 1984b, p. 193). Although Parsons and Bales (1955) believed that they had identified a universal, functionally-based family relationship that provides stability to modern family life, Lewin concludes that they "put the stamp of social science validation upon a midcentury historical and economic *fait accompli*, the linking of the instrumental to the male and the expressive to the female roles, which they mistook for a universal element of social structure" (Lewin, 1984b, p. 195). Lewin attributes Parsons' shift in thinking in part to his own reverence for Freud and his experience as a years-long patient in psychoanalysis. Lewin's interpretation makes Miriam Johnson's attempted rehabilitation of expressivity-instrumentality that was discussed in Chapter 1 all the more ironic.

18 See, for example, Williams and Bennett (1975) for an early gender stereotypes study and Deaux and Kite (1993) for an overview of research on this topic.

19 See, for example, Brody, Hay, and Vandewater (1990), Conway, Giannopoulos, and Stiefenhofer (1990), Ganong and Coleman (1985), LaFrance (1993).

20 Spence (1993) argues that these various independent attributes contribute differently to each individual's sense of a gendered self because developmental histories vary from one individual to the next and each individual is influenced by a variety of sources that may or may not be related to gender. See also Koestner and Aube, 1995.

21 West and Fenstermaker (1995), Deaux and Major (1987), Risman (1998).

22 Similar emphasis on the individual's role in actively creating her or his identity has become a significant theme within personality psychology. McAdams (1995), among others, suggests that individuals fashion their identity through the telling and enactment of their life stories. The enactment and negotiation of gender is one part of this creation of identity. The dramaturgical notion of self and gender obviously owe much to Erving Goffman's concepts of deep acting and surface acting in social interaction.

23 My emphasis is on the part played by the social meaning of emotion in the construction of gender. Nancy Chodorow (1995), in a feminist psychoanalytic mode, proposes a role for themes of experienced emotion in the

construction of a person's individual sense of gender. She distinguishes the social construction of gender from gender's "personal meaning," describing personal meaning as the psychological experience as it is constituted by the psychodynamic processes described by psychoanalysis, in particular by emotion or affect and by unconscious fantasy (p. 517).

24 One may also self-consciously manipulate that gendered enactment (Smith, 1994; Worcel, Smith, and Shields, under review).

25 Philosopher Robert Solomon (1993) points out that it is precisely the belief that emotion is a barely controllable state blinding reason that makes emotion effective. "I couldn't help myself" makes it possible to make one's demands on the world through emotion without having to take the full responsibility for those demands.

26 These and other studies are described in Saarni (1999). Adults respond differently to girls' and boys' expressive style, particularly rewarding girls' expressive behavior when they are friendly and talkative, that is when they behave "like girls" (Cantor and Gelfand, 1977).

27 This idea is discussed in more detail later, especially in Chapters 5 and 6.

28 Overviews of emotional socialization can be found in Gordon (1989), Saarni and Harris (1989), Brody (1999), and Saarni (1999).

29 My description of gender schemas does not suggest that there is a single, fixed gender schema as in Bem's (1981) gender schema theory. I am using the term because it, for me, captures the organized yet fragmentary nature of gender ideation as expressed in the multidimensionality and performativity of gender.

30 Martin, Fabes, Eisenbud, Karbon, and Rose (1990).

31 See Feldman Barrett and Morganstein (1995) and Feldman Barrett, Robin, Pietromonaco, and Eyssell (1998). Reviews of the research literature have also revealed an effect of reporting context on the extent to which women's and men's responses are gender stereotypic (e.g., LaFrance and Banaji, 1992; Shields, 1991a, 1995). Like the actor-observer bias more generally, the emotion stereotypes are more readily applied to others than to oneself.

32 There is evidence that the implicit causality of some verbs is in part a function of gender (e.g., Henley, Miller and Beazley, 1995; LaFrance, Brownell, and Hahn, 1997). Differences in conceptualizing the self versus others is also manifested in contrasting verb types that are used in natural speech (McGuire and McGuire, 1986).

CHAPTER 4

Sentiment, sympathy, and passion in the late nineteenth century

W. B. Carpenter was an eminent nineteenth-century British physiologist. He was also an enthusiastic exponent of the then new physiological psychology that proposed that events previously classed as purely psychological actually had their basis in the functioning of specific brain and nervous system loci. He published several well-regarded works on physiology and psychology, one of which, *Principles of Mental Physiology* (1874), became quite popular and went through a number of editions. Like most other men of science during that period, he came from a wealthy, well-educated family and was a privileged man of the upper classes. Also like other men of science, he found in the relationship of the sexes a pleasing symmetry of function based on the innate, biologically-driven proclivities of each sex. In *Principles of Mental Physiology* Carpenter lays out one example of the superb arrangement of nature:

> There is nowhere, perhaps, a more beautiful instance of complementary adjustment between the Male and Female character, than that which consists in the predominance of the Intellect and Will, which is required to make a man successful in the 'battle of life,' and of the lively Sensibility, the quick Sympathy, the unselfish Kindliness, which give to woman the power of making the happiness of the home, and of promoting the purest pleasures of social existence.[1]

Carpenter's illustration of the complementarity of the sexes is immediately recognizable as a statement of emotion stereotypes given a positive inflection: She is valuable because she is warm and sensitive, whereas he is valuable precisely because he is not. This chapter and the two that follow examine images of female emotionality/male non-emotionality at two historical moments – late nineteenth century and late twentieth century – as a strategy for unraveling the gendered expression of emotion stereotypes. These two periods exhibit striking parallels and contrasts in their respective conceptualization of the relationship between emotion and gender. The late nineteenth century witnessed the first self-consciously scientific attempts to explain gender differences at a time when, on both sides of the Atlantic, women's rights were increasingly becoming a public issue. The late twentieth century has seen a

69

resurgence of interest in gender as a result of a new wave of feminist activism. In both periods science borrows gender stereotypes to develop an explanation of the psychology of each sex, especially emphasizing differences between them, and then uses that explanation to confirm the "validity" of the stereotypes. The contrast between images of emotion and emotionality at these two points in time shows how the prevailing emotion stereotype rests uneasily on a changing, often paradoxical, set of beliefs about gendered emotion that shift from one historical period to the next. No matter in what way these beliefs about gendered emotion change, a constant core remains. The core is the identification of "emotionality" – ineffectual, misdirected, or trivial emotion – as distinctively "female."

Women and emotion

The identification of the feminine with emotionality is a long-standing tradition in Western thought. The supposed character of feminine emotionality has, however, shifted and changed over intellectual epochs. The Christian church fathers of the first millennium, for example, identified female emotionality with a tendency toward sexual incontinence. Women's emotionally-driven sexual insatiability *de facto* made them a risk to men's state of grace, an occasion of sin. Later, Thomas Aquinas' thirteenth-century commentary reaffirms Aristotle's use of women as an example of wantonness, but adds that women's weakness is the result of a defect in intellect, not of character alone: "for the most part, reason flourishes very little because of the imperfect nature of their body. Because of this they do not govern their emotions in the majority of cases by reason but rather are governed by their emotions."[2]

One legacy of the Enlightenment was the gradual transition from the belief in general inferiority of females in nearly all capacities (intellectual, perceptual, moral) to a notion that the mental and moral faculties inherent in each sex are complementary.[3] The development of this modern conceptualization of gendered traits was accompanied by a major shift in the meaning of female emotionality. Genevieve Lloyd (1984) sets the mid-eighteenth century as the beginning of a turn from a belief in general inferiority toward complementarity insofar as rational thought is concerned. She notes that the earlier tradition emphasized female intellect as an imperfect version of the male and that with the Enlightenment came the notion that women have their own distinctive kind of intellectual character which is the "natural" complement to distinctively male reasoning capacity. Even in the diverse theories of Rousseau, Kant, and Hegel (and others), she identifies a common characterization of the respective intellectual spheres of the sexes: the rational male world, which is objective and general in scope, and the particularistic, common-sense female world. Note that reason is ascribed to both sexes; the difference between the sexes lies in the innate intellect that is sex-determined. Reason is not construed as an exclusively male domain; rather, highly-valued, creative, expansive reason, in short the *better* form of reason, is identified as a male attribute.

With the advent of evolutionary theory in the mid-nineteenth century, variation came to be seen as the source of evolutionary progress. Complementarity of the sexes was the ideal way to explain how variation could operate while the stability and continuity of the species was maintained. In 1890 Patrick Geddes and J. A. Thomson promulgated their metabolic theory of sex differences, which was based on the proposition that females and males exhibit opposing types of chemical processes in every cell of the body: she is passive, submissive, and biologically economical; he is active, enterprising, and biologically profligate. They reasoned that differences in biological economy yield parallel differences in intellectual and temperamental traits. Indeed, they confidently concluded: "That men should have greater cerebral variability and therefore more originality, while women have greater stability and therefore more 'common sense,' are facts both consistent with the general theory of sex and verifiable in common experience."[4] In the US the notion of complementarity was most completely expressed by the variability hypothesis, the assertion that deviation from the average was more likely for males than females.

The idea of complementarity has special consequences for the representation of gendered emotion. To assert that one sex is *inferior* to the other in any area of competence conveys a sense of impairment or dysfunction in the inferior sex. To assert complementarity is to restore order to the world by allowing for qualitative as well as quantitative differences. In complementarity, kinds or types of emotion may be identified as more typical of one sex than of the other and purported sex-related differences in emotional temperament are automatically documented as natural and functional. The British physiologist, Alexander Walker, took up the topic of *Woman Physiologically Considered* (1850), arguing that despite the vast differences between the brains and minds of women and men, women are compensated for their intellectual limitations by a superiority in instinct. Indeed, he proposed that instinct governs women's lives, citing as evidence various truisms of the day, such as women's susceptibility to the manipulations of animal magnetism.[5] The complementarity model of gendered intellectual and psychological attributes characterizes a general movement in the nineteenth century toward belief in functional complementarity which is also evident in the private sphere/public sphere dichotomization of woman/man, family/work, and consumption/production.[6]

It is conventional to describe Victorian notions of masculine and feminine as complementary opposites: He is public, she is domestic; he is active, she is passive; he is rational, she is emotional. The last pairing – reason versus emotion – is not the relationship suggested by complementarity between the sexes. The binary opposition of male-rational, female-emotional, is, in fact, incompatible with a complementarity model and is an inaccurate representation of what was believed to be the ideal and the natural state of gender relations by late Victorian British and American middle- to upper-class scientists and laypersons.

Reason and emotion were actually viewed as attributes of *both* sexes, albeit distinctively gendered by "natural" differences between them. The Victorian lady was depicted as possessing an ideally domestic type of rationality which was complemented by a feminine form of emotion, a sort of delicate, yet somewhat unstable sensitivity of feelings. In their highest form, female/feminine reasoning capacities were of the intuitive, practical, common sense variety. The down side of female capacities in women of all social classes was the tendency for their weaker reasoning capacities to become swamped by the power of emotion.

Male/masculine reason in its highest form encompassed a certain broadness of scope and capacity for objectivity and abstraction and was expressed in creative thought and planning. Both sexes were believed capable of rational thought, but truly creative cognition was a male prerogative. Similarly, an idealized masculine version of emotion stands in contrast to an idealized feminine version. In its feminine form, emotion is portrayed as a somewhat unstable sensitivity of feelings toward oneself and others; masculine emotion, in contrast, is pictured as a passionate force that is as evident in the drive to achieve, to create, and to dominate as in sexual drive. Male/masculine reason was, in its highest form of expression, believed to be powered by a distinctively masculine emotion.

The complementarity of the sexes: Female emotionality/male passion

With the rise of evolutionary theory, the late nineteenth century saw the gradual replacement of the doctrine of general female inferiority with a biologically-grounded doctrine of complementarity. Charles Darwin himself cleaved to the belief in general female inferiority, noting in *The Descent of Man*, his first extended application of evolutionary theory to humans, that

> The chief distinction in the intellectual powers of the two sexes is shewn [sic] by man's attaining to a higher eminence, in whatever he takes up, than can woman – whether requiring deep thought, reason, or imagination, or merely the use of the senses and hands. (p. 858)

Darwin did grant that women exhibit more of some qualities, among them "greater tenderness and less selfishness," as well as greater powers of intuition, rapid perception, and imitation. However, he also surmises that "some, at least, of these faculties are characteristics of the lower races and therefore, of a past and lower state of civilization" (p. 858). Although Darwin altered his views of sexual selection between publication of the first and second editions of *Descent*, he retained the basic ideas about sex differences he had originally laid out. Darwin adopted a Lamarckian position in suggesting that traits acquired in adulthood were more likely to be transmitted to same-sex offspring, with these traits remaining latent until offspring had reached maturity. For Darwin there was some possibility that there was a remedy for female intellectual inferiority in young women's education: "In order that woman should reach the same standard as man, she ought, when nearly an adult, to be trained to energy and perseverance, and to have her reason and imagination trained to the highest point; and then she would probably transmit these qualities chiefly to her adult daughters" (Darwin, 1897, p. 565). In contrast to Darwin's views on the education of young women, others considered "too much" education harmful. For example, G. Stanley Hall believed that rigorous education during adolescence would impair the "normalization of the lunar cycle." To Hall it seemed that young women's education jeopardized whether there would even *be* future generations! [7]

According to male American and British scientists of the time, the psychological traits of each sex were a direct consequence of biology. And the biological exigencies of sex mirrored social realities. Woman was biologically conservative, less variable, neurally underdeveloped, and physiologically vulnerable. She was also genteel, unimaginative, perceptive, modest, coy, and dependent, and all of these traits were manifestations of her emotional nature. Although the specifics of any individual account varied somewhat, and despite the fact that each of these accounts was fraught with logical inconsistencies (never mind physiological inaccuracies), the account generally followed this line: Because of innate biological factors the human female's nervous system was limited (or prevented from its full development) either by the simple fact of being female or because of the biological demands of development and maturation of the female reproductive system. The end result was a nervous system that was less capable of sophisticated higher mental processes (most notably creative thought and rational insight) and which comparatively accentuated development of the lower mental processes (most notably emotion and certain aspects of perception). What was not dictated developmentally was insured by the menstrual cycle and by maternity. It was even seriously proposed that the needs of the uterus took precedence over other organs, and so blood that might ordinarily support brain functioning was, at puberty, diverted to service of the uterus. Later in the young woman's development, pregnancy and maternity insured that the instincts for caregiving would manifest themselves fully in her as a mother and come to dominate her whole person. The power of this physiological explanation of female psychology was so great that it persisted well into the 1920s, after behaviorism and a rejection of instinct theory had already come to be major themes in American psychology.[8]

Female reproductive physiology was presumed to exert the same limitations on the development of women of all races and classes, but it was only the middle and upper-class white woman who was further described in terms of the resulting constellation of traits: gentility, perceptiveness, and emotional lability. These three features intertwined were the foundation for the moral and intellectual character of the Victorian woman. Although female biology seemed to occasion women's moral inferiority, it was clear to scientists that the true Victorian lady was one of great delicacy and refinement. She was religious and interested in spiritual matters and appeared to possess a moral high-mindedness uncharacteristic of ordinary men. It was equally apparent to the scientist, however, that because she lacked the requisite cerebral capacity that could support the development of a true sense of justice, her moral judgment was best exercised in the mundane, accessible (and so easily understandable) moral dilemmas of everyday life. A true appreciation for moral order, a true ability to administer justice objectively, and a true capacity for faith (as opposed to simple religiosity) were beyond her capabilities. Likewise, women's perceptiveness seemed just as obviously directed to the mundane and immediate, and more than one male scientist was moved to point out the similarities between adult women and less developed individuals. Psychologist and instinct theorist William McDougall (1923, p. 391), for example, opined that, not only do some women possess a great deal of intuitiveness, but "young children, whose command of language is very slight, may exhibit it; and even in the higher animals, especially the dog, it is not altogether lacking." Humble cleverness, rather than creativity, characterized woman's insight.[9] Emotionality, usually portrayed as emotional lability, completes the triad. Emotional lability, however, was rarely characterized as maenad-like frenzy, but rather as a kind of childishness that manifested

itself as frivolity (as in too much love of parties and financial extravagance) or a too-sensitive sentimentality (as in the propensity to weep
or blush too readily). Feminine sentimentality was generally regarded
as a kind of misdirected feeling. For example, James Martineau's (1898)
analysis of ethics and emotion describes at length the difference between
high-minded compassion and mere sentimentality. Sentimentality, he
wrote, is a perverted compassion, with attention directed toward one's
own experience rather than the object of the sentiment. Sentiments
"direct themselves upon *ideal relations*, objects of apprehension or
thought that are above us, yet potentially ours" (p. 151), whereas derivative sentimentality is "a self-regarding play" with objects of true sentiment, such that, "instead of Compassion, there grows up a taste for
exciting and indulging Pity" (p. 177).

Together these three qualities framed the character of Woman, who
bore a remarkable resemblance to the ideal bourgeois and upper-class
lady: She was a girl of delicate sensibilities who grew into a lady of
devoted maternity. In the ideal case, she was guided throughout her
development by a calm, even temperament and gentle emotion that,
though it was her major natural weakness, was a powerful force for
the good, if well-managed. Her emotional vulnerability first subserved
the "mating instinct" by eliciting a "protective instinct" in the male; as
a mother, her innate concern with the immediate situation (read mundane trivialities) and with the helpless, prompted an irresistible rush of
maternal feelings that insured her care for the infant and her happiness
within the home. These "unreasoning tendencies to pet, coddle, and
'do for' others," psychologist Edward Thorndike noted, were "the chief
source of woman's superiorities in the moral life" (1914, p. 203). Within
the context of evolutionary theory, the concept of maternal instinct took
on greater social significance. Maternal instinct was the perfect vehicle
for the nineteenth-century scientists' understanding of female nature because it appeared to explain so much (even as it was explained by them):
woman's biological conservatism, her limited intellect, her emotionality.
Two widely-respected Italian criminologists speculated, for example,
that women were more prone to lying and that two important reasons
for this were women's natural modesty and the duties of motherhood
which fostered an evasiveness needed for answering children's sometimes inappropriate questions.[10] Even those who eschewed the general
concept of instinct accepted the instinctive component of maternal behavior. Many echoed Herbert Spencer's belief that woman's "love of
the helpless, which in her maternal capacity woman displays in a more
special form than man, inevitably affects all her thoughts and sentiments" (1902, p. 346). G. Stanley Hall, putative father of developmental

psychology, waxed especially poetic on the qualities of *Das Ewig-Weibliche* [the Eternal Womanly], "woman at her best never outgrows adolescence as man does, but lingers in, magnifies and glorifies this culminating stage of life with its all-sided interests, its convertibility of emotions, its enthusiasm, and zest for all that is good, beautiful, true, and heroic" (1918, p. 293).[11]

Whether males possessed a corresponding parental instinct was only infrequently considered, and then it was often viewed as an expression of a general instinctive response to protect the helpless. The added element of protectiveness, according to a number of scientists, had its basis in the father's sense that the child was his own offspring.[12] Men's protective tendencies were thus partially explained as the manifestation of the pride of ownership. Expression of the paternal instinct was not confined to offspring, however, but extended to all those in need of protection. Paternal instinct vis-à-vis grown women was manifested as an impulse to protect the more vulnerable female, no matter what the cost to the male himself. Alexander Sutherland (1898, p. 354), for example, romanticized the male's sympathetic tendency in the style of Victorian science – stripped of any sexual sentiment.

> [and] when, within the doomed vessel whose bulwarks are almost awash, he willingly helps to fill the last boat with the women, though fully realising that in a few minutes he himself will in consequence be a drifting corpse in the deep sea, in such cases, he proclaims how, after a long story of slow development, that sympathy which was originally the finer side of mere sexual feelings has spread and spread till at last it extends to every one that bears the shape of a woman.

The supposed asexuality of masculine protectiveness was not accidental. Idealization was perhaps a reaction to the increased participation of women in work life outside the home (Lerner, 1979). Social concerns regarding female sexuality in particular were apparent in a number of social institutions. Restrictions most often appeared in the guise of measures to protect the female's moral sensibilities. For example, the maintenance of proper moral standards dictated that physicians only rarely examine female patients, that delivery be accomplished in darkened rooms with the mother fully draped to protect her modesty, and so on (Dye, 1980). The reality of late-nineteenth-century women's life bore little resemblance to the sheltered and comfortable ideal portrayed in scientific publications and popular tracts. The ideal, the chaste Angel of the Household, if she existed at all, was to be found only in the upper classes. Even though middle-class women would have had the assistance of a full-time housemaid, their daily life was consumed by cooking, cleaning, and childcare. "Washday," for example, was more likely an affair spread over several days every few weeks because its labor-intensive components, preparing the clothes, boiling water, starching and ironing and more, disrupted all ordinary household activities. Nannies were also a luxury. A family whose income was not much more than £300 per year could not afford to pay the going salary of £25 to £35 per year.[13]

Emotion out of control

Control of emotion/passion was a valued standard and goal for both sexes. Successful control, however, was specific to each sex insofar as the sexes were believed to differ in emotional endowment. Nancy Armstrong's (1987) study of women's conduct manuals from the sixteenth century to the early nineteenth century illustrates the move toward consensus in a definition of the feminine emotional ideal. The transition centers on women's increasing identification with their place as the center of the household. Most of the manuals that Armstrong examined confined themselves to the "how tos" of running a successful household, but in those books that describe the personal attributes of a woman who has achieved successful domesticity, the image of emotional temperance and equanimity is at the forefront. Emotionally, the successful household manager manifests calm mother-love and unruffled housewifeliness. That such emotional temperance was not simply a by-product of domestication, but a goal to strive for in and of itself, is clear from those manuals that discuss the proper education of young women. One influential late eighteenth-century book on young women's education written by liberal thinking Erasmus Darwin, for example, identifies the ideal woman's "charms which enchant all hearts" as "softness of manners, complacency of countenance, gentle unhurried motion, with a voice clear and yet tender" (Armstrong, 1987, p. 80). Women's naturally limited capacity for reason seemed to have its most constructive application in controlling emotion. Ideal feminine emotion, that is, well-controlled natural feminine emotion, provides the gentle, constant temperance of spirit that is the comfort to the husband and the heart of the home. In one American advice book on love and relationships, Ella Wilcox (1894) instructs women that moderating emotion is crucial to pleasing men. She writes that men do prefer women "of sympathetic feeling and affectionate nature," but intense emotion must be avoided. A woman prone to emotion "needs to wear an armor of control and repose, no matter what it costs her to do so, if she would be pleasing to man. Let her nature be suspected, and it fascinates; let it be discovered, and it *ennuies*" (p. 80).

The "right" sort of uncontrolled emotion, blushing, was taken as a sign of good character.[14] But out-of-control emotion that takes the form of frivolity or oversentimentality or both was scorned as childish and impractical. Uncontrolled emotion explains the intemperate wife who becomes too fascinated with fashion and entertainment, as well as the over-sentimental woman who is over-sensitive and prone to weeping (presumably spoiled by reading too many novels or over-indulging maternal instincts), and whose domestic life suffers as a result. The first ruins her home (or her chances to have one) by profligate use of her time and money; the second does so through insufficient control of otherwise laudable tendencies. The femme fatale who figures so prominently in the literature and art of the nineteenth century appears not at all in scientific discourse.[15] However, the feminist, the "bachelor woman," and other women with acceptable morals who eschewed the so-called natural role of women of the comfortable classes, were described in treatises on the psychology of the sexes. References to emotion portray these women as frivolous or oversentimental like the uncontrolled domestic version, or as lacking proper emotional qualities altogether.

The concept of decisive action invested with, and so made stronger by, powerful feeling is the essential quality of idealized male emotion. The complementary masculine counterpart to nineteenth-century feminine emotionality is passion, not solely in its sexual sense, but more broadly, a deeply felt commitment to a cause, an idea, or an experience. Though problematic in its capacity to overwhelm reasoned behavior, well-controlled masculine passion is energy focused on "the battle of life" in business and protection of the domestic sanctuary. As such, male passion plays a crucial role in evolutionary theory. In Herbert Spencer's (1902) version, primitive man's passion made survival of the fittest possible. He notes that

> In the course of the struggles for existence among wild tribes those tribes survived in which the men were not only powerful and courageous, but aggressive, unscrupulous, intensely egoistic. Necessarily, then, the men of the conquering races which gave origin to the civilized races, were men in whom the brutal characteristics were dominant; and necessarily the women of such races, having to deal with brutal men, prospered in proportion as they possessed, or acquired, fit adjustments of nature. (p. 342)

Spencer's account – like other evolution-based accounts of the time – placed masculine competition at the *center* of emotion theory. In other words, male emotional attributes were asserted to have evolved in response to men's competition with other men; female emotional attributes, by contrast evolved in relation to men's. When passion takes the form of commitment it is the quality that enables men (and *not* women) to transcend the world of pedestrian ideas and experience. Male passion out of control is rarely acknowledged except in descriptions of criminals or the peoples these scientists elected to name "savages." Out of control passion is depicted as intemperance of the worst sort: uncontrolled sexual behavior or intemperate rage and wildness of the savage beast. Female sexual insatiability in earlier times had been believed to be the source of men's sexual weakness, but by the eighteenth century sexual insatiability came to be identified with masculinity. The idealized woman, that is the northern European woman of the upper classes, was one who did not have a strong sex drive, though "common" women were still portrayed in art and the public imagination as potential victims of their own sexual promiscuity.

That female emotionality is a weaker, more narrowly focused counterpart to male passion is wonderfully illustrated in the novel *Robert Elsmere* (published in 1888), which was extraordinarily popular on both sides of the Atlantic.[16] The story, written by novelist Mary Ward (more widely known as Mrs. Humphrey Ward), portrays the title character as a man of "passionate nature" who struggles with questions of religious faith in the course of the novel's several hundred tedious pages. In the course of the story, Robert Elsmere undergoes a profound crisis of his Christian faith and ultimately replaces his loyalty to the Anglican Church with activism in the form of a secular charitable society. His passionate struggle and rational resolution to his turmoil is contrasted in the novel with the emotion-based faith of Elsmere's wife Catherine, who, without leaving the church, becomes a zealous proponent of Elsmere's society after his death. Her conversion to a secular religion is not, however, predicated on an intense internal (i.e., passionate) struggle, but is a simple displacement. Her emotional attachment to the church is redirected to the charitable society which bears her husband's name. Former Prime Minister William Gladstone, who took time away from his governmental duties to review the book, noted: "The work may be summed up in this way: it represents a battle between intellect and emotion. Of right, intellect wins; and, having won, enlists emotion in its service" (1888, p. 768). In *Robert Elsmere* male passion is the foundation for effective and broad social action; female emotion is particularistic and so inevitably limited in impact. It is not emotion per se that is devalued, but rather its ultimate ineffectuality, an ineffectuality indigenous to feminine character or to a masculine failure to harness passion's power.

This account of gendered emotion represents a fairly select segment of society. Scientists of the nineteenth century were, for the most part, upper middle-class males and included some independently wealthy amateurs. Those affiliated with universities had students who also represented a fairly select portion of white male society. It is not difficult to understand how scientists could acquire and, with no effort, maintain a limited view of the day to day operations of society. Evolutionary theory was a powerful descriptive and explanatory framework altogether suited to the scientists' world view. The progressive man of science was one who embraced the Darwinian (or, more likely, the Spencerian) principles of progress through competition and increasing differentiation with evolution. The relative value ascribed to male and female forms of reason and of emotion neatly mirror the social hierarchy of race, sex, and social class.

Darwin construed sexual selection as the driving force of evolution. At its face, a theory for which reproductive activity has an important explanatory function is not immediately compatible with a presumption of female passivity. Nor do the constructs of sexual selection, natural selection, and adaptiveness *require* a presupposition of feminine passivity. Nevertheless, evolutionary forces were presumed to be expressed in sex-related biological roles. The female was the conservative, stable element which maintained the species over time; the male was the more mutable, variable element, and so the source of differentiation and species development. Female sexuality was neutralized by emphasizing the female's maternal role over her conjugal role. The mother who could become a mother only through sexual relations was neutered by science (and years earlier, by Christian religion): Victorian science did not know what to make of women, so women were made into mothers.

The image of Mother as the ideal and true Lady suppresses acknowledgement of the sexual female as well as the socially or intellectually passionate female. Accounts of the Victorian lady emphasize her emotionality, but the descriptions do not convey an image of emotion as passion (a deeply felt commitment to a cause, an idea, or an experience); instead, passion is a masculine prerogative and is identified with a distinctly nonfeminine emotion operative in intellect and through sexuality. Intellectual passion motivates achievement and combativeness, and is the source of the capacity to conquer frontiers. At its most spiritual, passion enables transcendence and the experience of the sublime. Thus, to construe women as *merely* emotional obviates the possibility of their being effectively passionate.

Where is gender in the study of emotion?

Despite the pervasiveness of emotion as a theme in scientific descriptions of the sexes, gender (in the form of sex-related differences) is a theme that is curiously absent from another popular topic in turn-of-the-century psychology: emotion. The formal establishment of psychology as a discipline is typically placed at 1879. That year Wilhelm Wundt set up a laboratory of experimental psychology in Germany (although some credit William James for beating Wundt to it at Harvard the preceding year). The various themes of romanticism, empiricism, evolutionary theory, industrial capitalism, and expansionary colonialism are all visible impulses in the foundational themes of this new science.

Emotion was one of the premier issues during the formative years of formal psychology. Charles Darwin and William James were two of the more prominent British and American figures, but many other notable and less notable scientific men were similarly concerned with emotion.[17] Evolutionary theory and the scientific method offered to psychologists a way to study a most central human feature without recourse to the dramatic romanticism that dominated artistic and popular emotion discourse. James, in fact, explicitly presented his emotion theory to provoke scientific debate and theorizing about emotion.[18] As predominant as the theme of female emotionality is in the writings of many of these scientists, it is quite curious that supposed sex differences in emotion and emotionality do not figure in emotion theory itself. Several of the more influential emotion theorists who elsewhere made comparisons of female and male psychology, and who emphasized emotion-based differences in those comparisons, make only passing remarks about gender, and in those comments, gender is clearly treated as a minor matter, not at all central to explaining how emotion works. Charles Darwin's (1872) book on the expression of emotion makes just one gender-based reference. (In a comment about the location of blushing in English women he asserts that it does not extend below the "upper chest.") Nor does William James mention gender similarities or differences in the chapter devoted to emotion in his landmark *Principles of Psychology* first published in 1890. Elsewhere in the book, however, he discusses evidence of the maternal instinct in the human female, and emphasizes its affective nature. James, like other founding fathers of psychology, believed male/masculine and female/feminine were manifestations of distinctively sex-specific physiology. For example, in discussing acute self-consciousness, James observes that like other emotions considered in his theory, acute self-consciousness is a bodily state that is expressed in behavior, in this case leading to "a certain rigidity in most men," but "in women to various gracefully shy poses" (James, 1884, p. 25).

Though gender is mentioned only infrequently in nineteenth-century psychological treatises on emotion, the way in which it is incorporated into examples is very revealing. References to gender in connection with emotion appear almost exclusively in examples which are themselves ostensibly unconcerned with gender. These references reveal the belief that feminine emotion has a different relationship to reason than does masculine passion. The dissociation between formal discussions of gender differences and formal treatments of emotion is possibly nowhere better illustrated than in the work of philosopher and social theorist

Herbert Spencer, the originator of the "survival of the fittest" doctrine.[19] Intending to apply his theory of evolution to major fields of study in a series of ten books, Spencer completed this monumental task over thirty-six years. Spencer devoted a substantial number of pages in his volumes on psychology, philosophy, and sociology to the question of emotion. No comparisons of male and female emotional patterns appear in Spencer's analysis of emotion, although he does explicitly distinguish between the emotional capacities of "civilized" and "uncivilized" human races. It is only in other chapters that review sex differences, differences in which he places great social importance, that a distinction is drawn between masculine and feminine emotional capacities. In *The Study of Sociology* (1902), for example, Spencer dedicates an entire chapter to discussion of emotions that exert an effect on sociological beliefs. He describes how sentiments (to be differentiated from sentimentality) such as "loyalty" and "awe of power" can impair and impede clear rational thought. Spencer focuses his discussion on the political and military levels of social organization, but instead of drawing an example from that realm, he chooses to illustrate his point with a more palatable gender-based analogy, one that represents the debilitating effects of emotion as a feminine condition. He likens the way in which "awe of power" blinds reason in society to the effects of maternal instinct which leads women to idealize their offspring and fail to see flaws in them (p. 144).[20] As in discussions primarily concerned with gender, Spencer here equates a distinctly female form of emotion with ineffectual emotion. His point is not that offspring are powerful, but rather that maternal emotion (like awe of power) is simultaneously natural (which, indeed, makes mothering possible) and the enemy of true rationality.

Like Spencer, other theorists of emotion distinguished between male passion and feminine emotion implicitly in the examples they used: For them, feminine emotion was geared to nurturance, but was deficient for other purposes. In fact, the concept of gendered emotion is only made explicit when sex differences, not emotion, are the focal topic. In a later chapter in *Sociology*, Spencer goes on at some length concerning gender differences that need to be taken into account in sociological study. Spencer adhered to the view that the female, by virtue of her more rapid rate of maturation, achieved physical adulthood at a comparatively arrested stage of intellectual development compared to males. As a result, "the mental manifestations [of females] have somewhat less of general power or massiveness; and beyond this there is a perceptible falling-short in those two faculties, intellectual and emotional, which are the latest products of human evolution" (p. 341). He felt that women's emotional deficiency is particularly observable in "the most abstract of the emotions, the sentiment of justice – the sentiment which regulates

conduct irrespective of personal attachments and the likes or dislikes felt
for individuals" (pp. 341–342). Spencer believed that, because women
were doomed by a limited intellect, other emotion-related skills more
prevalent among women, such as the ability to disguise one's feelings
or "to distinguish quickly the passing feelings of those around," are not
the special endowment of females, but simply the result of a power differential – which he interpreted literally as a function of difference in
physical might: the weaker female honed these skills as a survival strategy: "the weaker sex has naturally acquired certain mental traits by its
dealings with the stronger" (p. 342). "Ordinarily, this feminine faculty,
showing itself in an aptitude for guessing the state of mind through
the external signs, end simply in intuitions formed without assignable
reasons" (p. 343). In nineteenth-century thinking, female emotion is
ineffectual in part because feminine rationality is not competent to employ emotion's services.[21]

Given twin interests in emotion and in gender differences, which
were largely understood to be fundamentally expressed in emotion and
emotion-related traits, why was so much made of emotion in discussions
of the sexes and so little made of the sexes in discussions of emotion?[22]
What accounts for the dissociation between theoretical discussions of
emotion and descriptive summaries of sex-related differences in which
emotional qualities serve as markers of gender?

Psychological science, as a project to explain the *terra incognita* of basic
psychological processes, was concerned with generating explanations of
the generalized adult human mind. Apparently the generalized adult
human mind was male, and the emotional phenomena that were to
be explained were those characteristic of masculine passion. Theories
of emotion were directed to explaining emotion as passion. It is as if
mere feminine sentimentality was not authentic, whole emotion. Thus
to Spencer and his cohort mere emotionality (in contrast with passion)
clearly represented an unfolding of biologically-dictated feminine impulses, requiring no explanation beyond description of its sources in
female biology. In considering emotion, what was to be explained was a
nominally de-sexed passion that was, nevertheless, identified with the
natural, typical, and ideal masculine.

From the nineteenth century to the present: The elusive emotional ideal

The story of nineteenth-century gender and emotion helps to focus the
discussion of bedrock beliefs and the prevailing emotion stereotype.
Not only is the prevailing emotion stereotype remarkably resistant to
change, but, more important, the constituent beliefs comprise an often

self-contradictory set of paradoxes that shift markedly from one historical period to the next. Victorian notions of masculine and feminine
were grounded in the belief that distinctive styles of reason and emotion characterized each sex. These sex-specific capacities were viewed
as nothing more or less than the ordinary and healthy manifestation of
natural, that is, biologically-based and physiologically-mediated, differences between the sexes. In the nineteenth century, idealized feminine and masculine emotion was, in fact, a positive inflection of gender
stereotypes, believed to have its source in nature and, thus, to represent
the typical.

In the view of nineteenth-century scientists, ideal emotion was natural, typical, and *de facto* masculine, unless ruined by bad character. In
comparing that century to our own, perhaps the most immediate and
striking contrast lies in how the relations among natural, typical, and
ideal emotion are formulated. For scholars and scientists then, male
emotion (natural emotional endowment) was essentially equivalent to
masculine emotion (typical emotional behavior) which was essentially
equivalent to manly emotion (ideal emotional behavior). The natural
and the ideal were as one, with a clear distinction drawn between the
complementary provinces of masculine and feminine. Today, natural,
typical, and ideal are not equated, but are regarded both in academic
study and in the public imagination as having a more complicated relationship. As in the nineteenth century, ideal emotion is emotion that
is well-managed. And ideal emotion is still marked as a manly quality;
however, it no longer is viewed as an effortless and natural manifestation of one's biological status as a male.

With benefit of historical hindsight, the account of the gender-emotion
relationship in the nineteenth century has a kind of coherence that we
do not see in present-day scientifically-based accounts. Moving to the
present, we find a different relationship between accounts of gender
and the representation of natural, typical, and ideal emotion. Today,
as in the nineteenth century, theories of emotion do not, by and large,
incorporate a discussion of gender. In contrast, gender is deeply involved in literature written for the popular audience. In Robert Bly's
Iron John (1990), which spurred a men's movement devoted to exca-
vating a lost manliness from overcivilizing influences, the idealization
of natural emotional differences continues to play a significant role. In
popular advice literature that is directed toward reclaiming authentic
manhood or womanhood, there is a celebration of emotional difference
along with the exhortation to "get in touch with" those manly (or womanly), hence "true" feelings. Mary Crawford's (2000) analysis of John
Gray's *Men are from Mars/Women are from Venus* books and the couples
counseling industry based on the premise, reveals a vision of emotional

differences between the sexes that is not much different from that of the comfortable Victorian classes. Today, however, the assertion of vast differences in the emotional lives of women and men is typically accompanied by a detectable tension between emotion standards and emotion stereotypes. This tension is particularly evident in contemporary pathologizing of the "inexpressive male" and a seemingly paradoxical celebration of masculine emotion which I discuss in Chapter 6.

"Ideal" emotion as manly emotion

So what does the "right" way to do emotion look like? First, it may be easier to spell out what the ideal is not. Ideal emotion is not identified with natural emotion (in the sense of natural as what "happens to" a person). While much is made of getting in touch with one's true feelings, the aim of getting in touch is to get in control. I propose that it is, in fact, possible to identify an emotional ideal that prevails in contemporary dominant culture. It is not a state of stoic inexpressivity, but rather, the expression of deeply felt emotion under such control that it can be telegraphed by the minimal gesture, tone of voice, language, or facial movement. This style is especially evident in positive images of masculinity, the raised eyebrow, the quiet snarl, the explosive "yesss!" all signal that strong feeling is present and that it is controlled and directed by the experiencer.[23] Manly emotion is not male emotion. That is, manly emotion is not simply an expression of normative or natural emotion; rather, it is a goal, an achievement, a sign of manhood. It is the standard for "appropriate emotion" for both sexes. In the following chapter I look at the extent to which the question of appropriate emotion is a gendered question in children's development.

If manly emotion is the standard of appropriate emotion, how is it that everyone, girls *and* boys, women *and* men, does not become proficient at this highly valued, focal behavior? First, consider the defining features of manly emotion: it is intensely felt, genuine, goal or context driven and time limited, and most important, expressively economical. It is quite a tall order to perform manly emotion impeccably. Manly emotion calls for a measure of deep passion and consistent self-control that is hard to imagine outside of a Hollywood film. A second feature, explored in the following chapter, considers the social contexts in which boys and girls, women and men practice emotion. In particular it considers how sex-segregated children's groups and contexts for play foster the education of the emotions and emotion practice. For example, do competitive sports encourage manly emotion? Does playing "house" (and other scripts from everyday life) foster an expressive and nurturant emotional style? How do different peer group experiences help to shape the individual's emotional style and expectations of how others will respond to her or his emotions and how she or he should respond to others? The following chapter takes up these questions as a matter of the education of the emotions.

Notes

1 Carpenter, *Principles of mental physiology*, 1894, p. 417. The first US edition was published in 1875. Bruce Haley (1978, pp. 36–37) notes that, because of his respected stature among physiologists, Carpenter's opinions were given considerable weight. *Principles of mental physiology* was an expanded outline of psychology that he had included in *Principles of human physiology* (1842).

2 See, for example, the writings of Tertullian (CE 155–225) and Augustine (CE 354–430). The Aquinas quote is from a translation by Litzinger (1964, p. 642).

3 In this chapter I draw from my earlier research on the history of the psychology of women (e.g., Shields, 1975a; 1975b; 1980; 1982; 1984).

4 Geddes and Thomson (1890, p. 271). Though still advocating their "metabolic" theory of sex differences in a 1914 edition of this book, they renounce the variability hypothesis as a "dangerous" generalization. See Shields (1982) for the history of the variability hypothesis and Shields and Mallory (1987) for Leta Stetter Hollingworth's response to it.

5 Walker was ahead of his time in thinking about the reasons for women's psychological vulnerability. Although he emphasized organic differences as the basis for women's greater susceptibility to insanity, he also observed that because women are "exposed to more disappointments, and have fewer resources; they become oftener the victim of circumstance, while men are more favoured by nature and society to choose their situation" (p. 336).

6 See Russett (1989), Richards (1997), and Erskine (1995) for discussions of the ways in which Victorian science promoted the notion of separate spheres. The paradox of this dichotomization is illustrated in Margaret Homans' (1998) fascinating study of Queen Victoria as monarch and wife.

7 Sexual dimorphism of form and character were viewed as the distinct sign of evolution. Comparisons based on race typically noted that the physiognomy and temperament of women and men were far more similar in "lower" races than in those more advanced. See also Stephen J. Gould, 1981.

8 The inherent intellectual and emotional limitations of women were noted by such leading figures in the formative years of American psychology as G. Stanley Hall, Joseph Jastrow, and James McKeen Cattell.

9 Feminists and proto-feminists wrote critical responses to theories of female inferiority that invoked evolution's principles. Eliza Burt Gamble's *The Evolution of Woman* (1893/1894) is representative of one tack taken by these authors. In the preface to her volume, she writes that, until she read *The Descent of Man*, she had been unsuccessful in finding "detailed proof that could consistently be employed to substantiate the correctness" of her hypothesis that "female organization is in no wise inferior to that of the male" (p. v).

10 Lombroso and Ferrero (1899).

11 Hall's ambivalent idealization of woman clearly draws on Goethe "Das Ewig-Weibliche zieht uns hinan" [the eternally womanly draws us (men) onwards (and upwards)]. See also Lesley Diehl (1986) for more on Hall's views

on women. Gail Bederman (1995) offers an intriguing account of Hall's efforts to explain the occurrence of neurasthenia among privileged white men, emphasizing the role of Hall's thinking about race and civilization as the basis for his concerns and his proposed cure for neurasthenia.

12 See, for example, Alexander Bain (1859) and Theodore Ribot (1898).

13 Drasnin (2001).

14 O' Farrell (1997). Nancy Armstrong (1987) argues that domestic fiction defined middle-class roles by encroaching upon aristocratic culture and seizing authority from it, before a middle class actually existed. Through underscoring gender differences on the basis of psychological differences men came to be defined as political and women as domestic.

15 See Nina Auerbach (1982) for discussion of the amoral and immoral woman in literature and art.

16 Thanks to Deborah Weiner for directing me to Ward's book and Gladstone's review of it. Mary Humphrey Ward espoused the complementarity model in her own life in, for example, her belief that women were fit to participate in local government, but that governance of the Empire should be left to men. Ward's enigmatic personality and philanthropic activities are discussed in D. E. B. Weiner (1994).

17 See Gardiner, Metcalf, and Beebe-Center's (1937) comprehensive history of emotion theories – from the pre-Socratics through early behaviorism. Among late nineteenth-century scientists who offered theories of emotion were Wilhelm Wundt, William McDougall, John Dewey, and Herbert Spencer.

18 In the first article in which he lays out the propositions of his new theory, James' final footnote identifies a case that has come to his attention that may provide evidence incompatible with his theory (James, 1884). He concludes that, even if proved wrong, the need for theory was great enough that publication of his theory would "have been justified." And his final comment underscores that point: "The best thing I can say for it is, that in writing it, I have almost persuaded *myself* it may be true" (p. 205).

19 Paxton (1991).

20 Spencer uses a second extended example to illustrate how awe of power can sway beliefs, this one describing the religious fickleness of "half-bred Portuguese Indians" (1902, p. 145).

21 Spencer underscores the essentialness of woman as mother in a footnote in which he faults the comparisons of the "minds of men and women." The implied target of his criticism are writers who assert the intellectual equality of the sexes. For example, he notes that an "erroneous impression" of women's ability stems from a tendency to compare the elite of women against the average of men. The "most serious error," however, is that of "overlooking the limit of normal mental power." He notes that "under special discipline, the feminine intellect will yield products higher than the intellects of most men can yield. But we are not to count this productivity as truly feminine *if it entails decreased fulfilment [sic] of the maternal functions.* Only that mental energy is normally feminine which can coexist with the production and nursing of the due number of healthy children" (p. 402, emphasis added).

One finds similar gender examples in James (1884, p. 33). In a discussion of "the moral, intellectual, and aesthetic feelings" (as opposed to the standard emotions which are the focus of his theory), James makes the point that these emotions are more allied to a judgment of *right* than to the evocation of bodily change. He distinguishes between the experience of the connoisseur and that of the "sentimental layman," illustrating the distinction with an English couple's reaction to Titian's "Assumption": "...all I overheard was the woman's voice murmuring: 'What a *deprecatory* expression her face wears! What self-abne*gation*! How *unworthy* she feels of the honour she is receiving!' Their honest hearts had been kept warm all the time by a glow of spurious sentiment that would have fairly made old Titian sick" [emphasis in original].

22 This is largely true of pre-nineteenth-century views on emotion and the sexes as well; of concern here is the particular sociohistorical relation between popular ideologies and scientific ideologies. Suffice it to say that many who are represented in Gardiner *et al.*'s history of the study of emotion are also known for their thinking about gender, for example, Aristotle, Aquinas, Vives, Schopenhauer, and many others.

23 Effortful economical expression may, in fact, be costly biologically. See Robinson and Pennebaker (1991) for a discussion of emotion symptoms and health.

CHAPTER 5

The education of the emotions

"The Thrill of Victory and the Agony of Defeat." The slogan of ABC's long-running Wide World of Sports program is so familiar and so often parodied that it is easy to overlook the intimate connection it makes between sports and emotion. Competitive sports certainly are about winning and losing, but the slogan reminds us that the *emotions* of winning and of losing make competition the powerful experience it is. By capturing this sense of excitement and immediacy the slogan reveals the importance of emotional intensity for players and spectators. Competitive sport is perhaps the most common public context for display of strongly felt emotion, and it is emotion that makes winning so utterly desirable and losing so terribly painful. Sport is the component of popular culture that cuts across boundaries of ethnicity, class, and geography. Through the very ubiquity of sports metaphors competitive sports touch the lives of all except the most uninterested. There is an enormous literature of popular books and scholarly research focusing on the significance of sports in American culture, ranging from the illuminating to the downright silly.

"The thrill" and "the agony" are not the only emotions practiced on the playing field. In the context of athletic competition the full range of emotions, and emotional intensity varying from mild to the most extreme occurs and is expected to occur. Emotion is not only condoned but required in competitive sports. A range of emotions and intensity of emotion are visible constituents of one's role as an athlete, coach, or spectator. Interviewers ask "How did you feel?" as often as they ask "how did you do it?" And interviewing winners and losers alike focuses on the emotions of the game and the emotions of the game's outcome. Emotions are what make competition, winning, and losing interesting. And the emotional moments are intensified for fans through their identification with players. A former boyfriend once commented to me as he struggled to stay composed while watching basketball legend Kareem Abdul-Jabbar's farewell game, "A video of sports star retirement tributes would be the guy equivalent of a three-hankie movie." The competitive situation clearly spells out the rules of emotional experience and expression. The rules of the game cover which emotions ought to occur under which conditions and how these emotions should be experienced and expressed. For example, winners should be proud and happy, but not arrogant; losers may be sad, but not without dignity. Indeed, the practice of emotion within the context of competitive sports enables rehearsal of the limits of "appropriate" emotional experience and expression for life outside the arena of sports.[1] Most prized is intense, focused, and controlled (but not over-controlled) emotion. Manly emotion is the goal; extravagant expressiveness is valued in some measure only for anger or joy, and then, within a very restricted, time-limited, and almost ritualistic fashion.

Competitive sports are also largely a domain defined as masculine – both in the sense of manly and in the sense of not-feminine. It appears paradoxical, to say the least, that the manly arena of competitive sports is so defined by its significant *emotional* attributes. As for the contradictions inherent in the New Fatherhood which is discussed in the following chapter, the simultaneous valorization of emotion and the pressures to ensure its containment are quite revealing in what they have to say about Western, especially American, emotional standards. The identification of sport with the masculine persists even though girls and women have made tremendous advances over the past three decades in rates of participation, spectatorship, and audience interest in their competition. This trend is traceable largely to the passage of Title IX in 1972, which prohibited sex discrimination for educational programs receiving federal funds. Since its implementation, there has been a sea change in girls' and women's sports participation. According to the US Department of Education, in 1971 girls represented only 7.5 per cent of all high school athletes, but by the mid-1990s the proportion had increased to 39 per cent. Women's participation has accelerated over the past decade and now women's collegiate and professional sports have a wider and growing audience that includes men as well as women. The present conditions of rupturing of the gendered character of competitive sports make the case of competitive sports particularly useful in outlining how emotion standards are employed in defining and maintaining notions of gender difference. From childhood through adulthood the context of competition in sports stakes out the boundaries of difference, even as those boundaries have become more flexible. In addition, as women and men of color, particularly African Americans, have come to be a notable presence in many sports – even some of those most associated with white privilege, like golf and tennis – new expressive styles are absorbed into the dominant emotional culture.

So *how do children acquire the emotional competencies expected of everyone within the various social milieus they inhabit and, at the same time, learn to reconcile competing demands of gendered emotion style? And how do they do this in a way that does not undermine their own sense of authentic identity?* I begin with a brief overview of the education of emotion and the influence of parents and popular culture on its gendered side. Peer group play is especially interesting as a site for practicing emotion, especially in gendered form, so the next section considers the pretense play of early childhood through the peer group activities of middle childhood. I then turn to the special case of competitive sports as a significant site for the education of the emotions and the perpetuation of a distinctively American "manly emotion" ideal. Competitive sports are a particularly useful model system. Because sports cross racial-ethnic, geographic, class, and age boundaries in contemporary American society, they are ostensibly "gender neutral" and universal. The final section returns to the theme of emotion and identity.

Learning to do emotion the *right* way

Emotion theorist Ross Buck (1983; 1988) has used the term emotional education as a way to express what is uniquely human about learning about emotion. He observed that just as the child acquires an internal, symbolic representation of the external environment through experience in that environment, she or he also acquires an internal (cognitive and bodily) representation of the emotional environment. Buck did not originate the term, but his description captures the way in which exterior life and interior experience are connected in learning about emotion. In using the concept of emotional education I include learning what it means to experience emotion, the variety of emotion-related expectations one should develop about oneself (or others) as persons, the signs and symptoms one should rely on to know one's own or someone else's emotion, and how to tell whether an emotion is genuine as well as appropriate to the context. What my account adds to this mix is the idea that education of the emotions includes how emotion expresses personhood, especially through gender. Emotion education includes not only "because you are a boy, feel/show X," but also "feel/show X in order to become a boy."

Standards for emotional performance can be quite explicit or they can be implicit or opaque. Explicit standards are a common currency of everyday life. What we think we know about emotion, however, can disguise important features of apparently explicit emotion standards. These areas of unexamined assumptions are revealed only through asking the questions about emotion that no one typically thinks to ask – after all, if everyone "knows" them to be true, what is there to ask?

To illustrate my point I would like to consider who or what exactly defines the difference between appropriate and inappropriate emotion.

Everyone agrees that the "right amount" of the "right emotion" is good and essential to the child's healthy development. At the same time, everyone agrees that too much or not enough emotion, or the wrong kind of emotion is very bad indeed. Consider this example from a mid-twentieth-century parent advice manual in which contradictory messages about emotion are delivered without acknowledgment of internal contradictions.

> Emotions are useful and valuable *tools*. Our goal for our children is not to help them become adults who never express strong feelings, but to help them learn to use their emotions constructively. We want them to be free of damaging emotional conflicts, of unreasonable fears and anxieties. But we want them, too, to be able to express anger at social abuses and injustices, to express compassion and sympathy for others, to be able to love selflessly, and to have enthusiasm and joy for their work and activities. In that way we help them become responsible, emotional mature men and women. (English and Finch, 1951, p. 48; emphasis in original)

This all sounds very good until we start to ask exactly how a parent is supposed to tell the difference between damaging, healthy, or neutral conflicts in advance. How can a parent recognize the child's "unreasonable fears" with confidence: should a bully be ignored, approached, reported to authorities? What exactly defines the appropriate expression of anger? When is anger justifiable and when is it a nasty, self-centered tantrum – and who decides? The answer, of course, is "it depends." It depends, not on the emotion *per se*, but on context.

How people learn to discriminate appropriate from inappropriate emotion, like other aspects of emotional education, is conventionally explained in terms of the process of socialization. Socialization, as psychologists and sociologists use the term, is the lifelong process of learning to be a member of one's culture.[2] Contemporary developmental psychology tends to view children as active information seekers who selectively attend to what they identify as meaningful aspects of the social environment and who routinely engage in "making sense" of that social environment. Emotional socialization takes place within environments in which a complex network of built-in, physiological, social, and environmental variables interact. Social factors (the factors I focus on here) encompass the details of social roles that are gender-coded as well as the social-structural features of power and status differences between the sexes that frame social interaction.[3] We learn about and practice emotion in a variety of affective environments, and at different points in life different agents of socialization become more or less central to that learning. An adult may be more influenced by reading, by co-workers, by education, and so inhabits a different social world than she or he did during childhood. The boy who understood one set of standards for manly emotional expressiveness at one point in life faces another set of standards as an adult, not only because the standards differ somewhat for grown-ups and children, but because cultural standards change over time, too. The individual changes with time, but so does the world. The emotion and gender standards against which the individual judges herself or himself and against which others judge that individual change as society changes. The evolution of the New Fatherhood discussed in the following chapter is a good case in point. The New Fatherhood circa year 2000 entails a somewhat different standard of emotional display and engagement than did the Not-so-New Fatherhood circa 1900.

Emotional education, at least as I am presenting it, questions the completeness of conventional accounts of emotional socialization. From a socialization perspective, development is described in terms of the individual's approximation toward and variation on culturally agreed upon norms of conduct. Developmental progress is defined in terms of achievement of a fixed mature state. In the case of emotional socialization the approach focuses on explaining how the sexes come to differ in emotional experience and display. For example, family and peer group cultivate a "nice girl" orientation in girls that obviates the expression of anger, while supporting or promoting the expression of happiness, shame, fear, and warmth. Boys on the other hand are encouraged in the expression of emotions that reflect a sense of entitlement – anger, contempt, pride, and so on, while other emotional expression is dampened. So far so good, but the education of the emotions is never really finished for the individual. Socialization theories assume that gendered emotion is fixed once the child has identified the gender "appropriate" way of doing emotion, and that the main objective of emotional education is accomplished once the boy learns to match "boy" emotion to his own behavioral repertoire, the girl matches "girl" emotion to hers, and both reject an emotional style associated with the other sex as unacceptable for themselves. New models of gender, however, such as those discussed in Chapter 1, call into question the notion that gender is attained as a secure status and alternatively suggest that gender is a more fluid construct, one that must be negotiated in relationship with others and that is challenged by changing social contexts. Gendered emotion is not a feature of an achieved gender role, but an always in-progress negotiation of gender practice.

Achieving emotional maturity involves more than having acquired a grown-up repertoire of things we can do with emotion. Carolyn Saarni (1999) considers how children acquire the emotional competence needed for mature functioning. What does it take to be mature at emotion, to demonstrate self-efficacy in the course of emotional interactions? Saarni identifies eight skills that comprise the foundation of emotional competence. Because doing emotion and doing gender converge at critical moments in the production of our social selves, I would like to take a brief detour into Saarni's discussion of emotional competence and then relate the concept to the education of emotions as it pertains to gender. The eight skills that Saarni identifies as comprising a mature level of emotional competence include skills we would ordinarily think of as reflecting good self knowledge, such as the capacity for awareness of one's own emotion (including the understanding that at times one may deny or be unaware of the nature of one's own feelings), the ability to discern others' emotions, and the ability to understand and use the linguistic and expressive vocabulary of emotion as accepted within one's cultural frameworks. A truly insightful dimension of Saarni's analysis is her grounding of emotion as foremost a *social* transaction. Saarni notes that "emotional response is *contextually anchored in social meaning*" which encompasses "the cultural messages we have absorbed about the meaning of social transactions, or relationships, and even our self-definitions" (p. 2, emphasis in original). Other skills of emotional competence therefore place the social processes of emotion at the forefront, most notably "awareness that the structure or nature of relationships is in large part defined by how emotions are communicated with the relationship," and "capacity for accepting one's emotional experience as living in accord with one's *personal* theory of emotion" (p. 5, emphasis in original). This last is a key point that bears on the education of the emotions and the influence that this education has on the individual's understanding of how and when one should experience emotion. The prescriptions and proscriptions are gendered, just as the prescriptions and proscriptions of gender are affectively defined or inscribed in terms of emotion. To me, Saarni's take-home message is that emotional efficacy involves an acceptance of the validity of one's emotional state – emotions don't lie, even when those emotions are not the ones we believe are appropriate to the situation. Concern with validating oneself and one's belief system through emotional authenticity is an important topic, and I will return to it later in this chapter and again in Chapter 8.

Conformity to folk theory occurs in quite specific circumstances, as we have seen in Chapter 2, one of the most predictable being global, retrospective self-report in which personal and cultural norms seem to play an inordinately strong role.

Moms, dads, and omnipresent TV

Many agents of socialization exert an influence on the child's emotional expressiveness and beliefs about emotion, including parents and family, television, the school setting, teachers, and, increasingly, the Internet. All in some way show the boy how to feel and show emotion as boys "ought" to and show the girl how to feel and show emotion as girls "ought" to. Parents, though, are the first powerful influences on social development, and notions of gender and of emotion play a significant role from the very beginning of the parent-child relationship. All the evidence points to parents having the same basic goals for children of both sexes. For emotion, parents aim to encourage the expression of positive emotion and the modulation of negative emotion (Lemerise and Dodge, 1993). Nevertheless, parents may differentially encourage and respond to sons and daughters in gender-stereotypic ways. Researchers who have invested the considerable time and effort that it takes to study natural conversation between parent and toddler do see a gender effect in those conversations. Talk about feelings occurs more frequently between mothers and daughters than between mothers and sons, at least in the toddler and preschool years.[4] As for gender, the one area that seems to show consistent differences (on average) in the way that parents handle girls and boys is in the area of toy choice and encouragement of "gender consistent" play over "gender inconsistent" play.[5] The long-term consequences of these sometimes subtle effects is still an open question; nevertheless, the consensus seems to be, as Susanne Denham (1998, p. 114) points out, that parents create "an ethos, an affective environment, that has far-reaching effects on the emotional organization of their [children's] personalities" (p. 114). There is little known as to how these various patterns might apply to families other than white, middle-class, and mostly intact families typically included in this research.[6]

A classic research study from the 1980s brings home the point that parents may unwittingly hold different standards for interpreting the emotion-related behavior of their sons and daughters. Because it was not explicitly about emotion, the study shows how gendered emotion beliefs permeate the definition of "real boy" and "real girl." It also illustrates how, despite the best of intentions to the contrary, parents can, without thinking, gender stereotype their children. Margaret Bacon and Richard Ashmore (1985) investigated how mothers and fathers categorize descriptions of their children's social behavior. They generated a very long list of social behavior descriptions (195 categories of behavior) from European American parent interviews about their 6- to 11-year-old children and how the children spend their time. This list was presented to another sample of parents who sorted these descriptions into categories that "go together" with respect to the parent's own child. Bacon and Ashmore then examined the structure and content of the categories the parents generated and the relation among these categories.[7] Though emotion was not the focus of the study, the authors found two intriguing patterns relevant to emotion. First, parents viewed the dimension pertaining to degree of normality as related to the dimension of evaluation for daughters. That is, good behavior was seen as normal for daughters and bad behavior was not. For sons, however, parents appeared to consider normal behavior as a dimension separate from problem behavior. The researchers offered two interpretations of this finding. First, parents may see the "normal" behavior of sons as less likely to be good social behavior that should be encouraged than the behavior they expect to see from their daughters. It is also possible, they suggest, that "problem" behavior is more a matter of concern when exhibited by a son. Bacon and Ashmore stress that the finding suggests a narrower range of "acceptable" social behavior for girls, even though girls may have greater latitude in how they express gender through appearance and interests, no matter which interpretation is adopted. "Boys may be allowed more freedom to experiment and explore, thus exhibiting "not normal" behavior without the implication that such behavior is bad" (p. 212). The second area in which they found sex differences amplifies this conclusion. They examined parents' judgments of the most problematic behavior and found that mothers and fathers agreed that items reflecting hostility and aggression were the most problematic for their daughters. A difference between parents showed up when parents described their sons' problem behaviors. Mothers named as many hostile/aggressive items for sons as they had for daughters, but fathers considered the category that suggested poor peer relations as more problematic for sons. So when fathers judged their sons they indicated that things like "gets pushed around" and "is left out of games" are more of a problem than "spits at other kids and hassles neighbors." They conclude that, apparently, in the father's eyes, it is worse when a son is a "wimp" – that is, not masculine – than when a son is aggressively obnoxious.

Whereas parents and other family members may vary greatly over time and across circumstance in how rigid, flexible, or unconcerned they are regarding their child's gender performance, material culture pertaining to children is relentlessly gender stereotypic. Capitalizing on children's capacities to categorize boy things as different from girl things, advertising, films, television, and toys – whether traditional or technological – sell gender behavior in very clear packaging. Television especially provides emotional models. The large majority of these models are male, and when expressing emotion, nearly all of them are sex-stereotypic in their enactment of emotion. While TV programs for the very youngest viewers, *Barney, Teletubbies*, and *Blues Clues*, may aim to avoid gender stereotyping, advertising and programming for the kindergarten-up set tends to reinforce gender stereotypes even as those stereotypes are challenged. The popular cartoon *Power Puff Girls* is a perfect example of the reification of gender stereotypes, even while nominally subverting them. The three girls – named Blossom, Buttercup, and Bubbles just in case we might forget they are feminine – are direct descendents of the 1970s *Charlie's Angels*, three very sexy, very attractive, and smart women who battled the forces of evil under the direction of male mastermind Charlie. Advertising is an especially potent medium for promoting gender stereotypes. Children may take these TV models and practice their emotion, particularly in that genre that ties together the TV program with toys and products. Stephen Kline (1989) described the emergence of cartoon stories that depict highly abstracted characters, personalities whose behavior is entirely explained by a single trait or single emotion. Kline also notes that with the increase in product tie-ins adults become even more alienated from the child's world of play. The product tie-ins limit the range of plots, and children stay plugged into television, imitating what they see rather than engaging in their own play inventions. This is the ideal laboratory for showing a stock range of emotion stereotypes, many of which are gender marked.[8]

Emotion practice as gender improvisation

The power of the prevailing emotion stereotype to reproduce itself in real people's behavior is undeniable, but it begs explanation of why and how individuals improvise beyond the constraints of narrow gender choices. Gendered imperatives are neither as inflexible nor as unambiguous as they might at first appear to be. As we have seen in earlier chapters, the prevailing emotion stereotype is fraught with internal contradictions. For example, the previous chapter probed the notion of manly passion as idealized emotionality in the nineteenth century. How does the person maintain a sense of emotional authenticity in the face of these contradictions? You may recall from an earlier chapter that research only rarely yields a gender difference in knowledge about emotion, but *use* of that knowledge is another matter. Gender differences in emotion seem to reflect a discrepancy between knowledge and performance, not a gender difference in actual understanding of emotion. The key to understanding how emotion and gender converge is not in describing what each sex knows about emotion, but in explaining when and how that knowledge is deployed. By itself, the socialization model, with its emphasis on fixed, mature outcomes of development, does not help elucidate the processes that produce variability across time and situations, either within or between individuals. In other words, socialization by itself doesn't explain why or how people can so adeptly change gendered "emotional registers" when the situation demands.

In thinking about the education of the emotions it is crucial to be mindful that The Child (or The Boy or The Girl) risks overgeneralization. At the end of the day we are aiming to have a better way to understand how individual children in particular social contexts navigate the various and often conflicting messages that communicate how to be a *real* boy or girl and how to feel and display emotion in the *right* way at the *right* time. To do this we need to be attentive to the ways in which patterns play out, are disrupted, or transformed depending on social class, ethnicity, location, and historical time. Individual histories of experience in turn are located within a dominant culture in which the rules and limits of how one ought to do and to experience emotion, and how one ought to do and to experience gender, can be at odds with local culture or with individual talents and temperament.

Two concepts provide the means to extend and expand what the research on socialization can tell us. The first is an appreciation of gender as an ongoing practice, rather than simply an achieved trait. If gender is considered as *negotiated* in relationship with others, a practice that is fortified as well as challenged through those negotiations, we can discern the outline of the give and take of those negotiations. Focusing on gender in this way throws into relief the sometimes elusive and often arbitrary standards against which the success of individual gender practice is appraised. It also helps us to understand why changing social roles (or the persons who occupy them) by itself does not transform the structures that keep gender hierarchies in place. As far as emotion is concerned, gendered emotion is a practice in the always in-progress negotiation of constructing gender. Interpersonal context (perceivers' expectations and the nature of the situation) is integral to gender performance; it is not simply the medium within which gendered behavior occurs. Kay Deaux and Brenda Major (1987) proposed that gender-related behaviors are influenced by three aspects of the context: expectations of perceivers, self-systems of the actor, and situational cues. Deaux and Major's model is a medium for predicting variation within and across individuals and situations. Thus, interpersonal context (perceivers' expectations and the nature of the situation) is construed as integral to gender performance, not simply the social space in which gender performance happens. More important, Deaux and Major conceptualized gender-related behavior as a socially-embedded negotiation of identity that aims at self-confirmation and self-presentation. The crux of "performing" gender is persuading oneself and others that this performance is no performance at all, but natural, normal – in other words, an authentic expression of a real self. Cross-cultural research has shown us the great variety of ways in which "masculinity" and "femininity" are defined and also, importantly, that standards for what is considered typical or desirable for these features are linked to age and status. Jack Katz (1999, p. 170) reminds us, too, that, "in any given society, gender, age, and status characteristics are usually enacted as already there . . . One learns how to enact fundamental features of personal identity in ways that suggest that the features are inherent, natural, matters of grace, and not products of years of culturally guided practice."

A second important concept concerns how expectancies shape the individual's interpretation and performance of social mandates regarding gender and emotion. Focus on the child as an active self-socializer adopts a retrospective stance, that is, it builds on the fact that we base plans and current understanding on past events and consequences. Work that considers the child's self-socializing conventionally focuses on the development of cognitive capacities through infancy and childhood that enable one to build on past experience. Questions asked from this perspective, for example, concern how children categorize information at different ages or how the capacity for abstract reasoning influences the judgments they make about others. Saarni (1993) adds to this the importance of the child's prospective stance in emotional development. Emphasis on the prospective adds a means to express in psychological terms the processes by which individuals become active, even self-conscious (though not necessarily deliberate) in their engagement in gender-through-performance as a constituent of one's own identity. In other words, doing gendered emotion is a way to seek and create meaning for the self, and is more than a simple reaction to the pushes and pulls of personal history or current circumstances. This observation is quite powerful when applied to gendered emotion. "Performance" of gender creates gendered emotion; "practice" of emotion creates gender and reinforces the notion of gender as difference.

To summarize, we can think about children's experience of doing gendered emotion in relation to the sites in which the practice takes place, and also in relation to the function of emotional exchanges in children's lives. Developmentally significant sites are those in which children practice emotion in play and in competition. In the following section I consider the ways in which emotion practice occurs as gender improvisation in play. Play, especially play in the peer group, illustrates how performance of emotion scenarios serves as a framework for practicing gender. The complicity of gender practice in emotional education and of emotional education in gender practice underscores the dynamic complexity and continuity of the development of a social self.

Practicing emotion in play

Greta Fein (1991, p. 144) points out that children's play, despite adult intervention, is truly a child's world: "Play is something contented children do when adults are not bothering them to do other things; and play is something adults tell demanding children to do to get them out of the way." Adults can shape where and how children play, and the play materials that are available, but it is the child or children themselves who directly determine the course of the action and content. There is general agreement that play based on the exercise of imagination rather than rules has a special function of allowing children the free space to practice emotion, whether to re-live and tame specific emotionally challenging situations or to rehearse more mundane aspects of everyday emotional life, such as leave-taking. "Pretend play," because it involves pretense of character, setting, and/or objects, permits children to work through and practice alternate ways of experiencing and handling emotionally vivid situations.[9] Most researchers who consider pretend play do so from the perspective of how that play reflects and promotes the child's cognitive development, that is, skills of problem-solving, language, perspective taking, planfulness, and the like. From this perspective it is as if successful development involves learning how to use all the tools in a toolbox: there are correct and incorrect ways to use the tools, and the best way to gain expertise and dexterity is through practice, practice, practice. The cognitive-developmental perspective, which at present is the dominant theoretical camp within developmental psychology, can be contrasted with the social constructivist view of child development which is more prevalent in anthropological and sociological studies of childhood. The constructivist is interested in the child more as a meaning maker, less as a meaning discoverer. Taking a constructivist perspective, Kane and Furth (1993), for example, assert that for the growing child, reality is something to be playfully created rather than revealed. Using the toolbox analogy again, the constructivist perspective focuses more on what is built with the tools than on the mastery of the tools themselves. From this perspective, the fabrication of realities is not peculiar to pretend play because meaning-making goes on in all activities. Play, however, may offer special incentives or advantages for practice and invention because it is not so constrained by the limits imposed by the physical world. Race car driving and helicopter piloting aren't things a six-year-old can do "really" except in the context of play.

The mastery meta-language of the cognitive-developmental view runs throughout the literature on children's play. This cognitive-developmental framework conceptualizes the child's developing relation to his or her own emotional understanding and experience in terms of the goal of emotional self-regulation. That is, the endpoint of development is identified with the capacity for successful control or containment of emotion through self-understanding and the capacity for behavioral self-restraint. Hall (1986) emphasizes the importance of language in the child's successful development of self-control. Advocating that the child be encouraged to use words to "master strong emotions," Hall infers a progression from directly acting on the impulses generated by strong feelings toward the use of language to substitute for action, to achievement of self-control through clarifying, tolerating, and containing feelings through language. Compare this perspective with Saarni's emphasis on emotional competence, which identifies emotional self-regulation as just one of several skills foundational to the achievement of emotional competence. There is a striking difference between treating emotional development as ever more sophisticated ability to contain or express emotion and one that incorporates emotion into the larger themes of personal value systems and social interdependence.

"Cooked babies": Pretend play

The earliest signs of pretend play emerge between 18 months and two years, which is about the same time that preference for sex-typed toys appears. A useful distinction between pretend play and nonpretend social play is that pretend play is a nonliteral treatment of objects, setting, and/or identity, as conveyed primarily by the child's verbalizations, as in "I'll be the Mom, you be the baby" (de Lorimier, Doyle, and Tessier, 1995). The use of pretense can thus be distinguished from ordinary conversation, as well as unframed teasing or "acting silly." Goncu (1993) maintains that age three is a landmark in the development of verbal shared understanding (the technical term is "intersubjectivity") in social pretend play. By this age children can adopt a shared pretend focus and begin to mark their interactions explicitly as pretend play, that is, state that what they are doing is make-believe or pretend. And they can relate to one another's intentions within the pretense with increasing degrees of relevance to what their play partner is acting out or signaling as an intention to act out. In other words, play based in pretense is not unstructured play. The rules may evolve as the play progresses, usually when one participant judges the play partner to have violated the rule: "You can't do that!"

Pretense, however, is not just practicing what is already known or rehearsing the rules of everyday life as dictated by grownups. Rather, it transforms these events and rules. Fein identifies the challenge in explaining the relation between the literalness of mundane situations represented in pretend play and the spin-offs, elaborations, and imaginative applications, as "how to explain how a mind built from external events mapped onto it, can become a mind that subverts these very events" (p. 155). Pretend play is an opportunity to challenge reality and the values that adults try so hard to inculcate. Even if stones are used for money and dirt for food in a game of "store," arguments about who can and cannot play which role and what can and cannot be bought are vigorously disputed. Pretend play is not a literal scripting of real-life situations; whereas there may be elements of actual daily events, they are not necessarily played out fully or in sequence. Younger children's pretend play is particularly disjointed in connecting real with pretend. Fein observes that "even though sequences are detailed, ordered, and familiar, meanings may be startling" (p. 155). She brings home the point by describing one play sequence of 3-year-olds who put a pot on the stove, turned on the burner, and proceed with the pretense to cook, then slice and eat a baby! The upshot of this is that while the situations of pretend play may be outrageous, the emotions they generate or simulate are true to real life. Pretend play fosters no great distinction between emotion as practiced in play and as it occurs in everyday life outside of the play setting.

Earlier play theorists viewed pretend play as somehow less sophisticated than organized, rule-based games. Whalen (1995) exemplifies more recent thinking that emphasizes the cognitively sophisticated and socially subtle interactions that characterize pretend play and consider it no less advanced than the rule-governed play that comes to prevail later on in the middle childhood years. Pretend play takes a certain social maturity, and, in fact, differences have been observed between children who initiate pretend play and those who are nonparticipants. In one study of 4- and 5-year-olds, those children who were pretend play initiators were, compared to their less playful peers, more friendly, popular, expressive, cooperative, verbal, and creative, less impulsive and aggressive, and more likely to take the perspective of others (Fein and Kinney, 1994).

Jeff Parker and John Gottman (1989) trace a developmental progression in how children handle emotion in pretend play contexts. They identify the earliest use of play to maintain behavioral organization in the face of high arousal. The child then advances to be concerned with appropriate emotional displays in social contexts and, later, to an integration of logic and emotion into a coherent understanding of how emotions function in social discourse and relationships. Fantasy play involves calling forth, both expressively and experientially, the emotions to be practiced. Successful practice in the play situation requires children to have the capacity to regulate their own emotional experience to some degree and to control their own emotion-related action. An example cited by Parker and Gottman to illustrate emotion practice is a scenario of two friends pretending to drive their sick child to the hospital. The pair pretend to be frightened in this imagined life-or-death situation, and actually *are* frightened in rehearsing it. If some fear were not evoked by the situation, the researchers argue, the pretend scenario would not be an exciting, engaging play adventure. In pretend play children can come to understand their ability to control to some degree their experience of hedonically negative emotions. Through the story line they can express those troublesome emotions of anger, fear, or distress, and experiment with how these emotions can be shown, what can cause them, how others react, and what sorts of things can exacerbate the intensity of the feelings and the resources needed to shape the experience rather than have it overwhelm one (Singer, 1994).

A single pretense episode can contain multiple instances of individually experienced emotion and communication about that emotion. Indeed, these instances of emotion play a significant role in establishing the pretense and seeing it through its course. Verba (1993) points out that the "socioaffective aspect" is especially clear at the start of an episode when partners establish contact and the premise for play. During play, emotion's operation as an interpersonal phenomenon is evident in its use to sustain play when difficulties and conflicts arise that would otherwise lead to a breakdown in the play episode. The interpersonal nature of emotion is evident both in the style in which children deal with conflict, and in its function of creating an emotional bond of shared laughing and smiling that can forestall the appearance of other conflicts. Pretend play offers children a context for indirectly trying out different identities and emotional styles with minimum social risk. The approval or disapproval of others toward the tried-on role is at some remove from the child's own actual identity, and already here we see a common gambit in childhood and in later practice of emotion – that is, ignoring or disavowing the statement or the emotion expressed as if it was "just" an emotional response or as if it hadn't happened at all.

Much of pretend play is very obviously gendered. For example, gender one-upmanship is a common feature of unstructured play situations, especially in boys' play. One early study (McLoyd, Warren and Thomas, 1984) showed that whether the theme is every day life or space alien monsters, young boys are quite explicitly concerned with maintaining a boy play space through taunts and teasing "sissy" behavior, and demonstrations of strength and physical prowess. The extent to which children rehearse conventional gender roles (or class positions or ethnic traditions) in play is partly constrained by the play materials and environments available to them. The models of the "right" way to play are also prominently featured on children's television programming, especially in advertising. TV commercials show girls and boys interacting differently with toys (Goldstein, 1994), and the physical features of toys suggest play possibilities that incorporate stereotypic gendered styles. G. I. Joe® and other boys' action figures do not have long, stylable hair, and classic Barbie® is famous for her lack of joints at elbows and knees. G. I. Joe's® expressions show focused determination, while

Barbie's® is vacuously pleasant. Integral to the right way to play at gender is the right way to play at emotion.

"Cooties" and "cry-babies": Peers as enforcers of gendered emotion

Just about every grown-up who thinks back to school days can remember some version of a playground game in which the girls would chase the boys, the boys would chase the girls, or both. The rules of the game were vague, if indeed there *were* any rules. The object of the game was as obscure to the players themselves as it would have been to anyone watching. The charged combination of excitement and aversion that accompanied the game, though, made it very, very popular.

Children's self-imposed sex-segregated play and the role of play as a vehicle for children's socialization are each topics that have been studied and written about extensively. From early toddlerhood children choose to play with same-sex playmates if they are allowed to choose and enough near-agemates are around.[10] A number of other researchers have observed this preference pattern. Although adults can intervene and reformulate the play group, and although children will play with other-sex children if same-sex children are not present, there seems to be a very compelling interest in same-sex play partners. Eleanor Maccoby (1988; 1998) suggests that in the early years girls play a big role in establishing the sex segregation. Girls would rather play with girls because boys are pushy and obnoxious. It is not simply a matter of "politeness" – but boys are pushy and obnoxious in a way that ensures that their preferences take precedence over girls'. Nor is it the case that girls are nice and boys are not, rather, when girls and boys are together, girls' leadership is challenged and girls' interests are marginalized. Nevertheless, girls go along with boys' less mature play styles in mixed sex groups. It is not at all clear whether this is because girls are less physically aggressive, they find it easier to avoid conflict, they find other activities more attractive, or some other combination of motivations. Maccoby's analysis of sex-segregated play acknowledges the variety of factors that may bias the choices of children, from parental encouragement to engage in sex "appropriate" behavior and provision of play materials and opportunities that foster appropriate play, to sex-related differences in the ways in which aggression is manifested and styles of physical activity in play. In Maccoby's view, the most important factor in fostering the sex-segregation toward which children gravitate is the child's recognition that gender is a significant social category and the resulting classification of oneself as a member of the category "male" or "female." Maccoby's contribution is in pointing out how group gender differentiation can contribute to setting up the conditions for gender-exclusive peer socialization opportunities. She suggests that by the end of the second year, one can already see the basis of same-sex play group preferences being exhibited by looking at the toddler's choice of friends. Girls initially instigate this separation, but by the age of five or six, boys' groups are more vigorous in maintaining segregation – through name-calling, both of girls and of boys who would show interest in playing with girls. Within these sex-segregated groups different types of play predominate. For boys it is rough-and-tumble play within which the establishment and maintenance of a dominance hierarchy is a major motif; for girls, the emphasis is on thematic play within which leadership roles are more freely exchanged. Maccoby suggests that this is a strong universal pattern observed in a variety of cultural environments and is independent of other childrearing considerations (e.g., strict versus permissive; degree to which cross-sex cooperation is encouraged within formal and informal play structures). The relevance to emotion is quite striking. By establishing gender-exclusive play groups children set up and maintain gender-specific performance and rehearsal space for emotion. For example, the narrative themes and multiple characters that are the features of doll play afford situations to think about and practice emotion openly as a dimension of relationships and social exchange. Further, the conditions within the groups are such that different expectations are established regarding which emotions ought to occur and how they should be reacted to. Expectations even extend to the centrality of emotion to the group's interaction, including how much and what kind of emotion is needed for successful negotiation of play. Contact team sports, for example, may create more situations in which the anger-aggression connection is at the forefront and fewer in which acute self-consciousness or empathy are involved than in games and sports in which turn-taking and individual performance are highlighted.

The same sex/other sex distinction relies on children identifying themselves categorically with one sex or the other. And if the child feels at home in neither camp, that child is compelled, nevertheless, to acquiesce to the fact that two categories only are acceptable (not equivalent in value, mind you, but expected and able to be "dealt with"). The pressures and preferences to divide the gender world into two are found across play contexts, and across ages from toddlerhood to pubescence. Children's tendency to be attentive to gender-as-difference has had a narrowing effect on theory. Jacklin and Reynolds (1993, p. 207) note that "an underlying assumption of all the viewpoints of childhood gender socialization is that there are two sets of behaviors for children to learn . . . a central problem of all these viewpoints is that there are really more than two sets of behaviors to be learned."

Girls and boys learn about emotions in organized sports and games, but that which is conventionally identified as "girl play" is less boundary defined and more fluid with everyday situations or offers more opportunities for real-life to weave into the play momentum. Playing house or playing Barbie® means that you must make up the details of the narrative as you go along and the events of daily life can easily be made fodder for advancing the storyline. Girl play may therefore offer more opportunity to practice emotions as they are encountered in the ordinary give and take of social interaction. Boys engage in interpersonal dramatic play, too, both in mixed-sex and all-boy groups. The interpersonal affective dimension of boy-group play, though, may take a backseat to other play themes – killing or crashing, for example. The difference between the play of small, informal groups with that of formal rule-governed games and sports (that both girls and boys engage in) is the relation between emotion and play rather than the range of emotions practiced. Leslie Brody (1993), for example, adopts the "separate cultures" approach to explaining gendered emotion styles. She works from the generalization that "girls tend to play in intimate small groups that value verbal communication and cooperation and that minimize hostility and overt conflict," while boys "play in larger, hierarchically organized groups in which criticism, teasing, and status-oriented competition are commonplace" (p. 97). From this she concludes that different styles of sex-segregated play lead "girls to learn to value the expression of emotion (although not direct anger) and boys to learn to value the expression of only those emotions related to competition" (p. 97). This representation of children's play patterns and their rehearsal of emotion in play, however, is not as universal as it is sometimes assumed to be. Barrie Thorne (1993) has persuasively critiqued the separate cultures interpretation of sex-segregated play, pointing out that the model implies that girls' and boys' separation is the prevalent mode of children's social life and it "gives no theoretical attention to the moments of 'with' and comfortable sharing" (p. 90). The "static and exaggerated dualism" (p. 91) that the separate cultures interpretation emphasizes fits so comfortably with prevailing gender stereotypes it rarely is examined for the many occasions and kinds of play that it does *not* encompass. Moreover, the treatment of sex-segregated play patterns as typical and normative tends to overemphasize the social arrangements characteristic of popular children, marginalizing other groups and individuals. Thorne's conclusions are based on the rich results of her ethnographic study of two elementary schools (one in the mid-1970s and one in the mid-1980s). That work revealed a great deal of variety in group size, hierarchy, and play activities. Thorne observed that girls-play/boys-play organization was more evident among the most popular children and that other organizations of dyads and triads, and other non-gender-stereotypic play patterns commonly occurred, especially among children less firmly established in the popularity hierarchy. She warns that "a skew toward the most visible and dominant" silences and marginalizes others. That said, it is the good-looking and popular children who model ideal gender types in group play situations.

Girl-group play is far from nonhierarchical or noncompetitive. Linda Hughes (1988) critiques analyses of children's play preferences that characterize girls' games as passively cooperative games and boys' as more aggressive, competitive ones, pointing out the circular reasoning that gives rise to that conclusion: "Girls are more cooperative, so they play more cooperative games, so they become more cooperative" (p. 670). She observes that the dichotomization of cooperation and competition by researchers leads to the conclusion "that girls not only emerge as cooperative, but also as noncompetitive, and with few apparent opportunities to break out of the pattern" (p. 670). According to Hughes, a concomitant pattern of crediting aggressive, competitive play with fostering cognitive development fashions cooperation as an impediment. Her own observations of 4th and 5th grade girls playing Foursquare (a nonteam ball-bouncing game whose outcome depends on a combination of luck and skill) revealed a distinctive style of keen competitiveness. There was strong pressure for "being nice" to friends by helping them in the game, and less obligation to do so toward nonfriends, to the point of being "mean" to nonfriends in order to assist friends. Clearly, interpersonal concerns are a dominant theme in girls' play, but not to the exclusion of selective noncooperation or competitiveness. Hughes concludes that the interpersonal orientation of girls may shape their ways of competing, but not whether they compete at all.

Peer play enables the child to build skills that are involved in managing how we look in front of others. In the play situation, the child has a circumscribed environment in which to practice self-presentation and impression management, and with this the capacity to shape their behavior to create the desired social impressions of themselves for targeted others within the social environment. The projected social self involves both management of felt and displayed emotion as well as felt and displayed gender-coded behavior. Concerns with others' views of one's acceptability intensify at about the time that peer groups become resolutely sex-segregated. Parker and Gottman (1989) point out that children are often insecure about their social position and acceptability to other children from whom they want approval, and so spend considerable energy in the play situation to maintain status and to guard against rejection. The visibility of emotional display and the readiness with which children identify others' "inappropriate" gender-coded behavior ensures that one's own practice of gendered emotion is carefully monitored so that corrections can be made before anyone else notices. The child who doesn't pay attention to the boundaries of doing gender is the one who is an easy target for rejection from the group. Emotional behavior is an especially effective target for controlling peers – the appearance of emotion of whatever sort is a signal that there may be some added vulnerability to control. Calling someone a big baby or cry-baby is guaranteed to get results if some signs of strongly felt emotion are already evident. Indeed, the same strategy works well with adults, too, although "cry-baby" is likely to be replaced by "No need to get emotional."

The efficacy of emotion name-calling is asymmetrical with respect to gender. No one wants to be called a cry-baby and both girls and boys are vulnerable to the epithet. What does it mean to be called a cry-baby? For a girl it means you are acting immaturely; for a boy it means you are acting immaturely like a girl. While girls may chastise another girl for angry or fearful or giggly displays through name calling or even application of a specific emotion label, the message of the teasing is that she is acting immaturely or inappropriately, but she is still a girl. If a girl picks a fight, she's called "mean," not "a boy." When boys resort to name-calling and reference to emotional appropriateness in play setting, the name-calling explicitly identifies inappropriate emotion and explicitly or implicitly identifies that as "girl behavior." So monitoring others' emotional displays is a great strategy for exercising some degree of control over that person. It is also a way to underscore behavior that fails to meet correct gender standards. While signs of true emotion are the main target, there is also a preoccupation with shaping what felt emotion and displayed emotion ought to be present. Not getting angry when entitlement is violated is something that increases the child's vulnerability, whether girl or boy, to others' exploitation. However, being a "wimp" and under-displaying, or by inference under-feeling anger, tells a girl that she is undervalued, has a shaky status within the group, and is not tough enough. It tells a boy that he is ineffectual because he is acting like a girl. The power of the peer group (in childhood as well as in adulthood) is that others do not necessarily need to express their approbation or condemnation. We just have to *believe* that they hold those values and *think* that they might express them.

The special domain of sports

Competitive sports are a bridge between the earliest rehearsal of gendered emotion in pretend play and the ongoing practice of gendered emotion in later childhood and adulthood. I have written earlier on the idea that emotion makes the effect of winning and losing so powerful. The emotional features of sports help us understand how the emotion practiced in that arena differs from emotion in pretend play and, more significantly, the ebb and flow of emotion in every day life. Emotion *per se* is not a constituent of the game as it is in pretend play. In sports, the setting is well-defined and clearly distinct from the rest of everyday life, whereas the boundaries between pretend play and real life are far more fluid. The emotion of competitive sports is also very public emotion, and the rules of expression, and the violation of those rules or deviation from the guidelines, are matters of public discussion. A case in point is the controversial major college basketball coach, Bob Knight. His many years as coach at Indiana University were punctuated by his dramatic public displays of anger toward referees, the other team, or his own players. Episodes of strong emotion were played and replayed, discussed and analyzed in the sports pages and on television – even comic strips. Ultimately, a particularly intense physical display of anger toward one of his players led the president of the university to place Knight on a "zero tolerance" probation – one more outburst and he would lose his job. That outburst came, and Knight was dismissed after twenty-nine stormy years as a winning coach. For Knight, the question of emotional control was played out in a very public way, and his case is only one among many striking examples of emotion as public currency in sports.

Athletic participation is not the only field for practicing emotion, of course. Many private pleasures offer the opportunity to try on what a new emotional experience might be like or to relive and "do better" an emotional opportunity from one's past. Reading fiction, for example, can serve as a private form of practicing emotion. What is special about competitive sports is that emotions are interpersonal, as in the private sphere, but they occur within the context of an explicit set of rules that govern the timing and progress of a game or contest that itself is not about emotion. Emotion is framed by the rules of contest or competition and there is predictability as to when and which emotions should happen, and how intense those emotions should be. In tennis, for example, if a player expresses too much emotion, either positive or negative, the umpire can penalize that display either with a fine or by giving points to the opponent. In that regard the nature and form of expression can be a decisive factor in the game itself. The peaks and valleys of emotion are tightly linked with the contest's progress. In regular life, the moments of emotion are not so predictable and the boundaries that signal the likelihood – and appropriateness – of emotion are much sloppier. Moments of abrupt emotional intensity can occur when least expected ("Where did you say you parked the car?") or in the stray remark that is taken personally ("So you really think I look fat in these jeans?"). Emotions, in fact, commonly arise in the course of negotiating other social complexities that may seem to have nothing to do with instigating the particular emotional reaction.

The deep connection between sports and the education of emotion is a gendered connection. Sports education literature, whether it is aimed at justifying Little League or intercollegiate athletic programs, emphasizes that participation in organized sports contributes positively to the development of the whole individual – "good school spirit, group loyalty, and esprit de corps" as well as "the ability to give that little extra" – and emotion is the essence. One educator of the early 1960s describes the manly ideal this way:

> On the football field or the basketball court the athlete learns how to take hard knocks without whimpering. He learns to control his temper, not to lower himself to get even with the fellow who has taken a mean advantage. He learns to stand up to the strong and to protect the weak. The lesson is taught in contact sports never to kick a man who is down and always to back up one's teammates.[11]

Whereas the emotional foundation of character was emphasized for boys, girls' programs had quite a different emphasis and promoted a noncompetitive, "be nice" version of femininity. The pre-Title IX position of the Division for Girls and Women's Sports of the national sports educators' group was that girls' programs were in place "not to find the best team or player but to give opportunity and pleasure to all participating" (Ley, 1963, p. 24).

Much may have changed regarding girls' and women's sports participation since the 1960s, but sports education still aims to promote conventional masculinity. Michael Messner laments the negative aspects of sports in the young man's sense of himself as a success or failure. He views sports as a site for practicing "traditional" notions of masculinity, defined as notions of success, power, and superiority over the feminized segments of society. Though much emphasis is placed on the "emotional tempering" that the pressures of competition and giving one's best can stimulate, a minor theme in sports education is advice to parents and coaches not to underestimate the emotional investment of the young player and advice on how to handle the emotions of the young player.[12] Gary Fine's (1987) ethnographic study of Little League baseball vividly shows the significant role that emotions play in the Little League experience. In a discussion of emotion work among the players, he observes how seriously emotional display is taken. If one does not adhere to the emotional rules, Fine notes, one risks being labeled a "girl" or a "faggot."[13]

What is it like for the boy who doesn't have the opportunities to participate in male sports culture? Boys who don't become immersed in sports via television or who lack the chance to watch or play experience this as a disadvantage, even a shameful missing link to manhood. Boys whose access is limited by virtue of social class background or competing expectations of their ethnic culture, are *de facto* ineligible for the highest status. Sports are supposed to occupy an important place in the life of the normal American male. "Real" boys are expected to know and care at least a minimal amount – other boys and girls expect it of them, as do the adults who encounter children. Compulsory interest in sports demonstrates that one is normal, a "real" man, that is, not female, not feminine. Confessional pieces that take as their theme lack of interest in sports contain a strong assertion of heterosexual virility. In one such confessional piece that begins, "I've decided to come out of the closet," one man discusses the many situations in which he is disadvantaged because he has no interest in or knowledge of the manly world of sports.

> Even after three marriages, three children, and some in-between love affairs, plus the sure knowledge that I adore women, I still feel, from time to time that, somehow, I must be lacking in the right male genes.[14]

The expectation is that a real man knows something about at least some sports even if he elects not to participate, and the same expectation is not applied to women or girls. In other words, a boy would need to grow up on another planet in order for him not to be somewhat affected by the emotion models that are provided by competitive sports. Competitive sports do not create gender, they help to create the circumstances for defining gender as difference, and in the contemporary US, for drawing a line between masculine heterosexuality and anything that might be seen as threatening it.

The education of the emotions and social identity

Doing emotion the "right" way, which is often a gendered way, serves as verification of the authenticity of the self. Not "I feel, therefore I am," but "I feel as I believe I ought to, therefore I am the person I believe I am." Gender may be marked by any of the other major categories of social identity such as age, class, or racial ethnicity, as well as other distinctive features that come into play in forming public and private dimensions of identity – attractiveness, status, disability, to name but a few. The point is that the combination of gender and emotion is an enormously potent identifier, and when we talk about the multiple components of an individual's identity, gender is inevitably implicated.

The education of the emotions is about how to know one is experiencing emotion and how to tell whether that emotion is *authentic*, as well as appropriate to the context. Arlie Hochschild's (1983) landmark exploration of *feeling rules*, the culturally defined conventions for assessing the fit between felt emotion and the situation, and the efforts we make to conform to feeling rules, marked a turning point in emotions research. Before Hochschild, the emphasis was almost exclusively on management of one's expressive behavior, that is, on *display rules*. Display rules (Ekman and Friesen, 1975) identify when, how, and by whom specific kinds of felt emotion should be displayed. The idea behind display rules is that the main thing we need to worry about in emotion management is how we appear to others: You can feel whatever way you want to, just make sure you show the right kind of emotional demeanor, in facial expression, voice, gesture. In this school of thought, "Wipe that smile off your face" literally means just change the expression – I don't care what you think or feel, just make sure that your emotional deportment is in line with expectations.[15] Hochschild, drawing on Erving Goffman's distinction between surface acting (getting it right on the outside) and deep acting (getting it right on the inside), persuasively argued that in many situations we are expected to engage in deep acting to create the right kind of felt emotion, as well as the right kind of emotional display. Her particular focus in this original work was on the transformation of felt emotion into an unacknowledged product of labor, one that can be psychologically costly to produce. In many service occupations management doesn't want the employee to treat customers with perfunctory efficiency, but to radiate genuine care and concern. Hochschild's portrayal of the commodification of emotion in paid labor has transformed how emotion in the workplace is thought about and studied.[16]

What I find especially useful is the psychological dimension of the questions Hochschild raises. There are many external pressures to make sure that our feelings are in line with what they ought to be. When a person fails to follow the rules, other people signal the violation in a variety of ways, through looks, by making a statement, by making a show of behaving "correctly" themselves, and so on. But even when we fool others into believing our surface acting, it can feel as though that is not enough. When the emotional stakes are high people will go to great lengths to shape their felt emotion to conform to what they believe to be an emotional state more appropriate to the situation. Why isn't it enough to have the right emotional appearance? Your friend has won a prize and you don't feel as happy for her as you want to – so you work at changing your felt emotion. Your best friend works hard to stay "in love" with his romantic partner; your neighbor worries aloud that the death of her favorite aunt hasn't touched her as she believes it should. Why go through the efforts to "fix" emotion when, through clever management of our words and expression we could fool everyone else? Hochschild suggests that through *emotion work* we deliberately shape our felt emotions and we are motivated to do this not simply because of social pressure, but more importantly to "stay in character" with ourselves. The wrong emotion, or too much or too little, makes us "out of sync" with ourselves – we engage in emotion work so that we can continue to believe in ourselves.

A number of different ways of conceptualizing identity have been developed by psychologists and sociologists. Kay Deaux (1993; 1996), whom I have mentioned above in connection with the gender-in-context model, discusses identity in a way that is especially helpful in linking gender and emotion to a concept of self. Deaux sees identity as comprised of a set of social categories in which the person claims membership and the personal meanings that the person attaches to each of these categories. In other words, people create a personal identity out of the meanings and experiences that they attach to their identification with groups or social category. To one person, for example, self-identification as a Roman Catholic incorporates elements of spirituality, pride, faith, and security. For another it may reflect ambivalence about authority and doubt. The individual belongs to a set of distinct groups that comprise a sense of one's social self, and identification with each group may be more or less central to the individual. If Brian identifies himself as a Wiccan, for example, that identity may signify a central, organizing feature of his social relationships or it may play a minor part among the various other social identities that he claims: older brother, vegan, member of the Green Party, philosophy student, musician.

The social identity perspective is an alternative way of asking questions about gender than the long-standing convention of investigating gender in terms of gender difference. What is the problem with construing gender as difference? I've covered this in more detail in Chapter 2; here it might be helpful to review the idea in terms of a specific example, namely the contrast between extravagant expressiveness and the telegraphed style that characterizes manly emotion. The lament "Don't just tell me that you love me, say it like you really mean it!" calls out for extravagant expressiveness. The subtext of manly emotion is strongly felt emotion under control, and the stronger the felt emotion, the more clearly visible is the control of that intense experience. Each of these two emotional modes is defined as and defines a gendered style. Both modes, however, are also the "correct" standard of felt emotion and emotional display as defined by contemporary dominant culture. Extravagant emotion is a legitimate way to "do" nurturance;

"manly emotion" is called for in just about every other situation. The emotional double bind for women, then, is the expectation that they will be appropriately nurturant (as shown in part through extravagant expressiveness), yet also conform to the overarching standard of manly emotion. For men the bind is how to approximate the elusive ideal of manly emotion. The pushes and pulls ensure that resolution is not simple. Contemporary dominant culture in the US encourages men to be good friends, good lovers, and good fathers, which means "be sensitive" and risk being feminine. Contemporary dominant culture also requires manly emotional self-control, which is often understood as "be inexpressive" which is not only incompatible with the emotional extravagance standard, but more threateningly, is incompatible with being a genuine person.

The challenge of gendered emotion for both women and men is to become capable of reconciling competing emotional standards in a way that can be experienced as consistent with, or at least not undermining, a coherent sense of authentic identity. And one must be able to achieve this reconciliation while meeting the expectations and demands of others in one's various social roles. Keep in mind, however, that the double bind is not equivalent in its consequences for women and men. As the next chapter shows via discussion of the New Fatherhood, appropriation and recharacterization of features of feminine-identified emotion can actually reinforce the gender divide between manly and the merely feminine. For women, the double bind is a no-win situation. No small reason for this are the hurried transitions between emotion modes as one moves between personal/family responsibilities and those of work. More important, however, is the ever-present identification of female/feminine with the "merely emotional."

By the mid-twentieth century the notion of an idealized emotion in the service of reason was, in the US, replaced as a core emotion image defining masculinity by a pathological suppression of emotion and its expression. Whereas in the nineteenth century masculine emotional pathology was represented as a kind of brutishness uninformed by sensibility and uncontrolled by reason, the foremost emotional problem for the typical twentieth-century male came to be viewed as a problem of emotional deficiency rather than excess. The following chapter begins with the question of when and why a particular style of emotional display came to be considered *the* prevailing form of emotion in American men – ignoring the unique features of racial ethnic and social class contexts – and a threat to their physical and psychological health. What is masculine inexpressivity? And how did it come to be considered a pathology of masculinity? Through problematizing the "tragedy" of the inexpressive male (Balswick and Peek, 1971) and the emotional "hazards of being male" (Goldberg, 1976), it is possible to reveal the uneasy relationship among standards for ideal emotion and beliefs about natural and typical emotion in fragmented contemporary society.

Notes

1 This view works equally well for social constructionist models and fundamental/basic emotions theories. Zurcher (1982), for example, used a dramaturgical analysis to study emotional performances of football players before, during, and after professional games. Snyder (1990) focused on individual rather than team sport in his study of collegiate women gymnasts.

2 Socialization is accomplished through the same processes that account for all social learning: direct instruction by others, modeling one's own behavior on the behavior of others, and learning through reinforcement and punishment. While we might think of reinforcement and punishment for emotional displays occurring in very obvious ways, as, for example, in punishing tantrums, they can occur in subtle ways as well. Denham (1998) cites research showing parents' desire to discourage their sons' sad and fearful responses and expectations that their daughters should inhibit anger.

3 Extensive reviews of emotional development can be found in Saarni (1999), Denham (1998), and Brody (1999). As I mentioned in Chapter 2, comparisons of gender effects in emotional development across the lifespan are quite difficult because adults and children are rarely included in the same research projects, and research on children and adults tends to use different methodological strategies. See also the bi-directional model of emotional socialization outlined by Nancy Eisenberg and her colleagues (Eisenberg, Cumberland, and Spinrad, 1998).

4 Mothers and fathers report or are observed to differ in their emotion-relevant interactions and talk with sons and daughters. See, for example, Dunn, Bretherton, and Munn (1987), Cervantes and Callanan (1998), Fivush, Brotman, Buckner, and Goodman (2000), Garner, Robertson, and Smith (1997). Eisenberg (1999) observed that gender patterns in emotion talk were similar in Anglo and Mexican American samples. She concluded that social class is associated with the context in which feeling states are discussed, and ethnicity is related to the content of such talk.

5 For example, Leaper, Leve, Strasser, and Schwartz (1995) found that mother-child communication patterns were affected by whether the play activity was gender-stereotypic or cross-gender stereotypic.

6 See also Leslie Brody's (1999) discussion of the subtle sex differences in infant behavioral style and developmental timetables that could pull parents toward a more gender-exaggerated interactional style. Some researchers have observed, after early infancy, that the angry display of sons is taken and noted for what it is – dealt with – whereas that of daughters is deflected or ignored. Radke-Yarrow and Kochanska (1990), for example, found that mothers responded differently to the anger displays of preschooler sons than of preschooler daughters. Mothers responded to sons' displays of anger in gratifying ways, such as attentive concern, but they ignored daughters' expressions of anger or tried to inhibit the anger display. Robyn Fivush and her colleagues (Fivush and Buckner, 2000; Fivush and Kuebli, 1997) point

out that parent-child talk about emotions can promote gendered emotional socialization.

7 Among the categories generated by the sorting were Aggressive/Hostile versus Not Aggressive/Not Hostile, Normal versus Problem, and Typical versus Not Typical. The researchers also looked at the relation among these categories and between each category and parents' evaluation of the behavior.

8 See also Berry and Asamen (1993).

9 Many researchers have observed this, even in the very earliest pretend play. See, for example, First's (1994) discussion of playing "I'm leaving and you cry" by two-year-olds.

10 Choice of playmates is but one area in which same-sex preferences are the rule. Children as young as one year of age choose toys conventionally associated with their own gender (e.g., Bradley and Gobbart, 1989).

11 This and previous quote are from Harper (1963), p. 87.

12 See Messner, Dunbar, and Hunt (1992), Messner (1996), and Bruns and Tutko (1986). The goal of the ideal athlete is not emotion control in the sense of dampening experience and expression. Rather, the sports exhortation literature from the nineteenth century to the present shows that this is anything but the case. In fact, this continuity between the Victorian era and our own can be compared to the other major changes in representations of gendered emotion noted in earlier chapters.

13 The effectiveness of emotion models is illustrated by Fine's description of one pitcher who modeled his performance on the pitcher's mound after major league players. Not only did the boy emulate the pitching style, but he also clearly understood the expressive understatement of manly emotion. Fine's field notes include the observation that this boy "will sometimes throw his hands slightly in the air and mutter a quiet 'yay' to himself. Most of the time he is pensive and serious, and is totally wrapped up in the game" (p. 45).

14 Mark Goodson "Lousy at Sports." *New York Times Magazine*, 1986, p. 48.

15 The concept of display rules has come under considerable criticism (e.g., Fridlund, 1994). Beyond the obvious and general (e.g., smile when you get a gift) display rules are often identified *post hoc* and so involve a certain circularity.

16 A large body of research work on emotion labor was stimulated by Hochschild's work. See, for example, a special issue of *European Journal of Work and Organizational Psychology* (1999, number 8) on "Emotion at Work."

CHAPTER 6

Ideal emotion and the fallacy of the inexpressive male

Think back to Super Bowl XXIV in 1990, the San Francisco 49ers versus the New York Giants. The 49ers, the previous year's champions, were the strong favorites and dominated the game from the beginning. As the game wore on, the TV cameras sought out visuals other than the overwhelming defeat on screen. Personal triumphs also marked the event and so, late in the game, with the score 55–10, commentator John Madden focused on 49er nose tackle Jim Burt. Burt had been released by the Giants the previous fall because of back problems and was bitter about being fired, making no secret of his desire for payback. He had subsequently been picked up by the 49ers and was enthusiastically welcomed by his former rival team. During the ramp-up to Super Bowl Sunday he made it plain that he would do nearly anything to be in uniform for the showdown with the Giants. Late in the fourth quarter the camera picked up Burt at the 49er bench with his nine-year-old son. Burt had scooped up his son into his arms and was kissing him full on the lips and face. Madden could not resist the moment and in his signature heartiness and good humor, he enthused: "How about Jim Burt bringing his son out there, giving him five kisses in a row and then handing him his helmet and telling him to sit on the bench. That's Super Bowl Celebration . . . He's getting more kisses from his son! That's a Super Bowl record. I remember when he played for the Giants he brought his son down then and it was head butts in those days. Now a few years later it's . . . it's *kisses.*"[1]

Jim Burt's kisses contrast sharply with the prevailing emotion stereotype that equates masculinity with inexpressivity. The kisses were replayed on national television and mentioned in the sports pages of newspapers across the country. I followed the story closely, curious about the reaction that such a nurturant, expressive, loving display – on the football field, no less – would garner from the press and the sports-viewing public. But what, at another period, might have caused an uproar about the fragile state of North American masculinity caused nary a ripple. And not only was Jim Burt's show of fatherly tenderness not interpreted as unseemly, nor was it regarded as a breakthrough in emotional intimacy, even though manly kisses had replaced manly head-butts. The record number of Super Bowl kisses played as little more than a touching human interest story, footnote to another blow-out football game. How do we reconcile the general nonreaction to Burt's kisses with the rigid standards for masculinity implied by an emotion master stereotype which equates masculinity with inexpressivity? Had popular culture changed dramatically by 1990 without anyone noticing? Was there some special dispensation for fathers?

This chapter begins with contemporary notions of "masculine inexpressivity" and explores how inexpressivity came to be viewed simultaneously as a handicap and as an almost inevitable ingredient of masculinity. Paradoxically, the *absence* of emotion defines the masculine emotion stereotype, but notions of ideal masculinity in popular culture and everyday life *require* emotion. If inexpressivity is not an ideal, then what is? The key to answering this question is first to recognize that emotion is not inevitably devalued; rather, "appropriate" emotion is encouraged and valued. Emotional variety and intensity are important and even *required* components of significant masculine-identified activities, such as competitive sports. Pick up the sports section, tune into ESPN, or listen to sports talk radio on any given day and you will hear repeated reference to the importance of emotion to successful athletic performance. When I started this project I began to collect examples from *Sports Illustrated*, newspapers, and more. I was soon swamped with examples. It took very little time to see that – far from being rare gems, references to emotion, both the full range of specific emotions and "emotion" as a general term, were both common and indispensable in competitive sports. Sports talk is saturated with emotion talk.[2] So, in some respects, the Burt kisses fit easily into a sports culture that stresses the centrality of emotional experience and display in competitive performance. Appropriate emotion helps you win; inappropriate emotion helps you lose.

The chapter then moves to the question of the "right way" to do emotion. Ideal emotion is not gender-neutral, but, in fact, is a standard of "manly emotion." Manly emotion is not just "emotion done by males," but, rather, a standard for expressing "passion in the service of reason," a standard against which both women and men are evaluated. Indeed, with growing frequency the theme of masculine inexpressivity is subtly joined by its converse, a celebration of masculine emotion. What is going on? How has the appropriation of emotion, linked with the "merely" feminine for so long, become a vehicle for asserting manliness and the rights to power and privilege that accrue to masculinity? To work out the tensions between masculine passion as strong and genuine emotion, and feminine emotionality, I consider one significant area in which emotion's gender boundaries in the contemporary US appear to be in a process of renegotiation: the so-called "New Fatherhood." Nurturance and caregiving entail a style of "extravagant expressiveness" which is at cross-purposes with the economical expressiveness that is the hallmark of manly emotion. How does one successfully meet the demands of these competing standards – and why is it compelling to do so?

Inventing the problem of masculine inexpressivity

Everyone knows, or so says the gender stereotype, that men are emotionally inexpressive. Expert and lay literature alike have typically equated masculine inexpressivity with constricted emotional range, suppression of felt emotion, and diminished intensity of emotion. Worry about masculine inexpressivity was at its height in the mid- to late-1970s, around the same time as the popularization of androgyny and the first wave of the "men's movement," itself a reaction to the revival of feminism in the previous decade. Titles of articles and books about American men and emotion, mostly written by men, left no doubt as to the belief in the prevalence or seriousness of the problem: "The Inexpressive Male: A Tragedy of American Society?" (Balswick and Peek, 1971), "The Inexpressive Male: Tragedy or Sexual Politics?" (Sattel, 1976), "Some Lethal Aspects of the Male Role" (Jourard, 1971), and *The Hazards of Being Male* (Goldberg, 1976), to name just a few.[3]

The image of the inexpressive male is as much a component of the emotion master stereotype as is the notion of the emotional female. That is, inexpressivity is the popularly imagined normative condition of males regardless of age (beyond early childhood).[4] James O'Neil proposed that conflicts are inherent in the male gender role in post-industrial societies. His model of "sex role strain and conflict" considers restrictive emotionality one of two primary outcomes of masculine socialization. For O'Neil, restrictive emotionality encompasses "having difficulty expressing one's own feelings or denying others their rights to emotional expressiveness ... difficulty in being vulnerable, self-disclosing, and in understanding and integrating the complexities of emotional life" (1981, p. 64). Other outcomes of masculine socialization that he describes, namely concerns with control, power, and competition, also imply emotion antecedents or consequences. For O'Neil and others it is not the expression *per se* that seems to be the problem, but what the expression stands for. When viewed as a manifestation of a generalized manly distrust of emotion, inexpressivity's source seemed a direct outcome of defining masculine as the antithesis of feminine. O'Neil (1981, p. 67) observes that one learns that for the manly man, "vulnerabilities, feelings, and emotions in men are signs of femininity and to be avoided." Note that he distinguishes among "vulnerabilities," "feelings," and "emotions," and that the simple occurrence of these states is presumed to be misjudged as feminine weakness. The consequences of expressiveness are grave: "If a man *is* tender . . . if he weeps, if he shows weakness, he will probably regard himself as inferior to other men" (Jourard, 1971, p. 35, emphasis in original). Likewise, successful achievement of masculine inexpressivity was believed to carry serious risks with it. At least one critic of masculine inexpressivity drew a causal connection between emotional style and male mortality rates, linking inexpressivity "to man's faster rate of dying" (Jourard, 1971, p. 35). Despite dire warnings concerning the negative effects of inexpressivity, the evidence supporting such a conclusion is nil.[5]

When is emotion not "emotion"?

The portrayal of masculine inexpressivity is not consistent in its details. Tracts on the "inexpressive male," which were especially popular in the 1970s and early 1980s, include among masculine traits many items that clearly designate felt emotion or include some emotional component (e.g., sexual interest, aggressiveness, competitiveness, anger), or specifically refer to the intentional suppression or management of emotion (feelings or expression) already present. But these descriptions of emotional display are not labeled as emotion, and, more notably, they appear side-by-side with statements that describe emotional incapacity or lack of expression as a common condition of men. It is interesting that beliefs about emotion are used to define the manly even as emotion is written out. For example, in an epilogue to *Men in Transition* (Solomon and Levy, 1982), a good example of the genre, Wolfgang Lederer summarizes the image of American men as portrayed by therapists and researchers in the preceding chapters. He chides contributors for "a bias in favor of femininity . . . while the positive qualities of manliness are altogether omitted" (p. 476). According to Lederer, authors portray the stereotypical American man as one who, among other traits, is "aggressive, assertive," must aim to be "tough, cool, unemotional," is "afraid to cry," is "impatient and noncooperative" toward other men, and is "basically hostile" toward women (pp. 475–476). Ironically, Lederer does not see these traits as relevant to emotion and he concludes that the stereotypical man, as represented by chapter authors, "seems to be totally inexpressive of emotion unless he explodes with repressed anger" (p. 476).

Inconsistency in the meaning of inexpressivity is evident even in the most meticulous treatments of the question. Jack Balswick's (1988) study of inexpressivity is based on a combination of self-reports about the likelihood of discussing specific emotions with others and assessments of expressive behavior in the laboratory. In a general study aimed at identifying the specifics of gender differences in expressivity, Balswick found that among his college student subjects, women did report a significantly greater frequency of telling others about their feelings of love, happiness, and sadness, whereas men reported greater frequency of telling anger, although not significantly so. So far so good. This, as Balswick notes, is as would be expected from stereotypes. The problem comes in how Balswick interprets these patterns of general self-report. Although the items on his questionnaire asked about expression of emotion only in the most general terms (e.g., When I do feel angry toward people I tell them), he concludes that the self-report shows that "the inability or unwillingness of males to express love, affection, warmth, or tenderness may pose a problem, because these are characteristics prescribed by the male sex roles and yet are psychologically dysfunctional" (p. 97). His conclusions conflate what one believes one communicates emotionally, how comfortable one is in communicating emotion, and one's success in communicating emotionally. More important, there is a gap in reasoning that begins with self-report and moves to assertions about the dysfunctional aspects of "the masculine role." Balswick's attempt to provide a careful analysis of the inexpressive male ultimately shows that there is no single notion of who the inexpressive male is or what he shows, feels, can describe, or values.

A look at the evidence

Studies of masculine inexpressivity conventionally begin with the assumption that inexpressivity is a trait, that is, a fairly stable attribute of personality which may be innate, learned, or both. A corresponding assumption is that to properly understand inexpressivity, we should measure how much of the trait a person has, and how we can help people who have too much or not enough of it. These are all very good things to do if it is accurate to presuppose that masculine inexpressivity is a coherent, stable "thing." Quite a different investigative strategy makes sense if, instead of focusing on the causes and consequences of masculine inexpressivity, we problematize the notion of "inexpressivity" itself. What exactly is masculine inexpressivity? And why did this expressive style come to be considered a problem? For whom and in which contexts? Does inexpressivity, in fact, invariably characterize "masculine" behavior?

The basis for asserting an epidemic of masculine inexpressivity seems mainly to come from clinical impressions of individual writers. Assertions regarding the negative health consequences of "pent-up" masculine emotion seem to be based on the familiar metaphor of emotion as contained energy that, if not carefully released, can build to toxic levels. The hard evidence regarding restrictive emotionality, when cited, is self-report. Self-report gives us a very good picture of what people *believe* to be true about themselves, but it cannot tell us what people actually *do*. Self-report tells us in this case that men (at least those who participate in research and who are mostly white, mostly college students) believe that they – like women – feel more than they show, and – unlike women – they profess no great interest in talk about emotion. This pattern is essentially similar to a general tendency for gender differences to occur in self-report about emotion generally. As discussed in Chapter 2, there is a comprehension–performance gap between what women and men (as well as girls and boys) know about emotion and how they apply this knowledge to global assessments of others or general judgments about themselves. So, for example, the sexes are equally knowledgeable about the social consequences of showing emotion (or failing to), yet each sex is aware of the different standards for expressiveness accruing to it. Janet Stoppard has conducted several studies of gender-differentiated norms for expressing emotion. One of her intriguing findings is that women expect negative social sanctions if they do not express positive emotion toward others, but men expect no negative consequences for failure to express positive emotion toward a friend's success (Stoppard and Gunn Gruchy, 1993). The research I reviewed in Chapter 2 showed that women and men appear to hold the same beliefs about emotions, their causes and consequences. Indeed, one of the few consistent noteworthy differences in American women's and men's beliefs about emotion is a pattern of research results suggesting that men are less interested in talk about emotion and, unless prompted, are less likely to incorporate social-relational themes in their accounts of emotion. Once again we have to be careful with generalizations, because this conclusion is based almost exclusively on white, European Americans. Still, research so far seems to point to one solid conclusion: Men don't necessarily *feel* less emotion than women do, but – in general – they don't much like to talk about those feelings as much as women do.

Why inexpressivity?

Masculine inexpressivity is most often identified as a problematic result of adherence to masculine social roles and so, as a "problem" of acquiring a valued role, inexpressivity is considered neither intrinsic to maleness nor a fault for which the individual ought to be held accountable. According to these accounts, if he has a problem with emotion, the

American male has that problem only because he has learned to be a man and thus it is a problem that the individual shares with all well-socialized or oversocialized men (i.e., *real* men). Blaming socialized in-expressivity, of course, absolves the individual man of responsibility for his emotional difficulties. It also ignores those aspects of emotional be-havior that cause difficulties for others (aggressive acting out; battering or psychological abuse). If we fail to recognize, label, and acknowledge aspects of masculine behavior as "emotional," the emotional component of problem behaviors can be misconstrued. If fear, hostility, and rage are not identified as emotion, they are omitted *de facto* from the range of emotion-relevant concerns to be dealt with in the therapeutic context. A man undergoing counseling thus may be encouraged to excavate a new set of feelings instead of being pressed to name and examine feelings, such as hostility, that may already dominate his consciousness. The emphasis on searching for feelings obscures the problem of what one should do with the feelings that, although unnamed, are already vividly present. The one emotion-related problem that *is* acknowledged is anger, an emotion that I consider in greater depth in Chapter 7.

Isolating the problem of inexpressivity from individual accountabil-ity is typical even in the rare efforts to understand the phenomenon as a feature of social context. In an early commentary on how best to un-derstand masculine inexpressivity, Luciano L'Abate (1980) suggests that inexpressivity is not a universal masculine condition, but is situation-specific. In this brief essay he proposes that male inexpressivity may, in fact, be a limited reaction to an interpersonal situation in which the other member of the dyad is (comparatively) overexpressive. (For the moment I will bracket the question of who decides what constitutes "overexpressive.") Citing his own research on marital interaction and on conflict resolution, L'Abate concludes that "In our experience the more expressive the woman, the more inexpressive the man *may* be" (p. 230; emphasis in original). Although he notes that it is possible to find instances in which husband and wife reverse these expressive roles, he conceptualizes inexpressivity as a reaction to problematic *female* be-havior. By introducing the notion that gendered behavior happens in social contexts L'Abate presents a far more sophisticated analysis than do other tracts on masculine suppressed emotionality. Even in contex-tualizing the problem, however, he falls back on a view of male social roles as emotionally debilitating, and in so doing explains inexpressivity as a problem imposed upon men, rather than one generated by them. Whether inexpressivity/suppressed emotionality is viewed as a fixed constituent of masculinity or one provoked by social circumstances, the long-term solution for the problem is invariably viewed as an ad-justment in what is expected of men. Men are not held individually accountable for their emotional behavior because it is explained as a reaction to external pressure, whether masculine roles or female emotionality.

To sum up, what does this tell us? So far as "masculine inexpressivity" is concerned we find three themes. (1) In accounts of masculine inexpressivity historical time and culture are compressed, such that a stereotype of a certain subset of white males in the 1960s has come to be treated as a universal and enduring marker of masculinity. Particular men at a particular time may or may not have experienced this problem to some degree, but the notion has been inflated as a problem typical to *anyone* who is genuinely a man. (2) Emotional inexpressivity seems to have more to do with talking about emotion than showing it. In other words, inexpressivity does not generally appear to encompass the absence of feeling and showing emotion, but more accurately, reluctance or disinterest in emotion as a matter to be discussed (Jansz, 2000). And, perhaps most surprising, (3) emotion is often not counted as emotion. The stereotype of masculine inexpressivity, then, can only cautiously be applied to describing well-socialized masculinity. In fact, what self-report data tell us is that men in the US (and here I am overbroadly generalizing across age, ethnicity, etc.) believe that they feel more than they show (like women), and that they profess no great interest in talk about emotion (unlike women).

To be sure, some men (and some women) have a nearly incapacitating difficulty recognizing and acknowledging their own emotional states. For a significant minority this inability to express or label feelings may even lead to serious problems in maintaining interpersonal relations or achieving an adequate degree of self-understanding (Nemiah, 1996; Fischer and Good, 1997). What I wish to highlight is that the problem of inexpressivity, through its creation as *The Problem of Masculine Inexpressivity*, has come to be identified as the typical and normative state of masculine socialization. Emotional inexpressivity, by being "normalized" in this way, itself appears then to be a sign of normal, mature masculine functioning. The man who expresses his feelings, who thinks about emotion, is at risk for having attributes of his masculinity doubted.

Celebrating masculine emotion

Analyses of (and accompanying warnings about) masculine inexpressivity have continued to appear over the past twenty years, but most discussions have not brought in new analyses of the purported problem, and instead recycle the commentary of the 1970s. Although commentaries on the problem of male inexpressivity still occasionally appear, they more frequently contain a message that the way forward is through achievement of a uniquely masculine variety of expressiveness.[6] An interesting development since the mid-1980s is that the convention of masculine inexpressivity is often joined by its converse, a celebration of masculine emotion (though not usually explicitly identified as emotion). Largely a topic of the popular media and mental health literature, rather than of academic research on men and masculinity, this emerging view of manly emotion focuses on representations of male emotional nurturance, especially in the form of caregiving fathers. Nurturance, expressed through gentle physical contact and closeness, consoling and protecting the helpless, and expression of love, are themes common to this discourse. Even tears, which, more than any other expressions of emotion, have historically been identified with feminine emotion, have taken on an increasingly prominent role in representations of men's strong emotions in the US. Among the well-known American figures of the past two decades who have been teary-eyed in public are Presidents Ronald Reagan, George Bush, Bill Clinton, as well as General Norman Schwarzkopf, former Senator and presidential candidate Bob Dole, and assorted football and baseball coaches and star players.[7] Tears do not occur only in moments of great tragedy and mourning, for example, as we witnessed in the aftermath of September 11. They are visible in far less extreme circumstances too. When President-elect George W. Bush named Colin Powell his Secretary of State-designate, *both* men teared up. Former Representative Patricia Schroeder (D-Colorado), who came under strong criticism after publicly weeping, comments in her political memoir that the incidents of men's public tears are so numerous and so often treated positively by the media, that she has kept a file on men weeping ever since her own experience. Manly tears, however, are not indiscriminate, nor are they profuse. There are consistent conditions that mark the difference between manly tears or weeping judged to be merely emotional (regardless of the sex of the weeper). To put it somewhat differently, the manly ideal of rational mastery of nature that so characterizes post-Enlightenment discourse extends to the domain of emotion where passion is construed as not merely in opposition to reason, but as a force to be mastered by it. The special case of weeping is considered in greater detail in Chapter 7.

The current US version of the feeling male is markedly different from the quiche-eating Mr. Sensitive so disparaged in the 1970s.[8] The latter version achieves emotional capacity by adding feminine emotional style to the masculine repertoire. The aim is to be androgynous *and* manly, but avoiding campish parody. This is a tall order because simply grafting feminine emotionality on to the masculine role does not work: The man who adopts a feminine emotionality is not applauded as androgynous, nor congratulated for triumphing over constricted gender roles. He is viewed as weak or disingenuous. Former president Bill Clinton walked that fine line of sincerity whenever he declared "I feel your pain," and his uneven success gave late-night TV comedians an easy target. As historians of masculinity have repeatedly observed, masculinity (as an index of manhood) is never taken for granted as an achieved state, but must constantly be rehearsed and asserted.[9] The lesson from the 1970s is that, in the US, one cannot successfully retain masculinity and do emotion in the feminine way. In order to assert emotional superiority without relinquishing masculine privilege it is essential that the desirable or ideal form of emotion be distinguished from its weaker, ineffectual, or "merely emotional" version. It does not work simply to appropriate a style of emotional extravagance – the expressive style of nurturance that identifies the feminine prevailing emotion stereotype.

The current ideal of manly emotion is obvious in the exemplars of masculinity offered in popular culture. Media images suggest something other than a norm of inexpressivity for manly emotion. In fact, inexpressivity, in the form of absence of emotion expressed or inferred to be felt occurs far more rarely in depictions of strong male film and television characters than the prevailing emotion stereotype would lead us to expect. Expressions of strongly felt emotion are much more the rule.

Jerry Maguire and manly emotion

What is to be gained by appropriating feminine emotion? What motivates incorporating elements of "feminine" emotion into the performance of masculinity? Media images cannot tell us what people do, they can only tell us what people value or what they may strive (consciously or nonconsciously) to be. Hollywood films by virtue of their narrative form and their aim for mass appeal, are the perfect place to see how and when emotion is valued, and how emotion figures in the performance of an idealized mature masculinity.

The film *Jerry Maguire*, because of its focus on emotion and relationships, is useful for revealing some contemporary American bedrock beliefs about emotion.[10] *Jerry Maguire* was an enormously popular movie, both with audiences and critics. It made many "best" lists for 1996 (it was released in December of that year) and for the decade. It received five Academy Award nominations, including Best Picture and Best Actor (Tom Cruise), and Cuba Gooding, Jr. received the award for Best Supporting Actor. It had wide audience appeal beyond limited age, sex, and race market niches. "Show me the money!" and "You had me at hello" instantly became catch phrases that continue to circulate. *Jerry Maguire* also stands out as one of a fairly small proportion of Hollywood movies with strong leading roles for African Americans outside of action movies and films specifically targeted to African American audiences. From my perspective, though, it is the film's depiction of appropriate versus inappropriate emotion, emotional authenticity, "feminine emotionality," and racialized emotion that make it interesting as it reveals much about beliefs about emotion and its gendered enactment. Here I will mention just a few of the key themes that illustrate *Jerry Maguire's* celebration of manly emotion.[11]

The story is a variation on the Hollywood formula of self-discovery and romance, but it is more importantly a buddy picture. Sports agent Jerry Maguire (Tom Cruise) is paired with *two* buddies: the too-short Arizona Cardinals' wide receiver, Rod Tidwell (Cuba Gooding, Jr.), and the 6-year-old Ray, son of Jerry's love interest, the accountant Dorothy Boyd (Renee Zellweger). Through his buddies, the thinking-but-not-feeling Jerry finds the right path through connecting to the emotional honesty of the boy child, and the devotion to family of the football player. Conversely, the emotionally flamboyant and self-centered Rod, through Jerry, discovers that he must bring positive, focused passion back to his game to be successful.

Jerry Maguire (Tom Cruise) is a very successful and emotionally shallow sports agent. At a convention he has "too much pizza and too much conscience," which inspire him in a marathon writing session to produce a mission statement that outlines what's wrong with the business and the principle that should instead guide it: "Fewer clients, less money." After being roundly congratulated for his principles he is fired and leaves the mega-firm SMI ("Sports Management International") with only one idealistic accountant from the staff (the single mother Dorothy Boyd), and two clients, which soon dwindle to one. With Rod Tidwell his only client and his financial situation desperate, Jerry's need for emotional connectedness leads him to seek sexual solace from Dorothy and emotional resonance with her son, Ray.

The film blends elements of familiar Hollywood formulae: romantic comedy, journey of self discovery, social satire, and steadfastly heterosexual buddy picture.[12] Jerry can fake emotional authenticity, but is unable to develop a genuine emotional bond. His success as an agent is due in no small part to his ability to present himself as genuinely committed. He calls himself "the lord of the living room," a reference to his ability to settle deals on a handshake in the client's home. (Ironically, it is when the racist father of his first-round football draft client violates a handshake agreement that Jerry is left with Rod Tidwell as his only client.) Superficially Jerry exudes emotional heartiness, but he lacks genuine feeling. Two emotional outbursts that occur early in the film show his potential for strong feeling, but also show that he has no control over that strong feeling. Videotaped interviews of former girlfriends shown at his bachelor party are testimony that his success at faking emotional connection fools only those who do not try to get close to him. Ironically, Jerry's inability to be alone comfortably with himself leads him to reach out, first to Dorothy and then to her son Ray. Dorothy is a convenient temporary solution to Jerry's professional setbacks, but it is a private conversation with Ray about their respective fathers that sparks in Jerry the first step toward genuine emotional connectedness. Ray's Yoda-like look and precocious dialogue make his guru function in the film patently obvious. When Jerry eventually marries Dorothy, it is primarily because the relationship with her son has become so important to him. Although the child sparks Jerry's emotional redemption, it is up to another emotionally incomplete grown-up, Rod Tidwell, to help Jerry take responsibility for his marriage by moving beyond the bond with young Ray to participate fully in a grown-up emotion-based relationship. The late Dicky Fox, Jerry's sports agent mentor, appears as a different kind of Greek chorus on several occasions and underscores the film's emotion quest theme: "If this is empty [thumps his chest], this doesn't matter [slaps his head]."

Rod, in contrast, represents depth of feeling that is not "tamed" – genuine, but not controlled. The problem is Rod's attitude. He is truculent with the press, surly with his teammates, and has a wholly unrealistic and inflated view of his worth as a player. Rod is on a path of professional self-destruction because of, as Jerry says emphatically as he pushes on Rod's shoulder, "that rather large chip that you are carrying right *there*." It is clear to the audience that Rod's view of his own worth is unrealistic and it is not clear what has given rise to an increasing discrepancy between Rod's commitment to his family's well-being and his disregard for teammates and fans.[13] Rod's emotional connectedness to his wife and love for his family are unequivocal. Jerry's task, as agent renegotiating Rod's last contract, is to guide Rod to tame his emotion and place that emotion in the service of reason: Rod must rediscover his joy and love of the game and use that emotion to power his performance on the field and rebuild fraught relationships with teammates, the press, and fans.

By the film's conclusion both men do have an emotional epiphany, with the suggestion that the change the epiphany brings about is permanent and central to each man's character. Rod is knocked unconscious while making a game-winning touchdown, wakes to the stadium-full of cheering fans and reconnects joyously with his public. Jerry discovers at the moment of Rod's triumph that the experience is not complete without Dorothy and he returns home to reclaim his marriage. In each case the heterosexuality of each man is underscored and is an obvious but unacknowledged key to his successful negotiation toward emotional maturity as expressed through manly emotion.

Jerry's achievement of emotional authenticity can be contrasted with two other recurring images in the film, the first a women's support group and the second, his old SMI rival, Bob Sugar. Each of these reminds us of the intimate link between genuinely-felt emotion and true manliness. The first represents unreasoning emotion. Dorothy's sister hosts a support group for divorced women at their home. The women's group serves as a contrast to Jerry's legitimate emotional quest by being portrayed as dwelling on past hurts and as understanding emotion in terms of emotion cliché (e.g., " . . . then I got in touch with my anger"). The group's conversation occurs as a high-pitched din that Jerry must negotiate, first when he meets Dorothy for their first date, then at the film's conclusion when he comes to reclaim his marriage. In that latter scene, his entrance stops the group's conversation instantly, and they watch in silent and obvious admiration as he makes his declaration of commitment to Dorothy. For her part, Dorothy distances herself from the group's concerns and tells Jerry that no explanation is needed ("You had me at 'hello'") which signals that a *real* man doesn't have to talk about his genuine emotions, he just has to show that he has them.

The second is rationality uninformed by feeling. Bob Sugar is the classic mercenary sports agent ("It isn't show-friends, it's show *business*."). Openly disparaging of Jerry, Sugar disdains in his speech and in his person any connection between business life and a life of feeling. Indeed, he assembles the videotape of Jerry's exes to make Jerry squirm. In the film's account of life, however, rejection of emotion's role is bound to fail. The defect in Sugar's approach is revealed via a cameo appearance by Dallas Cowboys quarterback Troy Aikman. When Jerry and Rod accept the accolades of the press after Rod's post-concussion epiphany, Aikman turns to agent Sugar and complains, "Why don't *we* have that kind of relationship?"

Weeping, too, serves as an important signifier of Jerry's and of Ron's emotional development. Jerry sheds tears while writing his mission statement, when thinking about Dorothy's possible move to another city (and more importantly, the loss of Ray), and at the success of his lone client Rod. One critic cynically noted that when Jerry Maguire's feelings deepen, "Cruise starts doing that annoying trick he does with his eyes when he wants to convey big emotion. They get intensely shiny, like a lemur's."[14] Rod is brought to tears when he speaks of his family, and again on a sports TV show famous for bringing athlete guests to tears. In what begins as a winking nod to the commodification of emotion in sports, the TV show serves as an opportunity to reinforce the image of each man as having achieved emotional authenticity. In the end, Jerry's mission statement, prophetically titled "The Things We Think and Do Not Say," that sets the chain of events into play, is foremost an emotion manifesto. Despite Jerry's later reservations about the document, it propels the hero forward to find himself: "Hey, I'll be the first to admit what I was writing was somewhat touchy-feely. I didn't care. I had lost the ability to bullshit. It was the me I'd always wanted to be."

Jerry Maguire is, of course, only one film, and by itself it does not unequivocally demonstrate the pervasiveness of manly emotion as an ideal. Still, the film seems entirely believable as a masculine emotional saga and, when they see the movie, most people do not say "Wow! Men don't act like this in real life." It is the very *unremarkableness* of Jerry's and Rod's emotion that makes the film exemplary, and underscores the movie's potent depiction of manly emotion as *the* privileged emotion standard. I have chosen to focus on *Jerry Maguire* here, but any number of other films over the past decade, including many with less lofty artistic ambitions, illustrate some of the same themes: the need for a "real man" to get in touch with his true feelings and the superiority of manly emotion as displayed by the European American heterosexual male. Take just one such movie as an example, *The Replacements*, described by one critic as trying "to set some kind of record for regurgitating sports movie cliches faster than any film that's run before."[15] Released in 2000, it is of the same romantic comedy and buddy picture genre as *Jerry Maguire*. Ostensibly about a makeshift team during a professional football league strike, *The Replacements* centers on the hero's (Keanu Reeves) emotional saga: coming to terms with a significant past disappointment, emotionally bonding with his teammates, expressing the emotional strength needed to lead a team, and, not least, finding true love with the right woman (who happens to be a bar owner *and* a cheerleader!).

Competing standards for manliness and nurturance: The New Fatherhood

Although "manly emotion" is the overarching standard of ideal emotion, other context or role-specific emotional standards can compete with the requirements of this ideal. One site in which the tensions between masculine passion and appropriated feminine emotionality is most evident is in the representation of fatherhood. How has optimal fathering been redefined to incorporate more and more of the conventional hallmarks of motherly nurturance? By looking at the so-called "New Fatherhood" we can see what is at stake in contesting versions of gender-coded emotion. Caregiving requires expressive extravagance, a style of emotional expressiveness that is directly at odds with the requirements of economical, telegraphed, manly emotion that is the expressive ideal.[16]

The role of the father has varied along and across lines of racial ethnicity, social and economic class, and religion at all points in history, and the new father is just one among many images that capture how men today enact their position as fathers (Mintz, 1998). Lamb (1986) places the rise of the motif of the new nurturant father in the mid-1970s, although LaRossa (1997) locates the change as occurring between the two World Wars, and Griswold (1993) argues that in the 1920s the image of father as a nurturant pal was already commonplace. The new nurturant father, today a fixture of the lifestyle section of the newspaper and films and TV, is portrayed as offering emotional support to mom so that she can be a happier and more effective caregiver, but also and more importantly, he interacts directly with the children in caregiving and in play and emotional support. Lamb points out that most of the evidence for the new nurturant father that had been amassed by the mid-1980s was anecdotal. There was little actual research evidence regarding how consistent the image of the new father was with actual family practice. In fact, the little documented evidence on fathers' participation showed only that increased involvement of fathers with their children was largely in shared recreation. The image of the nurturant father is still strong as we enter a new century, but the data on actual paternal practices show that there has been only marginal advancement in the time that fathers spend with the children who live with them, and that the time still is more likely to be in play than in cooking, cleaning, and other caretaking. (See, for example, Hall, 1994; Ishii-Kuntz, 1995.) Marsiglio (1995a) points out the racialized nature of the positive image of the new father by contrasting it with the prevailing stereotype of the black father as "inner-city, hypermasculine males who are financially irresponsible and uninvolved in their children's lives" (p. 5). (Rod Tidwell's devotion to wife and family stands in noticeable contrast to the stereotype.) Marsiglio also cites Griswold's (1993) observation that the New Fatherhood is middle-class, and in that respect, adopting the New Fatherhood role is a strategy in which men accommodate to the realities of the two-job or two-career household.

Images of fatherly nurturance

The new father avoids the wimp construction by becoming a public symbol of commitment to caregiving as reflecting a progressive set of values. Gillis (1995) points out that the New Fatherhood is in some respects the restoration of an old fatherhood that emphasizes the father as the head who defines the family unit. The rites of the New Fatherhood – from participating in the birth, to pushing a stroller – serve to "reinforce the old provider role rather than form a fundamentally different relationship between father and child. By and large, good fatherhood is still mediated by good husbandhood" (Gillis, p. 22). There are notable exceptions, of course, from TV's psychiatrist *Fraiser* to well-intentioned but inept single guys in movies such as *Three Men and a Baby*. Marsiglio (1995b) outlines the interconnections between popular culture images of fatherhood and the actual practice of real fathers. Emphasizing the dynamic and negotiated nature of the images and practices of fatherhood, at the level of both the individual and the larger society, he encourages researchers and policy-makers to reframe the conventional and outmoded questions often posed about fathers so that social conditions can be created that would be more conducive to fathers – of all parenting styles and positions – to develop and maintain their commitments to their children's economic and emotional well-being.

The New Fatherhood both parodies and implicitly aims to subvert maternal emotional styles and concerns in what seems to be part of the celebration of masculine emotion described earlier. Even though there is a rush to reclaim the significance of parenting, fathers are not expected to adopt the emotional style that characterizes the mothering script. Fathering is, like every other masculine-coded activity, supposed to be done in a manly way. For guidance in this regard, the concerned father can turn to *Daddy Cool*, a book on how to be an effective father and at the same time preserve one's masculinity. Newspaper comics from well-known *Doonesbury* to cartoons less-widely syndicated portray fathers grappling not only with the activities of parenting, but also the emotional complexity of the role. In one typical Father's Day cartoon strip, a neighbor compliments Bruce on the tie that his son made for him and then notes that fatherhood must put its own special perspective on things. "You bet!" Bruce replies, "It's brought me in touch with feelings I've never known before – guilt, anxiety and the fear that I'll never measure up to his expectations."[17] Whereas jokes about maternal feelings of guilt have a long and poignant place in American popular humor, paternal guilt and anxiety is a relatively recent motif and here the research literature agrees that these emotions are part of coming to terms with this evolving definition of how to be a good father emotionally (e.g., Daly, 1995). News stories in the "Lifestyle" section of newspapers also focus on the emotional turmoil and triumphs of the new father, and though the frequency definitely takes an upturn around Father's Day in June, pieces appear all year round, and often in surprising venues. One of the more recent additions to my collection is a hip-hop magazine featuring a celebrity rapper father with his baby on the cover.

Sensitive, caring fathers have been a feature of prime-time television since the 1950s and 1960s brought us caring dads in *Father Knows Best*, *My Three Sons*, *The Courtship of Eddie's Father*, to name just a few. The 1980s saw *Cosby*, *Growing Pains*, and even more custodial single father households, such as *Full House*, *My Two Dads*, and *Sinbad*. The trend has continued into the new century, even as the proliferation of cable channels and decline of network dominance of prime-time programming continues to fragment the viewing audience. Print, too, celebrates the new father. The father who manages exquisitely to balance an open show of emotion toward his child with adherence to a standard of economical expressiveness is the rule rather than the exception. To be sure, 'Klutz Dads' who are inept at relationships still abound on the small screen in figures such as Tim Allen's *pater familias* in *Home Improvement*, a network television show that enjoyed a ten-year run in the 1990s. But even here, deeply felt, authentic emotion is essential to the character. The premise is that Allen, star of a fictional do-it-yourself cable TV show, is as inept at home improvement as he is in navigating the emotional needs of his wife and three sons. Aided by a father-figure next-door neighbor (whose face the audience never sees) and a good heart, however, he manages to be successful in achieving emotional communication while retaining his "regular kind of guy" distance from emotion. In other words, he is successful at what needs to be done in the way of emotional communication, but never so successful that he gives up the guy position of being somehow outside and above the emotional fray. Hollywood movies, too, portray a kinder, gentler dad and have come a long way since Dustin Hoffman struggled in a charmingly inept manner to manage a distraught child in the Oscar-winning *Kramer v Kramer* in 1979. As in television representations of family life, father is likely to be portrayed as competent not only in the activities of caregiving, but emotionally as well. The image of nurturing and nurtured males runs throughout *Jerry Maguire*. Chad, Ray's baby-sitter, is an excellent example of the film's emphasis on "appropriate" caring. No Mary Poppins he – he tutors his young charge on the jazz of John Coltrane and Miles Davis, exemplars of controlled emotion in the service of reason.

Lest we think that the New Father has pushed aside the Old Father, an interesting study of representations of masculinity in TV advertising tells us that, at least by the 1980s, this was not the case. Coltrane and Allan (1994) compared advertising messages from the 1950s and 1980s as a strategy for identifying how cultural symbolism about gender and families has changed in recent decades. Their findings regarding advertising parallel what is repeatedly shown for TV programs: men far outnumber women no matter when the data are collected. The biggest change they found since the 1950s was in the representation of women – with an increase in the proportion of women shown in work roles. On the other hand, emotionality (that is, being sensitive, crying easily, showing feelings, verbal self-disclosure, or expressivity) was the province of women in both eras. In the 1980s female advertising characters were three times more likely than male characters to be portrayed as emotional. As for images of parenting, the biggest change over time was in the proportion of men shown parenting – not in what they were doing as parents. In the 1950s men were less than one-third of all parents pictured, by the 1980s, they constituted nearly three-quarters of parents! So far as media images are concerned, the Coltrane and Allan study suggests that the New Father is not so much defined by nurturing *like* women, but – by sheer dominance of the imagery – as defining what nurturance is.[18]

Image meets reality

Moving to real life – what does the New Father do? Ralph LaRossa notes that we should not presume that the refashioned image of fatherhood actually represents a change or development in the scope and nature of fathering behavior. Rather, he suggests, we should distinguish between the *culture* of fatherhood and the *conduct* of fatherhood. The culture of fatherhood, like emotion culture, refers to the shared norms, values, and beliefs regarding fatherhood, whereas the conduct of fatherhood is what fathers actually do with their children. Across race and class lines women do two-thirds or more of the domestic work in marriages than do men, and women's well-being is more directly affected by the availability of childcare (Steil, 1997). Even when both parents have full-time paid work, mothers do much more with children than fathers do. Indeed, mothers spend about three hours to every hour a husband spends taking care of young children (Aldous, Mulligan, and Biarnason, 1998).[19] LaRossa (1988) argues that the disparity between culture and conduct is nothing less than remarkable considering the prevalence of the belief in the New Fatherhood. He points out that the notion that something has changed in the conduct of fatherhood has been popular among the general public as well as family experts and has gone on since the 1960s. The change in belief has, in fact, not reflected a change in the performance of fathering, it is the image of fathering that has changed, not the reality. LaRossa shows that much of what passes for paternal involvement in childrearing actually reflects a class-limited grafting on of fatherly duties of caregiving to an already set masculine agenda. For example, LaRossa describes "the technically present but functionally absent father" (p. 454) as one who places the baby's stroller trackside so that the baby can watch him run laps, or the father who takes a mini-TV to his child's Little League game.

The New Fatherhood is a particularly interesting phenomenon because it occurs within a long-standing Anglo-American bedrock belief, reflected in scientific and medical literature, that presumes the existence of a distinctively *maternal* instinct to care for the young. The crux of the belief is that women, by virtue of biology, are predisposed to caregiving, are more competent at it, and naturally enjoy it more than do men. The notion of a maternal, rather than parental, instinct sets up very different conditions for expectations regarding the competence and affect that accompany caregiving for women and men. "Instinct" suggests that all females are born with the behavioral capacity to understand and perform – without assistance – the behaviors that constitute good mothering. The female's supposedly limitless pleasure in mothering makes it possible to overlook the highly isolated and exhausting character of the mother's 24-hour days and to accept as "natural" the absence in dominant American culture of the kin group and the village or neighborhood community which shares the responsibility for childcare in many societies. The belief further promises feelings of guilt for any mother who allows a lapse in her maternal feelings. If an individual woman does not exhibit these behaviors to an appropriate degree, the inadequacy is diagnosed as indicating pathology or personality aberration. And, of course, a corollary to the belief in instinctive maternal behavior is the belief that defects in the mother-child interaction are a primary cause of later personality pathology in the offspring, a conceptualization of motherhood that sets the stage for what has been referred to as the psychoanalyst's favorite indoor sport – mother-blaming.[20] There is no corresponding "explanation" for the absence of an inclination to caregive by males.

The standard of manly emotion

Why has the New Fatherhood emerged as a masculine motif in the late twentieth century? What advantage is there for the real man to move into the emotional space of extravagant expressivity that defines nurturant femininity? What is the attraction of assuming a role of nurturance that has been so identified with the female parent that it is virtually impossible to escape the gendered-ness of the activity? James Doyle (1983) notes that the first and most fundamental lesson the boy learns in developing a sense of masculinity is to define it in terms of what is "not girl." This general rule certainly applies to what children learn about what it means to experience emotion, what kinds of emotion-related expectations one should develop about oneself (or others) as persons, the signs and symptoms one should rely on to know one's own or someone else's emotion, and how to tell whether an emotion is genuine as well as appropriate to the context. To be "not girl" does not mean to deny the fact of emotion, nor kinds of emotion, but instead to learn the circumstances "appropriate" to emotion's experiences and expression. Boys reject the feminine style of emotion and learn how to do emotion the manly way. They learn the "stiff upper lip" – a clear signal that one's intense emotional feelings are firmly under control. It is not a sign of absent emotion, but that the emotion is manfully contained.

If masculinity is put at risk by assuming a role that requires the antithesis of manly emotion, then something big must be at stake. Kimmel (1987) suggests that crises in masculinity, popular debates about what it means to be a "real man," are reactive to changing definitions of femininity. Stressing that masculinity and femininity are the products of role enactments as opposed to traits, Kimmel looks to broad changes in economic and social structures to explain why negotiation of gender relations takes on special prominence at particular historical moments. We can think of the New Fatherhood as a way, paradoxically, to reaffirm rather than blur the line of gender difference. As in every generation the social markers that mark the border between masculine/feminine are in constant negotiation and renegotiation. Appropriating emotion expressivity and displacing extravagant expressivity with telegraphed emotion, thus doing emotion the "right way" – as manly emotion – reclaims and reasserts a definition of "masculine" when gender categories are up for grabs. Indeed, in an era when neither "masculine" work nor "masculine" clothing unambiguously define gender as difference, emotion is one of the few remaining contested areas left in which drawing a line between masculine/manly and feminine still works.

In the following chapter I take a closer look at how the prevailing emotion beliefs create a context for one of the most transparent contradictions among bedrock beliefs about emotion. Ask anyone over the age of six to name four emotions and with little hesitation she or he will recite: happy, sad, angry, and afraid (or scared). Anger is a prototypic emotion and yet anger is stereotypically associated with the also stereotypically *un*emotional male. How is it that her anger is emotional, while his is, well, simply anger?

Notes

1 Superbowl XXIV was broadcast by CBS on January 28, 1990.
2 In fact, sporting events are often defined in terms of emotion. Peter Richmond, *GQ Magazine* sports columnist, for example, summed up the Super Bowl this way: "Well, in the Super Bowl, it's *all* about emotion" (Morning Edition, National Public Radio, January 26, 2001). The XFL, a football league

launched in early 2001, aimed to attract young adult men to viewership by promising to intensify the emotional involvement of the TV audience. Body microphones enabled fans to hear real-time expressions of pain on the field, disputes between coaches and referees, and conflicts between coaches and players. Whereas the NFL penalizes excessive displays after touchdowns and big plays, the XFL encouraged them.

3 Joseph Pleck (1984) sees a modern crisis of masculinity as beginning after World War II and notes that concerns about the deleterious consequences of the behavioral restraint required by the male role are expressed in two classic sociological studies of the times, C. Wright Mills' *White Collar: The American Middle Classes* (1956) and W. F. Whyte's *The Organization Man* (1956). Others have placed less emphasis on role demands and more emphasis on the men's movement as an attempt to reaffirm existing power relations in the face of social change.

4 As discussed in Chapter 3, the stereotype of the unemotional male is relative to the female stereotype within the same racial ethnic group, and the difference is most sharply drawn in stereotypes of whites.

5 A similar sentiment is expressed by Goldfried and Friedman (1982, p. 310). Snell, Belk, and Hawkins (1986), for example, examined correlations between scores on subscales of the Masculine Role Inventory and stressful life experiences. Despite their conclusion that "the masculine role was associated with elevated distress" (p. 359), the actual pattern of correlations is singularly unimpressive. Some (e.g., Pennebaker, Colder, and Sharp, 1990) have argued the therapeutic benefits of disclosing emotionally traumatic experiences. Work of Bernard Rimé and his colleagues shows that it is not the disclosure *per se* that has a beneficial effect, but more than likely, an impulse to sociability triggered by the disclosure accounts for the increased reported well-being (Rimé, Finkenauer, Luminet, Zech, and Philippot, 1998).

6 Levant (1995) adopts the restrictive emotionality model in his account of the male "ordeal of emotional socialization" (p. 236). Heesacker and Prichard (1992) take an approach derived from Robert Bly's (1990) construct of "male mode of feeling." They advocate the adoption of elements of Bly's pop-psych program in professional mental health counseling because they believe that most extant approaches to counseling emphasize "a female-oriented approach to emotion and emotional expression" which pathologizes "legitimate differences [from women] in men's emotional lives and ... expression" (p. 275).

7 One of the most revered moments in sports weeping was captured in photos of basketball legend Michael Jordan taken after the Chicago Bulls won their first National Basketball Association championship ever in a close final game against the Los Angeles Lakers.

8 A popular book spoofing the sensitive male, *Real Men Don't Eat Quiche* (Feirstein and Lorenz, 1982), gave a name to the general distrust of emotional expression by men.

9 See for example Seidler (1997). Peter Stearns has explored issues of masculinity in modern emotional culture in several of his books, beginning with *Be a Man!* (1979).

10 *Jerry Maguire* was written and directed by Cameron Crowe. In Shields (2001) I take an extended look at the film and other recent cinematic celebrations of manly emotion. *Jerry Maguire*'s emotion themes are touched on by many reviewers, including Tom Gliatto (*People*, December 16, 1996,

p. 25), Rocco Simonelli (*Films in Review*, January 1997, p. 87.), Brian Johnson (*Maclean's*, December 30, 1996, pp. 100–101). See also Cameron Crowe, "The 'Jerry Maguire' Journal" (*Rolling Stone*, December 26, 1996 to January 9, 1997, pp. 137–142).

11 Representations of manly emotion are quite common in major Hollywood films. Popular movies as diverse as *Shakespeare in Love* (1999), *Gladiator* (2000), and the animated *Shrek* (2001) all feature male leads whose strongly felt emotion is essential to the plot. In each, an emotionally-motivated quest drives the plot and the hero arrives at a higher and more mature understanding of his emotion by the film's conclusion.

12 Susan Jeffords (1994) traces the transformation of the popular culture image of idealized masculinity as "hard body" during the Reagan presidency to a "kinder, gentler" masculinity during the Bush years of the 1990s. She observes that by the end of the 1980s films began to focus more often on the theme of manhood divided and troubled, a need to reconcile outer strength with inner feelings. Fatherhood, she suggests, became the vehicle for achieving that reconciliation.

13 Arguably Rod's race is integral to the representation of unharnessed strong emotion. If one does a thought experiment, however, and imagines Rod to be of another race (white) or ethnicity (Polish), the representation of him as an emotionally immature and out-of-control athlete still works.

14 Tom Gliatto (*People*, December 16, 1996, p. 25).

15 Bob Strauss (2000) in the *Los Angeles Daily News* quoted at *www.rottentomatoes.com*. *The Replacements*, also starring Gene Hackman and Brooke Langton, was written by Vince McKewin and directed by Howard Deutch.

16 Thank you to Christina Jarvis for suggesting that war and sports provide the public model for manly emotion, while fatherhood provides the model for private life. George Roeder's *The Censored War* (1993) tells the story of how American public opinion about World War II was manipulated by wartime images. He notes, for example, that the war manual for reporters directed that men could not be shown crying in news photos.

17 *Miss Featherbee* by Leila Cabib, June 18, 1989.

18 Coltrane and Adams (1997) also examined TV ads from the 1990s and found essentially the same patterns, such as women more frequently portrayed as sex objects and less frequently portrayed as displaying active/instrumental behavior than men. And male characters were still outnumbered by female characters. Signorielli (1993) points out that the few highly visible counter-stereotypic examples may lead us to forget that the majority of representations of women of color and white women continue to be quite stereotypic.

19 Although there has been some shift to increased husband participation in housework and father participation in childcare, men are more likely to be involved in less frequent, intermittent, or "fun" activities of childrearing and home maintenance than are women. See also Coltrane and Adams (2001) and Orbuch and Timmer (2001).

20 For critiques of the modern conceptualization of maternal instinct and mother blaming, see Caplan and Hall-McCorquodale (1985), Chess (1982), and Shields (1984), for example.

CHAPTER 7

Emotional = female; angry = male?

"Anger has long been regarded as a basic element of affective life, a fundamental or primary human emotion. It is crucial for human survival, having important internal regulatory and social communicative functions. Physiologically, it prepares the body to initiate and sustain high levels of focused and directed activity. Psychologically, it is linked to self-protective and aggressive action tendencies. As a form of social communication, anger conveys distinct messages to others, forecasting predictable consequences, and eliciting affective and behavioral responses in others."

Craig Sternberg and Joseph Campos (1990, p. 247)

"To get angry is to claim implicitly that one is a certain sort of being... One claims that one is in certain ways and dimensions *respectable*. One makes claims upon respect."

Marilyn Frye (1983, p. 90)

The main questions I have tried to answer in this book are "Who gets called 'emotional' and what does that mean when it happens?" Early on in my work I was not surprised, but was fairly dismayed to see that the answer to these questions is almost always gendered. More unexpected, though, were the many instances I found of emotion, especially men's emotion, simply not being identified as "emotion." I remember a conversation a few years ago with the receptionist in the Dean's office at the university where I worked. I had stopped by the office to pick up a friend for lunch and, while I waited the receptionist asked me what I was teaching that term. She was quite interested that I was teaching the psychology of emotion and, laughing, said that her husband could really benefit from a class on emotion because he was so very unemotional. So I asked her, "Does he ever get pissed off about things?" "Oh, *yes*," she answered emphatically and without hesitation. "When he does," I continued, "is it hard to tell that he's upset?" Again, she did not hesitate, but answered just as emphatically, "Not at all!" At first it is puzzling that a woman who seems so attuned to emotion apparently does not recognize anger as emotion. How could she be oblivious to her husband's emotionality and at the same time be so aware of the fact that his anger is easy to read?

139

In some respects the question of anger is *the* fundamental paradox in the emotional female/unemotional male stereotype. The stereotype of emotionality is female, but the stereotype of anger, a prototypic emotion, is male. Why is it that anger, which is so often portrayed as childish (peevish, irritable, testy, sullen, cranky, touchy, irked), and the essence of the apparently uncontrollable, irrational character of emotion, is masculine? Is there a difference (either conceptually or behaviorally) between masculine anger and the anger of immature tantrums? Is anger, in fact, viewed as emotionality when displayed or experienced by adult men?

Anger is center stage in social and behavioral science investigations of emotion, and is accorded a position in research and theory that other emotions rarely have been, unless they are considered in terms of pathology. Fear is the object of extensive examination when implicated in phobia or anxiety. Sadness has gained attention because it is presumed to be a core feature of depression. Even love, celebrated in life, poetry, and popular song, has to be justified as a legitimate object for study in a way that anger does not.[1] The sheer quantity of published research on anger is daunting. Scanning the "pop psych" shelves in bookstores shows that anger is not just an academic preoccupation. Titles like "*How to Free Yourself from the Grip of Anger,*" "*How to Express Your Anger and Still be Kind,*" "*Dealing with Anger,*" and the ambitious "*A Comprehensive Approach to Anger Management*" reflect a general urge to harness, hide, work with, or subdue angry feelings and acts. As the Sternberg and Campos quotation above vividly expresses, anger enjoys special status in contemporary emotions research. It is treated as special because it is viewed as "crucial for human survival," and because it "prepares the body to initiate and sustain high levels of focused and directed activity" while at the same time it "conveys distinct messages to others." Anger is portrayed as problematic, but as a focused, purposive emotion with roots in evolutionary need.[2]

What makes anger special? Anger is deeply implicated in the exercise of power. Power is the ability to get what you want; anger is the means to exercise power when faced with the loss of or the threat of losing what you have. In this chapter I will consider the personal experience of anger as a sense of entitlement and link that to the sense of moral order which a society uses to justify existing status and power relations. By entitlement I mean the expectation that one ought to receive or retain something that one values. The next section lays out a framework for understanding anger as a kind of emotion – especially what elicits it and the consequences of its occurrence. I then examine the conditions that create beliefs about one's own entitlement that are prerequisite to experiencing anger, and making that anger effective. I then turn to how anger plays out in certain gendered contexts, and consider the relation between gender and internalizing or externalizing anger, and between gender and weeping.

Parsing anger

Emotions can be described in terms of what they are *about*. Emotions do not occur without reason, and usually we can identify some overarching theme that characterizes a particular kind of emotion or emotion "family." When the theme or "aboutness" of anger (and its emotion relatives) is put into focus, what consistently shows up is violation of what the individual perceives to be his or her rights. The important ingredient is the conviction that one is entitled to a particular state of affairs. Anger (and its emotion relatives such as resentment or jealousy) occurs when we believe that we have been or are threatened with being deprived of something we believe is rightfully ours – my wallet has been stolen, I didn't get the promotion, my boyfriend didn't phone, I am deprived of civil liberties that other people enjoy. Emotions of violated entitlement are involved any time one believes that a possession has unjustly been taken away or if there is the threat that it will be taken away. It is important to point out that just because *you* believe yourself to be entitled does not necessarily mean others agree. So they may not believe you are justified in being angry (or jealous, or irritated, or resentful, or . . .).[3] The theme of anger as a concern with rights or entitlement is one with a long history in Western thought that can be traced to Socrates and earlier (Kemp and Strongman, 1995). On what basis is the entitlement predicated? In each case the theme of the emotion is that one has had some privilege or right violated – whether it is that it has been taken away, there is a threat that it will be taken away, or it is in some other way disrespected. So the two-year-old who doesn't want to eat her peas is expressing, through her anger, some belief that she is entitled to make a choice about what to eat and what not to eat. The anger is a way of exerting a new-found sense of self that says, "I decide when and what to eat!" Any grown-up observer, though, sees the toddler's rage as willful expression that is very short-sighted and not in the best interests of growing up to be strong. After all, we all need to eat our peas. By the same token, romantic jealousy is *not* about loving too much, but, as Robert Solomon (1993) and others have pointed out, it is about guarding one's possession from being stolen. It involves a belief that what one has is vulnerable to being taken away. No matter what popular songs may tout, romantic jealousy is not about love or even about lust, but about possessing another.

Anger and its emotion relatives are an interesting set of emotions because, in many respects, they exemplify the built-in dimension of human emotion. Anger in some form seems to be universal among human societies, and anger appears early in the infant's emotional repertoire. Human anger expression parallels the appearance of aggressive behavior of our close and not-so-close mammalian relatives. At the same time, however, the theatricality of anger fits neatly into a social constructionist interpretation of emotion. I do not think that all emotions are equally well-served by a social constructionist account, but our understanding of anger, romantic love, and certain types of guilt and shame is enriched when viewed from a social constructionist perspective. James Averill (1982; 1991) presents a very persuasive social constructionist description of anger. He observes that any emotion can be described on any one of several levels of analysis. Anger, for example, can be described in terms of its experiential properties, its possible evolutionary history, or its codification in various social institutions and structures. The picture of an emotion differs depending on the level of analysis, and each level of analysis focuses on different facets of the origins, functions, and consequences of the emotion in question. No individual perspective is the single "correct" one because, after all, each is a level of analysis, not a stand-alone explanation. The capacity for anger, Averill argues, has a biological basis in humans' innate capacity for reflective self-consciousness, motivation to cooperate, and aggression. At the psychological level, it can be described as aiming to correct a perceived wrong, while from the perspective of interpersonal relations anger can be described as aiming to facilitate social order. The epigrams that begin this chapter illustrate the different levels of analysis. Both take a functionalist perspective, and both connect anger to the individual's capacity for living within complex groups. But while Campos and Sternberg consider anger as a product of primate evolution, Frye considers it within a distinctively human network of relationships.[4]

The social constructionist theory as advanced by Averill (see Chapter 1) defines emotion as a deeply acted transitory social role which includes the individual's appraisal of the situation and which is interpreted as passion, rather than action. It is very important to understand that "deeply acted" does *not* mean deliberate, disingenuous, or in any way superficial. Indeed, an important quality needed for emotion to "work" is that we believe it happens to us rather than that we make it happen. The enactment of the role is not strictly scripted, though the conditions for genuine emotion do conform to certain rules regarding what the emotion can be about, who is appropriate to experience and express it, what the time course is for the emotion, and so on.

Anger involves some appraisal that one has been deprived of or denied what one is rightly due, whether that deprivation consists of the theft of one's car, an attack on one's name, or concerns about endangered species. The loss can be very focused and concrete (rage against the driver who took our parking place) or abstract and global (rage against the senselessness of a war). Anger is always *about* something, but in order for it to be directed *toward* someone requires that the target of anger is presumed to be somehow responsible for the loss. People can be angry at themselves when they hold themselves accountable for negative consequences of failing to look out for their own interests. Anger toward another individual or entity similarly requires a belief in the agency of that other. I cannot be angry *at* the puppy for chewing my shoe unless I hold the notion that the puppy can control its action and failed to employ that self-control by sinking its teeth into the forbidden leather. Solomon (1993) describes the theme of anger as one of indictment and accusation, "a projection of our personal values and expectations on the world" (p. 227). If emotion is essentially "taking it personally" (as I defined it in Chapter 1), then anger is the quintessential emotion. The "taking it personally" in the case of anger concerns the interpretation of loss (or threat of loss) as a violation of one's sense of moral order: This *belongs* to me; I have a *right* to expect a certain state of affairs. Indeed, Solomon points out that our capacity to get angry over trivia is a means to "assert our right to assess and our need for legislative autonomy, much as a magistrate might levy contempt of court charges, not for the nature of a remark or a gesture itself but rather only because it was *contempt* of court, a denial of his own authority" (pp. 227–228; emphasis in original). Consider the scene that I described in Chapter 1: Socrates' impatience with his followers' lack of self-control. Socrates berates his followers for their failure to behave in a way consistent with their philosophy – and, worse, this occurred at a moment absolutely requiring composure! In Socrates' view, they were behaving emotionally and like women, which violated his sense of the right behavior for the situation as expressed through his philosophy. His reproach is aimed to restore the "right" way, that is, the manly, Socratic way, to die.

Focusing on the judgments that comprise anger helps to offset the cultural literalness that accompanies talking about "specific" emotions. A tendency to assume that the existence of similar emotion labels in different cultures indicates equivalent emotions, sometimes called "the fallacy of misplaced concreteness," interferes with seeing how points of universality are embedded within networks of cultural distinctiveness. James Averill points out that the universality of any given emotion depends on the breadth of the category. The more general the level of cross-cultural comparison, the greater the universality. "Anger" at the most specific level of individual experience is nuanced by the particulars of the evoking situation. At that level it is true that no one else could ever feel the way I felt when my car was stolen – that car, that time in my life, those specific circumstances surrounding its theft – all make the signature of that highly charged emotion unique to me and to my experience. At a more general level, however, the sense of having been wrongfully deprived of an essential possession, a possession with great monetary value and crucial to the ordinary conduct of life, is a state with which many can identify and which they (along with me) would label "anger." At an even more general level, the realization that one has been deprived of what one is due is an experience that crosses cultures, historical periods, age, and circumstance, and so is evidence of universality of anger as a broader class of emotion. How that experience is represented in language and the beliefs about what to do with the anger (such as what constitutes the appropriate response, the social consequences for acting on the anger impulse, etc.) do vary across time and culture.

Getting justice and getting even

Anger is associated with action, and even if that action consists of not much more than vengeful plotting, there is the impulse to act to change things. Nancy Stein and Linda Levine (1990, p. 65) suggest that what makes anger different from other emotions of loss is that the angry person firmly believes that he or she can institute a plan to restore conditions to what they were before the aversive state or loss occurred. In their view, anger is elicited when "a person experiences an unexpected loss, failure, or aversive state and refuses to accept being in the resultant state" (p. 65). "Refusing" entails the belief that the surrounding conditions can be "fixed." Many emotions involve some sense of loss or deprivation and not all are variants of anger. Sadness, for example, involves a sense of loss, but loss is experienced quite differently, as a sense of powerlessness or resignation to the immutability of the loss. Because the emphasis of anger is on the restoration of a prior state, they assert that motivations to destroy or injure the agent who caused harm are not a component of prototypic anger. So the revenge fantasy does not stem from a desire to ruin the perpetrator, but is a next-best solution to fixing the problem. "If I can't restore my marriage and my life to what it was (or what I now fantasize that it was), I can at least ruin *your* life, *your* finances, and *your* self-esteem as mine has been ruined."

The persistent threat of uncontrollability gives anger a special edge as an exercise of power. According to George Lakoff (1987) the central metaphor of anger in American English centers on the fact that anger "can be intense, that it can lead to a loss of control, and that a loss of control can be dangerous" (p. 386). Images of energy or heat building up within a container that need to be released in a focused way are characteristic of the way Americans describe their anger experiences. Advice about anger management expands on the metaphor and typically emphasizes the importance of releasing this potentially volcanic energy early enough in the phase of "heat build up" so that the release can be controlled. Lakoff notes that these metaphors also reflect the notion that anger is conceptualized as a mass: "it has a scale indicating its amount, it exists when the amount is greater than zero, and it goes out of existence when the amount falls to zero" (p. 386). The anger-meter is not an infinite scale, but when some quantity is reached, folk theory prescribes that the pressure must be alleviated or the pressure becomes dangerously uncontrollable. Indeed, the anger-as-volcano metaphor is found in many cultures throughout history.[5]

Carol and Peter Stearns (1986) propose that American society has developed a deep ambivalence toward anger over the course of the past two centuries. In early American society tight intimate community supervision provided behavioral control of anger expression, but in contemporary times methods of control have moved toward an emphasis on direct manipulation of emotions and, particularly, of anger.[6] I agree that American preoccupation with anger – what causes it, how it can be controlled, problems associated with it – does make it, along with romantic love, a focal point in emotion culture. However, I believe that the Stearns overstate the extent to which the suppression or elimination of anger stands as an ideal. Instead, the goal seems to be one of achieving an idealized state of focused and controlled experience and expression appropriate to the evoking circumstances. In other words, the goal is manly emotion. And although that standard may be the one against which all adults may be measured, the possibility of being found adequate to the standard depends on more than just how one expresses the emotion. Etiquette maven Judith Martin ("Miss Manners") reminds us that "civilization" after all "has developed a variety of restrained but effective methods of showing anger, from the glare to the lawsuit, depending on whether you want to freeze the other person's blood or capture his assets."[7]

Another issue that comes up in dealing with the aggressive expression of anger is the extent to which the enraged individual actually has control over anger expression. The plea such as "I just lost it" would seem to absolve the angry individual from responsibility for her or his actions. The "hot" content of emotion of violated entitlement seems to permit vengeance or satisfaction beyond restoration of the loss. If the expression is beyond my control, then I would have the advantage of owning the reason for the anger, but not anger's consequences. Patricia Greenspan (1987) identifies actions performed out of rage as exemplifying behavior that is "unfree" but for which the agent is still in some sense responsible. That is, the condition of anger, in a sense, narrows the range of what is expressed or the alternatives that the angry individual believes are possible or comfortable to express. For example, in anger it is difficult, if not impossible, to imagine finding any humor in the situation, showing genuine warmth toward the offending party, or believing that the offense is really no offense at all. In Greenspan's view, the person may be responsible for that behavior only when viewed from the larger context within which the rage occurs. For example, that person may have cultivated the disposition to exhibit rage. One may be responsible for the truculent attitude, the responsibility for making oneself unfree, but the rage, once elicited, narrows one's views of alternative actions. Researchers are careful to point out that anger is but one condition that may generate aggressive or violent behavior. Other conditions that stimulate aggression are pain and discomfort, and these, in fact, may be more direct and frequent causes.[8] In any event, as we saw in the previous chapter, the consequences of aggression and acting out are different for girls and boys.

Who is entitled to anger?

Emotion of entitlement is emotion of the status quo and of challenge to it. From this perspective, the tendency to link masculinity and anger stems from the privilege that adheres to masculinity: Anger per se is not a masculine prerogative; rather, a sense of *entitlement* is a masculine prerogative, and anger is the outcome of violations (or anticipated violations) of those entitlements. Power is the capacity to get what one wants, to achieve one's own goals. The use of power is aimed at restoring, maintaining, or acquiring what one values. Where gender is concerned, what is at stake is the *status quo* of social arrangements that inequitably benefit one sex over the other. "Benefit" would include achieving one's goal in the immediate anger-evoking situation, but more importantly, the longer-term maintenance of social structures and practices that preserve power inequities. Not surprisingly, the perspectives of the anger perpetrator and the target of anger differ markedly, highlighting the interconnections of power and status. One study compared autobiographical accounts of being angered and being the target of anger. Perpetrator accounts described the anger event as meaningful, understandable, isolated, and without long-term implications for the parties involved. From the target's perspective, however, the narrative described an entirely different emotion. Targets portrayed the event as arbitrary, not justifiable, and bearing long-term effects including harm, loss, and grievance.[9]

Who has a right to be angry, and about what? Explicit and implicit indicators of status, especially gender, class, age, and race, are important to include in any full account of anger's social meaning. Paul Freedman (1998), for example, tells us that in the late Middle Ages the peasant class in Europe was thought to be incapable of constructive or effective anger. The vast majority of writers from the thirteenth through the sixteenth centuries portrayed peasant anger as unthinkable for individuals and, when expressed by the group, as the worst sort of destructive irrationality. Peasant uprisings were viewed not as anger-based responses to perceived injustice or as aimed at social change but, rather as a natural outflowing of the peasant low nature that could boil over if they were not firmly held in check by their betters. Freedman observes that "cold, calculated anger, either for revenge or in defense of honor, was considered generally impossible for peasants" because their anger was simply "an instinct opposed to thought, the most dramatic expression of baseness more commonly evidenced by [their] mere boorishness" (p. 179). Of course, identifying peasant anger as irrational and potentially dangerous provided the nobility with every justification for quashing their demonstration of anger. The double standard reduces the emotion of those with less status to mere emotionality, while reserving for one's own class a belief that anger is a powerful motivator that can be harnessed for good (i.e., self-serving) purpose. Contemporary research confirms that status influences both when anger will be recognized as anger and judgments made about the legitimacy and meaning of anger. Tiedens and her colleagues (Tiedens, Ellsworth, and Mesquita, 2000) showed that status predicts the emotions that are anticipated after negative outcomes. Research participants read brief vignettes in which the boss or his assistant was responsible for a serious blunder: not having the materials for an important presentation and thereby making their client angry. Participants then estimated emotional reactions of each to the situation. Individuals in high status positions were perceived likely to feel anger in response to negative outcomes; people in low-status positions were perceived likely to feel sadness and guilt. Tiedens *et al.* argue that emotional differences between people at different social levels occur because people believe that status indicates ability, and this belief in turn influences attributions of responsibility for positive and negative outcomes. In a second study they showed that people also infer status from emotions: Angry and proud people are thought of as high status whereas sad, guilty, and appreciative people are considered to be low in status. In these studies the target individuals were male or sex was unspecified, so it is still an open question as to how evaluations and expectations play out when status plus gender plus ethnicity or class are contrasted.

Race and gender, in particular, converge at important points in the social meaning of emotion. Evelyn Nakano Glenn (1999) reminds us that race and gender share key features as analytic concepts. An important one is that both are *relational*. Categories within gender (e.g., woman/man) and within race (e.g., black/white) take their meaning in part from their relation to each other. In that regard, the dominant category serves as the standard, the *de facto* "normal," and the other stands in contrast as the "variant." By virtue of being the standard, the dominant category is nonproblematic and remains unexamined. Thus, for example, white seems raceless. Think about it: how often have you, the reader, thought about European Americans when I have mentioned the importance of looking at emotion in terms of racial ethnicity? Unless you happen to be a member of a nondominant group, I doubt that has occurred often, if at all. The relevance to anger of these chronic but unnoticed comparisons is twofold. First, gender and racial ethnicity will separately and together provide a framework for the individual to understand her or his scope of entitlement. Second, expression of entitlement by individuals in the "variant" categories may be evaluated differently (by oneself as well as by observers) than expression of entitlement by those in the nonproblematic "standard" category. One way in which the impact of stereotypes is studied involves "priming" research participants with stereotype-relevant information and then assessing the extent to which their subsequent judgments reflect the intrusion of those stereotypes. Priming typically is accomplished by embedding the stereotypes within a neutral set of information, such as a long word list, such that the priming occurs without the participant's direct awareness. Abreu (1998), for example, found that therapists who had been primed with African American stereotypes rated a hypothetical African American male client more negatively on hostility (but surprisingly, more favorably on non-hostility related attributes) than therapists who had not been primed. When one tries to suppress one's own tendency to stereotype, the stereotypes may paradoxically increase the stereotype's influences on one's social judgments. Wyer, Sherman and Stroessner (1998) showed this effect, finding that non-African American students' efforts to suppress African American racial stereotypes increased their judgment of a male African American target's hostility. How strongly these effects would show up for African American women targets or for male targets of other racial ethnicities (including Euro-American males) compared to African American males remains to be investigated.

One way to map the complexities of status variables in legitimizing anger is through gendered emotion stereotypes that change when race or class is added to the equation. The information here is very sparse. Even though there have been a number of studies of emotion stereotypes in recent years, the tendency has been to presume "woman" stands for all women, "man" for all men. Agneta Fischer (1995), for example, has shown that "powerful" emotions, that is emotions that involve attempts to gain or regain control over the situation, are associated with men, but "powerless" emotions, such as sadness, anxiety, and fear are associated with women. So far, though, we only know that there is an association with gender when the research participant is asked to *imagine* the target. In one of the few studies that have considered the interconnectedness of status variables, Lott and Saxon (1998) found that social class had a dramatic effect on judgments of emotional qualities. While they found no difference in people's ratings of Jewish, Latina, and Anglo women targets in terms of how unhappy, emotional, or assertive the woman was judged to be, when social class was varied, the working class woman was viewed as more unhappy and more emotional, but less assertive than the middle-class woman.

The basis for entitlement

Anger can be experienced as mixed with a variety of other emotions – for example, depression, fear, or relief. It is incompatible with emotions that would undermine or negate the premise of entitlement on which the emotion is built. Imagine that you are cruising along the freeway at 80 mph. The speed limit is 65 and a state trooper pulls you over and tickets you for speeding. Do you get angry about the ticket? If other drivers have been passing you at even higher rates of speed, or you just got a ticket last week, or you never speed except just this once – probably yes, because it is experienced as a violation of your entitlement *not* to get a ticket. On the other hand, if you – like many of us – drive over the speed limit frequently, but seldom or never get caught, it is easy to think of the ticket as a kind of payment that is "due" for all that "free" speeding. No sense of violated entitlement, so no basis for anger. Similarly, if I were to empathize with the needs or limitations of the offending party that in my view caused her or him to encroach on my sense of order, this would disrupt the assumptions necessary to anger. I cannot possibly be angry *at* the puppy for chewing my shoe if I believe that the puppy is not competent to control its own behavior, although I may be quite angry about the conditions that gave this irresponsible little dog opportunity for the snack. The premise of anger and its incompatibility with competing frameworks of understanding offer another angle from which to view the relation between gender and anger. If, in fact, girls are encouraged to prize interpersonal relationships and to be concerned with others' emotional well-being, the set-up for anger would be less likely to occur because "what I am due" is less likely to be at stake. Where there is a gender difference in anger, the difference lies largely in what women and men believe they are due, rather than whether anger occurs as a response to a perception of violated entitlement. Anger is a gender issue because who believes they are entitled to what is associated with the criteria that define status – of which gender is among the most salient. Social class, racial ethnicity, and other markers of status, too, will be implicated in marking the boundaries of legitimate and questionable sense of entitlement.

There is interesting work on the concept of entitlement that shows how, at least among young Americans in areas of compensation for work, women and men may begin with different assumptions about what they are due. Faye Crosby and her colleagues have studied this phenomenon in a variety of contexts, and have found that even when women acknowledge general inequities they do not perceive their own situation as exemplifying that general pattern. Crosby has dubbed this "denial of personal disadvantage." Such denial is not "simply politeness that accounts for people's greater willingness to voice discontent on behalf of their group than on behalf of themselves" (Crosby *et al.*, 1989, p. 92). Instead, even individuals who are acutely aware that their own group encounters discrimination, tend to believe that they personally have been exempt from this discrimination. The sense that one is personally exempt from discriminatory practices manifests itself in how deserving one feels of reward. Brenda Major and her colleagues have explored the general finding that women appear to feel entitled to less than do men who have done comparable work. Major has shown, for example, that in the absence of information about standards for pay or performance, women tend to reward themselves substantially less than men, to estimate a lower rate of pay as appropriate for work done, and to produce more work more efficiently than men for the same pay. The key is that this only occurs when women have no standard against which to evaluate the fairness of pay. In one set of ingenious studies, Major and her colleagues asked women and men to work by themselves on a task for a specified time period and then privately to take what they believed to be fair pay for the work from a $4.00 kitty. Some were given social comparison information, that is, information indicating how much money other participants had presumably paid themselves to work on the task. When women and men had social comparison information, there were no differences in what they paid themselves. In the absence of such information, however, women took an average of about 60 per cent less than men ($1.95 on average for women, and $3.18 on average for men). Major makes a good case that the difference "results, in part, from structural inequalities present in most contemporary societies, that result in women and men having access to and using different comparison standards to evaluate what they personally deserve" (p. 13). Occupational segregation of work gives one a same-sex standard of pay comparison and the concomitant undervaluing of female-dominated occupations insures that the pay standards for women are lower than men. Even in the same occupations women are underpaid relative to men and face restricted opportunities and demands of family and home responsibilities in a far greater way than do men. Major suggests that these structural inequalities produce sex differences in four types of comparison standards: "social comparisons, or beliefs about what others with similar contributions earn; self-comparisons, or expectations based on what one has earned or received in the past; normative comparisons, or beliefs about what people typically earn for doing the type of work one is performing; and feasibility comparisons, or expectations based on what is realistically attainable given the constraints one faces" (pp. 15–16).[10] The upshot of this line of research is that, without a basis for making some determination about entitlement, there is considerable individual difference in how willing one is to assert a certain level of entitlement.

The fact is that some people seem to have a more expansive notion of what they are entitled to than do others. A distinction can be drawn between anger as a situationally-specific response and as a general attitude, a trait that reflects a general readiness to experience events as relevant to one's sense of entitlement. In the popular late 1970s British TV import *Fawlty Towers*, resort hotel owner Basil Fawlty ("Monty Python" veteran John Cleese) spends his life ready to be frustrated or angered by the least provocation by his staff, guests, wife, or the world. Basil's wife, Sybil (Prunella Scales), described his style best: "You're either crawling all over them, licking their boots, or spitting poison at them like some Benzedrine puff adder." Psychologists have devised questionnaires that differentiate among anger "styles." Charles Spielberger's (1988) State-Trait Anger Expression Inventory (STAXI) was designed to assess people's reports about their experience of anger, including what appear to be two trait-like qualities (trait-like in that they appear to be manifested to the same degree by the individual across time and across situations). One, an angry temperament dimension (the Basil Fawlty dimension), represents "a general propensity to experience and express anger without provocation," while the angry reaction dimension (what we might call the "I'm not your doormat" dimension) represents "the disposition to express anger when criticized or treated unfairly by other individuals" (p. 1). People's responses to items tapping each of these dispositions are only modestly correlated. This shows that having the capacity to experience anger when one perceives oneself to be wronged stands separately from a more general propensity to view the world in terms of one's own personal entitlement. The dispositional tendency to experience anger is linked to a strong sense of entitlement and to high but "unstable" self-esteem, that is a strong positive regard for oneself that is easily upset – the more I feel I am entitled to and the less secure I feel about those entitlements, the more vigilant I tend to be with respect to potential violations.[11]

Weighing the consequences of anger

At least some of the prevailing notion of the absence of women's anger stems from who is and is not willing to openly express anger. Expression of anger is not a simple through-put of the experienced emotion. Both women and men report that they do not express their anger openly, and women, furthermore, may be especially aware of negative consequences that are incurred when anger is expressed openly. People do weigh the costs that go with anger.[12] Weber (1998) points out that theorists tend to overlook the pragmatic basis for people's ambivalence about anger. Simply put, people say they think about the appropriateness of anger at least in part in terms of whether anything will be accomplished by its expression – is it worthwhile to get angry? Thomas (1996), focusing on women's reports about their anger experiences, found that most reported that anger was generated within their closest relationships and that they weighed up carefully what could and could not be accomplished by letting that anger show.

Other factors that contribute to thinking about the consequences of anger expression emerge from the provoking context. Biaggio (1991) points out that, while the same kinds of situations and provocations elicit anger for women and men, some classes of provocation are more likely to be encountered by one sex than the other. Some early work (Frodi, 1978) suggested that women were especially irritated by condescending treatment. This might be because women are more often the object of it, because the condescending treatment is more pointed, and/or because they are more likely to identify certain behaviors by others as indicative of condescension. It may not even be on many men's cognitive "radar screens" to notice condescending treatment in some contexts, although Frodi found that men reported being provoked by condescending treatment from women. We are more likely to learn how gender and anger are linked if we look at and theorize context than if we simply enumerate the themes and frequencies with which women and men report anger occurrences. Miller (1991) asked undergraduate women and men to write scripts for conflict between friends and found no noteworthy differences in the narratives themselves, but consistent differences in how they represented the contingencies of their responses. The course of action in the men's scripts depended more on the offended party's initiation of conflict, but the women's scripts depended more on whether the offending party apologized. In Chapter 3 I described the "memory-work" technique that Crawford, Kippax, Onyx, Gault, and Benton (1992) used to examine the ways in which emotional experience is understood. After searching for common elements and meanings, they distill individual themes into a more general understanding of experienced emotion. They found that the key to understanding the differences between women and men's experiences of anger is through looking at how power and perceptions of power are distributed. They argue that, in a sense, if you *really* have power, anger is unnecessary. The subtlest expression of anger or threat should be enough to restore the situation to its desired state. On the other hand, "anger arising out of a sense of powerlessness takes on . . . an out-of-control, passionate, ineffective character. It is a response to strong judgements about unfairness, injustice, which remains unresolved. The anger of a person without power has a strong component of victimisation" (p. 348). In this regard, the frustrated male golfer who vents his anger on his golf clubs, and the harried working mother who loses her temper after coming home once too often to a mess, both use anger to make a claim of entitlement. And even though the objective "rightness" of each one's anger is vastly different, their capacity to bring about desired change marks both their claims as futile.

One of the important features of the analyses by Major and by Crosby is that they point to structural features that set up the circumstances for different ways in which women and men understand their place and develop expectations for the consequences of their circumstances. This is neither a blame-the-victim model that focuses on what women "ought" to be angry about, nor an exhortation to "get in touch with" the anger that is "really" there. It presumes that the individual's experience is legitimate even if the circumstances in which she or he operates are not. And, it factors into the explanation of anger the understanding that people have expectations regarding the consequences of experiencing (or expressing) emotion in particular ways at particular times. The empirical research here for the most part addresses explicit knowledge of the consequences of the outcomes of emotional exchanges. Margaret Clark and her colleagues, for example, find that expressions of anger decrease observers' liking for the angry other, whereas expressions of happiness increase liking for that person (Clark, Pataki, and Carver, 1996). Janet Stoppard's research has most comprehensively mapped beliefs about the costs and benefits we believe accrue to displaying (or withholding displays of) emotion. For example, Stoppard and Gunn Gruchy (1993) examined gender-differentiated norms for expressing emotion. Among other observations, they found that women believe themselves to be required to express positive emotion toward others and expect negative social sanctions if they do not, whereas men expect no negative consequences for failure to express positive emotion.[13] Clark (1996) also reports that the effects of expressing a specific emotion (happiness, sadness, or anger) on an observer's rating of the expressor's likeability is, in part, a function of the sex of the expressor and of the observer. For example, expressing sadness appears to increase the perceived neediness and to decrease the perceived likeability of the person expressing it, except in dyads in which a woman expresses sadness to a man.

What is there to get upset about?

Some stunning examples of the costs and consequences of expressing anger can be found in the research on marital interaction. Christensen and Heavey (1990) have shown that a spouse's tactic of using withdrawal or demand in resolving conflict depends on the outcome she or he desires. John Gottman and Bob Levenson (e.g., Gottman and Levenson, 1988; 1992) have described marital relationships as having a particular gendered pattern to conflict management, with wives more likely to seek engagement, while husbands withdraw emotionally. Gottman suggests that this pattern becomes exaggerated as conflict escalates. He explains this pattern in terms of men's management of their physiological arousal, but an alternative (or supplementary) explanation is based on the relative control of resources within the marriage.[14] Reasoning that desire to maintain or change the *status quo* should influence whether one opposes or withdraws from discussion of problematic issues, Christensen and Heavey rated the interactions of married couples on topics for which one spouse wanted to change the other. They found that the goal of the partner, rather than the sex of the partner, determined whether withdrawal or demand characterized the individual's style. Wife demand/husband withdrawal occurred most often when the wife wanted to change the husband; when the husband wanted to change the wife, the demand/withdrawal pattern was reversed. The overall appearance of a consistent gender-related difference in strategy can be interpreted as an artifact of who is in a position to desire change and who benefits from maintenance of the *status quo*. Thomas' (1996) qualitative study of women's anger found that the most pervasive theme in women's descriptions of the precipitants of their anger was the role of power, or lack thereof, especially within work and family relationships.[15] One respondent quoted (on p. 61) offers a perfect illustration of the demand strategy:

> I felt like my weekends were spent cleaning the house while his week-
> ends were spent playing, and I resented that. . . . Like I told him when
> I was angry, "You don't want to compare what you do and what I do
> because you'll lose, trust me. How many times do you do the laundry,
> and how many times do you fold and put up clothes, and cook the
> meals and run the kids?" He knows he doesn't do that. He knows I do
> most of it and he likes it that way and he wants to keep it that way.

The point here is that a serious discrepancy in privilege sets up the conditions under which, once a woman feels some degree of entitlement to an
altered situation, the experience of anger becomes a tool to bring about
change. Initiating change requires an assertive stance, a stance that appears as a "demand" strategy. Emotional withdrawal or stonewalling
may subserve physiological homeostasis, but it also is an efficacious
strategy for maintaining a *status quo* situation that advantages oneself at
the expense of one's spouse. In other words, in this example there is nothing for the husband to be angry about except threats to the household
chore organization as it currently exists. For the wife, on the other hand,
anger is inevitable once she identifies the situation as one that she expects
to operate differently. Janice Steil (1997) examines why, despite the general acknowledgment that equality is valued as a goal for contemporary
marriage, wives in most marriages still carry a disproportionate responsibility for the work of relationships, home, and children. Steil shows
how motivations to seek change are often impeded by spousal differences in the sense of entitlement. Conflicting views of who is entitled to
what are ripe grounds for evoking anger. One typical newspaper comic
strip takes on these issues when a boy tells his newspaper-reading father
that mom is being a grouch and asks "What's bugging her?" Dad explains it away as a peculiarly female problem "It's hormones . . . Makes
'em moody from time to time." Mom overhears, however, and angrily
objects "There's nothing wrong with me. I'm just sick of picking up after
you!" At which the son whispers to his father "I see what you mean."[16]
A cartoon, maybe, but it also captures another side of women's double-
bind described by Steil: pressing for change in the relationship is at odds
with one's role as the nurturer and relationship monitor.

Whichever partner is dissatisfied, there are predictable strategies
for expressing that dissatisfaction. Caryl Rusbult and her colleagues
(Rusbult, 1993) investigated the occurrence of responses to dissatisfaction in close relationships. They have identified four general types of response to dissatisfaction: exit, voice, loyalty, and neglect. One can leave
the relationship (exit), speak up through working to repair the relationship (voice), passively wait for improvement in the relationship conditions (loyalty), or simply allow the relationship to deteriorate (neglect).
Although they originally expected gender-related differences in the

tendency to employ a particular response pattern, over a number of separate studies they have, in fact, found no consistent or substantial gender-related differences in style. Once again, any gender effect needs to be understood as a manifestation of the context. In order to choose exit or voice and have that choice work, one has to have the resources that make that choice possible. To exit you have to have the power to leave and have somewhere to go; voice needs a dynamics of partnership that enables communication.

Privileged anger often goes unremarked, and not named as emotion. In other words, anger is treated as if it were a simple position statement or directive. The receptionist story that I used in the introduction to this chapter is a perfect example. She clearly understood her husband's angry expressions, but his behavior was not counted as "emotion." Persons in lower status positions exert power, too, of course – the stereotypes of the tyrant petty bureaucrat or power-wielding secretary are as well-known in real life as they are in cartoons and jokes – but their displays are not accorded the gravity of those of higher status.

When it comes to demonstrating authority through power, women and men may be evaluated differently. In one early study (Jacobsen *et al.*, 1977) women authority figures (e.g., professor, mother, police officer) were evaluated differently depending on whether the subordinate was male or female. Evaluation of male authority figures was not a function of the sex of the individual over whom authority was exercised. Women authority figures who were firm with a male subordinate were evaluated more negatively than their male counterparts, and when the subordinate was female and the authority was lenient, women were again evaluated more negatively than their male counterparts. It is not clear whether things have changed all that much in the past twenty-five years. Brody, Lovas and Hay (1995) found that both men and women reported feeling more anger toward a woman who was presented as being in an enviable position (e.g., getting a free airline ticket) than toward a man in an identical enviable position. They argue that the woman who wins is seen as less deserving of good fortune, by virtue of the lower status accorded by gender, and hence more appropriate as a target of anger. Lower status people, their research would suggest, will look less deserving, less entitled. Women are often caught unawares by the envy that men might have toward their success or good fortune. On the other hand, the implied status of gender is attenuated when other indicators of status are made more explicit. Karol Maybury (1997) examined the influence of sex and status of protagonist and anger type on observer judgments of anger displays. College students read scenarios that described the protagonist responding with either physical or verbal anger toward a co-worker of higher, equivalent, or lower status after that co-worker had committed a significant work-related error. Whereas sex of protagonist had few effects, the effect of protagonist status was substantial. High status protagonists' anger displays were judged as more appropriate, favorable, and situationally motivated than were those of low and moderate status protagonists. High status protagonists were also judged to be less likely to be fired for their anger display. Other researchers, also using vignette studies, have found that both gender and job status serve as cues for interpreting facial expression of anger (Algoe, Buswell, and DeLamater, 2000). Recall the research by Tiedens and her colleagues that I described earlier. We begin to see a picture of privilege begetting privilege through the exercise of anger.

This work again clearly demonstrates the power of gender emotion stereotypes. At the same time, however, this stereotype research is built with few exceptions on studies in which only target gender or status is identified, leaving open the question of how status as entitlement to anger plays out across racial ethnic groups. Jill Crowley and I have begun exploratory work on this question and it is obvious even in this early work that current notions of a one-size-fits-all anger stereotype is too simplistic to account for how stereotypes may filter understanding of others' emotion (Shields and Crowley, 2000).

Internalizing anger or externalizing anger?

One currently popular explanation for gender differences in anger is that males learn to externalize their anger, while females learn to turn it inward. On the one hand is the argument that women are compelled to unlearn their capacity for anger expression or divert it toward a kind of self-blame. Harriet Lerner (1985), for example, in *The Dance of Anger*, her best-selling book originally published in the mid-1980s (and one of the few practical advice books on the market that does not advocate simplistic solutions that entail women learning to "be nice"), suggested that "the taboos against women feeling and expressing anger are so powerful that even *knowing* when we are angry is not a simple matter. When a woman shows her anger, she is likely to be dismissed as irrational or worse" (p. 2). American society, she said, views women's direct expression of anger as unladylike, unfeminine, unmaternal, sexually unattractive, and strident. Women – at least the readers of the magazine *Self* – tend to agree. In an informal poll of readers, the majority agreed that "It's more difficult for women to show their anger than it is for men" – citing reasons like "It makes us look bitchy" and "We're perceived as being hysterical."[17]

With the perspective of another decade we ask *which* women under *which* circumstances say they are angry or show it or both? How is the language of anger (the one who is angry and the target of anger) a function of gender? It is easy to assemble anecdotal evidence of the loaded gender-specific language that is used to describe anger: He is angry; she is out of control. He is firm; she is a bitch. Not even high-minded etiquette guide Miss Manners escapes such gender bias. She, too, is subject to the gender-coded application of emotion judgments. She reports that she had once, after expressing her displeasure with a coldly raised eyebrow, later heard that she had been described as having had a "tantrum"! Instead of asking what is "wrong with" women's anger, we can identify the conditions under which women's anger will be unacknowledged or pathologized by others and the conditions that encourage anger's diversion or internalization. These are not necessarily exclusive of one another. Periodically a newspaper style section or popular magazine discovers women's anger, as for example, when in the late-1990s the *New York Times* identified "female rage" as the new "in thing." In *The First Wives Club* (1996) three women get together after twenty years of separation and decide to form a group in order to get revenge on evil ex-husbands. The popular comedy, starring Goldie Hawn, Bette Midler, and Diane Keaton, was heralded as a cinematic turning point because these angry women were not punished for seeking revenge or for having the audacity to live well. The ambivalence of punishment and praise for African American women is similarly evident in hip-hop and rap culture.

Alison Jaggar (1992) identifies as "outlaw emotions" those emotions that do not conform to the normative for a given situation. The lone woman at the board meeting who is embarrassed or angry when the others around the table laugh at a sexual innuendo is experiencing an outlaw emotion. If her reaction is visible, it is puzzling or comical or irritating to everyone else around the table because it does not fit their conception of an appropriate reaction. Her marginal status makes it more likely that she will not fit the emotion-defining framework. While the majority opinion is that the innuendo, for example, is (or ought to be) funny, the outlaw who experiences the unconventional emotional response for that situation "may be confused, unable to name their experience; they may even doubt their own sanity." Women, she observes, "may come to believe that they are 'emotionally disturbed' and that the embarrassment or fear aroused in them . . . is prudery or paranoia" (p. 131). Jaggar points out the costs that accrue to the individual whose genuine emotion is nevertheless outlaw. Some outlaws are more at risk than others. When the individual stands out in multiple ways as "different from" the group, by age or appearance, for example, it is easy to stand out as an interloper in others' emotional territory.

What do women say about their anger?

Whereas the language of anger reveals a striking difference in the way in which gender is linked to thinking about anger or evaluating others' anger displays, measures of anger experience do not. Self-report of anger, for example, tends to yield few gender differences in frequency or intensity of anger. Thomas (1989) found no differences between women and men in measures of either anger suppression (anger-in) or anger expression (anger-out). However, she found that women were more likely to discuss their anger, had more anger-related physical symptoms, and that trait anger, as measured by State-Trait Anger Scale, was strongly related to perceived stress, especially vicarious stressors arising from women's concern about others and their drive to care for them. Kopper and Epperson (1991) also found no gender differences in trait anger, anger-in, anger-out, or anger-control. Other researchers, however, have reported that girls and women report that they hide their anger more (e.g., Ramsden, 1999; Kopper and Epperson, 1996). They may hide anger for a number of reasons, but the research points to their perception of negative consequences attached to expressing anger openly. Sharkin (1993) maps out one consequence of overgeneralizing about the prevalence of anger-in versus anger-out for each sex. When the psychotherapeutic context is influenced by stereotypes that male anger is a control issue, female anger an expression issue, the actual situation of the client can be misread. He points out that women do seek counseling in order to control their anger, and that men seek counseling in order to learn more constructive expression of it. To this we could add that women's problem is explicitly identified as an "emotional" one, whereas men's is identified as a problem of self-control.

Differences do emerge, as we have seen, in the way women and men, as well as girls and boys, understand the consequences for using (or not using) emotion-relevant information in a certain way. Saarni (1999) concludes from the research that, among children, girls tend to use internalizing processes such as worrying, withdrawal, and self-blame when emotionally disturbed, whereas disturbed boys are more likely to act out through aggression, hostility, stealing, and so on. In a series of studies, Nancy Eisenberg and her colleagues have tried to unravel the complexities of the mutual influences of preschool children's temperament (that is, the typical behavioral "style" with which a person responds to change in the environment) and how well children manage challenge or obstacles (coping efficacy).[18] They have shown how the interweaving of adults' gender expectations, the child's temperament, and the outcomes of anger-provoking situations for these preschoolers sets the stage for how children later understand how to handle themselves and their anger. For example, in one study they focused on young children's anger reactions in the school setting. The children who tried to deal with the anger provocation with nonhostile verbal strategies tended to be the children who were less intense in their emotional reactions overall, and who were viewed by their teachers as generally more effective socially. So what the child brings to the table, so to speak, in terms of temperament, may make it more possible for the child to use constructive means for dealing with anger rather than just having a tantrum or bashing the provocateur over the head. Still, teacher reaction is also affected by the child's gender. Teachers viewed girls, but not boys, who tried to remove themselves from the situation, when angered, as socially skilled. From the teacher's standpoint, almost anything that keeps peace in the classroom is good. When girls dealt with their anger by avoiding it, they were as valued as when they stood up to provocation in a nonhostile way. Boys, on the other hand, were not viewed positively when they withdrew from the conflict situation.

If we look at what women say about anger, not in therapy, but in everyday life, the theme of entitlement plays a prominent role. Campbell and Muncer (1987) tape-recorded conversations among same-sex groups of adult friends. Although they obtained transcripts from only one group of women and one group of men, they were able to examine seventy accounts of anger episodes (about half from each group). Relevant here is the striking difference in the implicit model of aggression that structured the social talk. For women, issues of control and loss of control figured prominently, suggesting that anger and aggression were viewed as the result of breakdown of internal control that leads to a breakdown of normal social interaction: "The outward expression of anger was often referred to as 'losing it' and the women were acutely sensitive to the effect of such a loss. Tears, raised voices and blows were all discussed as embarrassing, silly, childish or threatening to the future of the relationship between the parties involved" (p. 507). In the men's group, the theme of appropriate management of aggressive encounters was significant, with judgment of appropriateness of aggression being based on the characteristics of the target rather than the breakdown of self-control or disruption of social relationships. "The men talked as if there were social rules which dictated whether anger should be acted upon or not and these implicit rules both outlawed aggression against much weaker targets and sanctioned non-aggression against much stronger or more threatening opponents" (p. 508).[19] A gendered account of anger calls attention to a difference between effective anger and anger that is mere emotionality. If tears are *the* sign of ineffectual anger, we would expect that tears would only rarely figure in the emotional displays of the confidently powerful. But that is not the case at all.

"It takes a real man to cry"

The American myth, at least since Edmund Muskie's emotional reaction in 1972 to a personal attack on his wife by a reactionary newspaper publisher in the New Hampshire presidential primary race, is that weeping is political suicide. Yet tactical tears have been part of the American political scene for decades. Vice-presidential candidate Richard Nixon salvaged his standing as Eisenhower's running mate in 1952 in part by showing controlled emotion – including a moist eye – in his Checkers speech. Muskie, then, seems to be an anomaly in the overall arc of public life.[20] In contrast, the "Muskie rule" certainly applies to women politicians. Indeed, Madeline Kunin (1995), when governor of Vermont, began her autobiography by acknowledging the power of tears: "'Don't cry,' I told myself fiercely, 'stay in control.'" When Representative Pat Schroeder announced her withdrawal from the 1988 Presidential race, the collective audible reaction of disappointment from her audience of supporters broke her composure. Her tears drew a strong response both from her critics and her supporters. Most of the print reaction centered on the responses of other women to Schroeder. Her Democratic supporters and Schroeder herself were most dismayed with what they viewed as the inevitable stereotyping of her response. As Schroeder observed, "Why must a woman be contained, controlled? It begins to sound like the ads they used to have for women and tranquilizers." Her critics, largely those on the other side of the political map, did indeed seize the opportunity to invoke the stereotype. One Republican pollster put the perfect partisan spin on it, saying Schroeder's "inability to command her emotions when she was making an announcement about the Presidency only served to reinforce some basic stereotypes about women running for office – those stereotypes being lack of composure, inability to make tough decisions."[21] The double standard was not lost on Schroeder, who pointed out "The good news for men is: crying is a badge of courage. The bad news is that for women it's still a scarlet letter." Schroeder is not alone in appreciating the costs of tears. Much anecdotal evidence shows that women are well aware of the dangers of tears. A survey of *Working Woman* magazine readers, for example, revealed that over three-quarters of respondents believed that the behavior *most* damaging to one's professional image was "crying in the office."[22]

In the immediate aftermath of September 11, 2001, however, the ordinary practice of tactical tears was completely overtaken by the magnitude and incomprehensibility of the events. People wept, and wept openly, because we found language insufficient.

What tears can say

Tears signal any number of different emotions, both positive experiences and the most personally devastating. Tears of sadness, joy, and surprise speak to overflowing emotion, uncontained emotion, but tears that go with anger are the most damning. Crawford *et al.* (1990) point out that powerlessness or a sense of victimization is part and parcel of both depression and anger, but the sense of impotence in depression "stems from within; knowing what activity we could and should engage in, we are yet unable to act." Angry tears come because "we cannot act because action is denied us – the forces which frustrate us are too powerful" (p. 342). Tears of anger signal not only uncontrolled emotion, but *ineffective* emotion. The negative consequences of angry weeping can be exacerbated in a spiral of misunderstanding and escalation (Cupach and Canary, 1995). A woman who expresses anger through tears may not be acknowledged by others present as having a legitimate claim to anger or its redress. She may then interpret the failure of others to recognize the anger as condescension and become even more angry, even more tearful.

Weeping, whether a simple moist eye or outright crying, when it occurs in front of others, embodies emotion as an interpersonal event. The power of weeping lies in the connectedness of weeper and observer. Tears are a powerful communicator of felt emotion, but are not specific to any individual emotion. Tears accompany joy as well as anger, accomplishment as well as loss. Jack Katz (1999, p. 197) characterizes tears as "a personally embodied form of expression that transcends what speech can do." Tears take over when we want or need to express something in the most profoundly physical way, but speech fails, is unavailable, is useless, or is powerless. Katz's theory offers another reason for the proliferation of high status men's public weeping. In the previous chapter I described how the appropriation of this stereotypically feminine emotional response reasserts the difference between the "merely feminine" and the "manly." Katz's analysis adds the insight that the discreet tear is a means to express genuine and heartfelt emotion without the burden of putting that emotion into broader expression or to name the feelings behind it. Controlled tears stand for the gamut of feeling – compassion, concern, sorrow, and so on – all rolled into one, but without words. Too many tears, though, and the tears begin to speak for themselves as a blatantly emotional act. The positive value placed on the wordless expression of emotion via public tears is not universal, and men of lower status and women cry in public at their own risk. The rules of emotion positively sanction the honest tear for public and powerful men.

In the US, researchers obtain a fairly consistent difference in the self-reported frequency of weeping, with women reporting more frequent crying than men.[23] The definition of weeping varies considerably from one study to the next. For example, one large survey asked about "crying spells" (which connotes a fairly strong reaction), others include everything from tearing to open weeping, and still others leave the definition of "crying" up to individual research participants.[24] Most research has focused on college-age individuals, which is problematic. The little information that is available on later adulthood shows that, at least with more dramatic forms of weeping, there is an apparent decline in overall frequency for both sexes, but a gender difference nevertheless (Ross and Mirowsky, 1984). For the most part, women and men report similar situations that elicit tears and the same range of emotions that accompany weeping.[25]

Strong emotion is potentially emotion out of control, and tears convey the potential for loss of that self-control. The signal of emotional intensity and potential for loss of control are two of the strongest indicators of the authenticity of the feelings behind the tears. Nevertheless, tears, like many other expressions of emotion, can be controlled. People have a remarkable capacity to control weeping in comparison to other signs and symptoms of emotional experience. Kraemer and Hastrup (1988) asked college student women to either hold back tears or to weep freely in response to a short, sad film. Women who had been asked to cry, cried far longer (an average of 4 minutes) than women who had been asked to try not to cry (an average of 30 seconds). Even genuine tears are not a simple "readout" of feelings. Delp and Sackheim (1987) generated happy or sad moods in research participants while measuring tear flow in both eyes. Mood induction worked equally well with women and men, and for neither was there a correlation between amount of tearing and reported mood. People are justifiably leery of the meaning of weeping in adults and on guard for false tears.

The potential for control gives rise to witnesses' ambivalence to weeping. Weeping in front of others can have a profound affect on them. The perception of the observer matters a great deal in how effective the tears are in changing the situation or eliciting help, sympathy, or support. All bets are off, for example, if the observer believes the weeper is deliberately or manipulatively crying. In his history of crying, Tom Lutz (1999) gives numerous examples of the suspicion with which women's tears are regarded, suspicion that seems to stem from the capacity for tears to be "faked" as a power ploy, that is, in order to obtain some desired result. Thus effective weeping is a contradiction in terms: It must communicate that one feels intensely enough to shed genuine tears, but not so overcome that one cannot still effect exquisite self-control. False tears and uncontrolled tears both damage the interpersonal connection that makes tears otherwise so powerful. The controllability of weeping is at odds with the features that speak to its authenticity as a sign of felt emotion. Unbidden tears also come at the most inopportune moments. Representative Schroeder's tearful exit from the Presidential race was clearly not what she had planned, but, as she explained to the press, "I got up to give the speech, and when the groan came from the crowd, *that* I was not prepared for. It hits you like a truck."[26] Tears, then, are something of a paradox: compared to many other signs of strongly felt emotion, tears are both easy to summon yet can surprise us by their occurrence; yet "crocodile tears" can appear to be as genuine, or even more so, than spontaneous unbidden tears.

Reactions to weeping depend how the weeping is done and who sheds the tears. As I have shown in the previous chapter, Mr. Sensitive as a manly emotional ideal did not work in the 1970s, because it simply involved grafting a "feminine" response onto the "masculine" repertoire. Emotional display is not gender-neutral, and to borrow tears without modification to the manly way of weeping will not have the same impact. What we see today in the revival of masculine emotion in the form of public weeping, is a strategy to selectively appropriate emotion as a sign of authenticity, honesty, sincerity, "heart." This is not a twentieth-century innovation. Expressive weeping was not only tolerated but characteristic of early- to mid-Victorian men. Only later in the nineteenth century did a standard of attenuated expressiveness become the sign of manliness; a standard which by the mid-twentieth century became mislabeled as the requirement to be inexpressive.[27] "Manly emotion," as I have shown, is a standard requiring that one show that "appropriate" emotion is intensely felt, but not extravagantly shown. It requires an economy of expression and containment within the situation. Done correctly it can be very effective – for the right person. When college-age men wept in front of a stranger during a sad movie, they were liked better than men who did not weep; women, however, were liked better when they did not weep than when they did (Labott, Martin, Eason, and Berkey, 1991).

The "Muskie rule" seems to apply to nearly all public tearful behavior by women. For men, however, tears can work to advantage. Ed Muskie's mistake may have been a too-profuse tearfulness, suggesting the possibility of uncontrolled emotion. More likely, though, it was the fact that the tears were an expression of anger. Muskie's political sin was not tears *per se*, nor his expression of the groundless attack on his wife, but the fact that those tears showed him powerless to act against and rectify a violation of entitlement. His tears signaled ineffective emotion. And the expression of ineffective emotion was his political downfall. "It takes a real man to cry," but a man must cry the right way at the right time. And tears of anger, for either sex, do not meet that criterion.

Emotional prerogatives

Because of anger's characterization as problematic, yet significant in human evolution, it has become the contemporary version of nineteenth-century passion. Anger serves as the double-sided emotion without which great deeds would not be accomplished, yet which holds the possibility of destructive power if not competently harnessed. The quotation from Sternberg and Campos that begins this chapter captures that sense of anger as serving vital functions for human survival, physiologically, psychologically, and socially. Yet Sternberg and Campos' description of anger is curiously lacking an acknowledgment that these physiological, psychological, and social functions take place within a meaning-making cultural system. Will anger's physiological preparedness be exercised constructively? Or at cost to the individual? Will anger's psychological links to self-protection and aggression result in benefit? Or in loss? Will anger's social communication be understood as aiming for change and as having the wherewithal to bring that change about? The decontextualized description of "pure" anger makes all anger equal, and effaces the politics of entitlement that are the framework of anger. Frye's observation, centered as it is on entitlement, cuts to the heart of what this chapter is about.

In one sense, idealized anger epitomizes the manly emotion ideal and the function of that ideal in maintaining gendered social arrangements. When anger is practiced by the "wrong" person (the female, the child, someone of another race), the rules for appropriate expression shift. Women's anger, for one thing, is often, but not always, represented in terms that emphasize anger's ineffectual form: petulant, bitchy (ergo about trivial matters), or diffusely out of control ("hysterical," ergo impossible to harness in the service of reason). What happens with anger specifically is what occurs for emotions more generally. That is, women do not report less frequent occurrence of anger than do men. And women's angry responses are not invariably believed to be less legitimate when they do occur. Rather, the *meaning* of anger and its expression is interpreted in terms of *who* expresses the anger. Anger's gendered meanings are context-dependent, local instances of emotion judgment as value judgment.

The discourse of emotion is fundamentally concerned with judgments about the authenticity and legitimacy of experience. Beliefs about emotion as correct or incorrect, socially appropriate or inappropriate, and healthy or unhealthy are themselves deeply implicated in creating and sustaining gender boundaries. The social meaning of emotion is about telling the boys from the girls. This chapter, by concentrating on anger, shows that judgments of correct or incorrect, socially appropriate or inappropriate, and healthy or unhealthy are themselves gendering acts. Who gets called "emotional" depends on who is doing the naming, who is named, and the circumstances in which emotion occurs. In the following chapter I take a closer look at what is at stake in drawing these gender boundaries and why emotion is contested at all. What, after all, is "appropriate" emotion, how do we know it when we see it, and why does it matter so much?

Notes

1 In the late 1970s Elaine Walster's (now Hatfield) National Science Foundation-funded research on romantic love was pilloried as a waste of taxpayers' money by then-Senator William Proxmire. His argument was that there were simply some aspects of human behavior that could not be understood and that would be better left to remain a mystery! Hatfield has since received a number of honors for her pathbreaking research.

2 Carol Tavris' *Anger: The Misunderstood Emotion* (revised edition, 1989), is an outstanding and readable introduction to the psychology of anger. It covers all the basics and more: Is it better to count to ten or to blow off steam? Does chronic anger cause health problems? Why is it difficult to control anger? Does anger necessarily lead to aggression?

3 Solomon (1993) posits that emotions can be described on a number of dimensions, including ones that reflect aspects of the relationship between the experiencer and the object of the emotion. In what I am calling the family of emotions concerned with a sense of violated entitlement, Solomon identifies the difference among anger, resentment, irritation, and contempt as being due to how we view ourselves in comparison to the emotion object. Whereas in contempt I view myself as superior to the emotion object, in resentment I view myself as inferior.

4 Other theorists (e.g., Izard) believe there is a much broader set of anger-evoking stimuli, including frustration and physical pain.

5 See Mesquita and Frijda (1992).

6 Peter Stearns (1992) identifies the 1920s as the beginning of a shift toward "more uniform, gender-unspecific control urged in actual socialization practices." Stearns believes that this change contrasts with the Victorian tendency to encourage pronounced gender distinctions in emotion. I believe he is correct in describing a historical change, but not toward a unisex standard that both women and men have an equal chance to achieve. One of the problems in trying to square their account with mine is that Stearns and Stearns often rely on evidence regarding aggression to make inferences about anger.

7 "Miss Manners," by Judith Martin, *San Francisco Chronicle*, September 25, 1989.

8 Averill (1982) argues that aggression is neither necessarily nor simply related to anger. Berkowitz (2000) offers a model of how aversive physical and psychological experiences may generate fear, anger, or aggression.

9 Baumeister, Stillwell, and Wotman, 1990.

10 Major *et al.* (1989). See also Bylsma and Major (1992).

11 Evidence regarding the low correlation between the Basil Fawlty dimension and the doormat dimension can be found in Fuqua *et al.* (1991). On vigilance regarding violations of entitlement see Kernis, Grannemann, and Barclay (1989). Roland Neumann (2000) has shown that prior repeated use of internal attributions (that is, I am at fault) enhances the tendency to experience guilt, whereas external attributions enhances the tendency to experience anger.

12 See Kring, 2000, for a review of psychological research concerned with gender and anger.

13 See also Stoppard (1993) and Timmers, Fischer, and Manstead (1998).

14 Gottman and Levenson (1999) more recently have cautioned against the implicit "blame the wife" dimension of their model and provide data to show that conflict processes in distressed couples are a systemic feature of the relationship, not simply the result of one partner or the other's behavior.

15 For other critiques of Gottman's model or discussions of power in marital relationships, see also Denham and Bultemeier (1993), Noller (1993), Steil (1997), and Coltrane (1998).

16 "For Better or For Worse," by Lynn Johnston (September 20, 1984).

17 "Your Answers on: Anger," *Self* (May, 1992, p. 28).

18 Eisenberg, Fabes, Nyman, Bernzweig, and Pinulelas (1994). See also Fagot (1995) for a discussion of the interplay between environmental factors and the child's own construction of the environment in gender development.

19 Crawford *et al.* (1990) point out that Campbell and Muncer represent the subject of their research differently when they discuss women's and men's accounts by using headings of "women and anger" and "men's aggression" respectively in summarizing results.

20 The apparent increase in "public" tears by men in positions of power or prestige has not gone unremarked, or in some cases unlamented, by pundits. From Russell Baker fussing about New York mayor David Dinkins' tears, former President George Bush's weepiness, and "New Age Guys [who] not only weep in public, they boast about it," to Calvin Trillen pondering the meaning of *Time* magazine's tally of President Bill Clinton's public tears, there is both open acknowledgment of the prevalence of public men's tears and concern regarding what the trend signals. Compare this to the welcoming acceptance of New York mayor Rudolph Giuliani's tears and other open display of strong emotion by public figures and ordinary citizens alike in the exceptional period following the terror attacks of September 11. Tom Lutz (1999) cites many instances of male public figures weeping throughout the twentieth century.

21 Muskie denies having wept. Some say it was the snow melting on his cheeks that gave the appearance of weeping; others contend that he grew teary eyed. The quote criticizing Schroeder is by Linda DiVall ("Are female tears saltier than male tears?" by Bernard B. Weinraub, *New York Times*, September 30, 1987, p. 12).

22 Rosch (October 1988).

23 See Frey, Hoffman-Ahern, Johnson, Lykken, and Tuason (1983); Lombardo *et al.* (1983); Williams (1982).

24 Ross and Mirowsky (1984) asked about "crying spells," while Frey *et al.* (1983) and Lombardo *et al.* (1983) used an open-ended definition of crying.

25 See Lombardo *et al.* (1983); Williams (1982). An additional complicating factor in evaluating gender effects vis-à-vis weeping is the prevailing notion that weeping is essentially a physiological and emotional catharsis. Recommendations for "having a good cry" are abundant in magazines directed to a female readership. Randy Cornelius (1986) has traced this catharsis model through popular magazine and newspaper articles from the mid-nineteenth century to the 1980s. The large majority of articles portrayed weeping as a positive human characteristic and emphasized the importance of weeping to good health, warning that holding back tears is perilous to one's health. Yet all published studies that have attempted to test that notion have failed to find support for it and weeping in response to a sad movie actually increased reported sadness temporarily (e.g., Kraemer and Hastrup, 1988). See also Vingerhoets, Cornelius, Van Heck, and Becht (2000).

26 Bernard Weinraub, "Are Female Tears Saltier than Male Tears?" (*New York Times*, September 30, 1987, p. 12).

27 See Haley's (1978) discussion of the way in which Victorian beliefs about health and competition shaped a modern notion of masculinity, and Ellison's (1999) study of relationships among politics, sensibility, and masculinity in Anglo-American culture from the late seventeenth to the early eighteenth century.

CHAPTER 8

Speaking from the heart

"Who Wants to Be a Millionaire?" is currently a hit TV game show around the world, and it is seen in countries as varied as Saudi Arabia, Turkey, Japan, and the US. In every country that it plays, it has the same structure and, indeed, the same "look." The premise of the show is that an ordinary person can work her or his way through a series of questions to win a huge pot of money. The show's format and style are, in fact, copyrighted and new licensees must sign an agreement that they will not modify anything without express permission. Some of the most closely spelled-out details pertain to the contestants. The selection process is specifically designed to be quasi-random and, for example, participants are not chosen for their attractiveness. The strict formula has been enormously successful across cultures with very different social conventions and popular entertainment styles. Why does the formula work? According to David Briggs, creator of the original series in Britain, it is all about emotion. He points out that the multiple-choice format is critical to the show's success because it enables the audience to see the exact moment at which the contestant knows that she or he knows the answer, or does not: "You can almost see inside their souls." Indeed, the drama of the show is entirely dependent on the authenticity of that moment, "It's about complete emotion. *Real* emotion on a television set. With *real* people."[1]

There is something extraordinarily compelling about witnessing genuine emotion. "Millionaire" draws viewers because of its emotional authenticity. Just as importantly, we rely on emotion to assure ourselves of our own humanness. We monitor what we feel, weighing it in terms of whether it is too much or not enough, and concern ourselves with emotions that do not seem right for the situation, what Arlie Hochschild (1983) called "misfitting feelings." It is hard work being human. Philosophers and artists remind us that a great deal of that work is concerned with being true to our emotional selves and authentic in our emotional exchanges with others. They point out that it is through experiencing emotion and aiming to understand our experience of emotion that we understand ourselves to be human. In the contemporary US there seems to be a special premium placed on demonstrating the truth of one's emotions as the basis for making claims on respect, loyalty, or belief in one's ability. In American politics, for example, a candidate's emotional connection often seems to be prized over knowledge – genuine emotion is shorthand for "character," leadership ability, and good judgment.

Doing emotion is being human

Earlier in this book I have made the case that to "do" emotion is to "do" gender. What I mean by this is that, through experiencing and expressing emotion in conformity with gendered standards, children and adults aim to approach the perfection of these gendered standards, and in so doing practice "gender correct" emotion. In other words, beliefs about emotion – the language of emotion, social conventions regarding emotion, and the like – inscribe and reinscribe gender boundaries. Gendered emotion tells the boys from the girls. Gender boundaries, in turn, map the limits of an emotionality that signifies frailty or imperfection.

I have also argued that we are very concerned about doing emotion the proper way because emotion and gender are deeply implicated in the creation of a self (gender) and in one's experience of authenticity as a human being (emotion). Simply manipulating the appearance of emotion is satisfactory only in the limited circumstances in which we are not held truly accountable for our feelings (Hochschild, 1983). Emotion experience tells us we are human; believing that others honestly and authentically experience emotion persuades us of their humanity as well. What is at stake, then, is not only gender boundaries, but who has claims to selfhood, to define what is and is not correctly felt emotion, and to define what emotions can and cannot be about.

The story of Socrates that began Chapter 1 brings home this point. Was Socrates angry with his companions because they were being emotional, because they were acting like women, or because they were acting emotionally like women? First, from this vantage point we see that neither "woman" nor "emotion" is a simple category. Which woman? What emotion? Second, we understand that something more is going on in this scene than a simple equation of either woman or emotion with inadequacy. Socrates was vexed by emotion done as women do it, that is, openly, as expressing caring-about and caring-for in relationships. Socrates was troubled not just because his friends wept, but by weeping, they emphasized an emotional connection with him. The story of Socrates' death illustrates both the long history of discounting women's capacity for ideal emotion – emotion in the service of "reason" – and the equally long-standing tension between emotion in the service of reason and emotion in the service of relationships. In fact, one could argue that the passion-versus-reason tension is not even about a male-versus-female dichotomy, but about a human (*de facto* male) capacity for attaining the "right" balance of passion and reason. Historically, females do not figure in mapping the domain of reason, nor, it would appear, the domain of emotion, except as demonstrations of the non-normative male, creating the "difference" that establishes the masculine as center.

On what grounds, then, can individuals make a public claim of the rightness of their own emotional experience? Or justify their evaluation of someone else's? What is at stake in the everyday give and take of asserting emotional legitimacy? And why is emotion contested at all? These interrelated questions have framed much of this book, and here I want to focus on their implications for everyday life.

What is at stake?

Even casual use of emotion language polices gender boundaries: Men get moist eyes; women weep; men *have* emotions, women *are* emotional. Bedrock beliefs are so embedded within the dominant culture that they seem unquestionably to embody the true nature of emotion. What maintains their deep connection to gender?

Sandra Bem (1993) has written about three "lenses of gender," hidden assumptions about sex and gender that shape our perceptions of social reality. The first is *androcentrism*, which describes the implicit definition of male as normative; the second is *gender polarization*, the imposition of gender difference as an organizing principle for nearly every dimension of human experience; the third is *biological essentialism*, which naturalizes and legitimizes androcentrism and gender polarization as if they were biologically-derived inevitabilities. Each of these lenses (as Bem calls them) can perpetuate gender emotion stereotypes and make them appear resistant to change or challenge. For example, the way in which genderedness of emotion stereotyping insinuates itself into our interactions with children makes it difficult to disrupt the *status quo* because the stereotypes implicitly seem so "right." We praise girls for being nice and serving as the peacemakers and we are disturbed when boys do not stand up in a manly fashion for their rights or oppose others' aggression. It is through simple daily interactions that gender as a system is practiced and reproduced and challenged. Dana Vannoy (2001) points out that "Every moment every day individuals have the opportunity to choose to behave differently – to resist gender expectations associated with control and deference," and yet we do not. In fact, even those of us who strive not to subscribe to gendered norms of inequality are caught up in the ordinariness of doing gender, such that "the taken-for-granted acting out of nearly invisible expectations usually re-creates gender inequality between men and women even if gender is irrelevant to the situation" (p. 511).

Why are the gender dividing lines so compelling, and why are they so rigorously monitored? How is it that we are complicit in the use of emotion to fortify existing gender arrangements? Barbara Risman (1998) speculates that any challenge to gender structure makes us question who we are. The predictability offered by gender structures anchors us to certainties of personhood, and without them we would be left floating, disconnected, without "gendered selves and interactional expectations to give meaning to our lives" (p. 151). Robert McConnell (1987) suggested that if this condition occurred it would constitute a kind of "gender vertigo." One need not look far to see how eager people are to observe gender categories. When we hear about a friend's new baby, one of the first questions is "Girl or boy?" Even family pets do not escape gender monitoring. If a visitor to the house calls Spot the dog "he" and Spot is a she, we are likely to correct that misperception.

What does it take for effective resistance to gendered conventions of emotion? The American view of oneself as a genuine human being, as "in character" with oneself, invariably creates a tension between measuring oneself against the impossible standards of manly emotion and the demands of conforming to other expressive styles (e.g., nurturance as extravagant emotion) or emotional communities to which one owes allegiance (e.g., urban African American; east coast Italian American). And the overriding reason for worrying about this at all is the need to be "emotionally authentic" as oneself. Envisioning alternatives to gendered standards is made more vexing because a particular form of privileged white, heterosexual masculinity always insinuates itself back to the center of the discussion. A huge frustration in writing this book is that each time I try to shift the focus expressly to women, to men of color, to children – the silent, but often quite obvious, comparator is a stereotypic or idealized white, heterosexual adult male standard. Existing research literature is of little help in this endeavor. For example, as I have noted in an earlier chapter, research on gender emotion stereotypes is quite frustrating in its failure to explicitly consider that gender emotion stereotypes may be racialized, or implicitly heterocentric.

I want to turn now to three areas in which gendered emotion has broad and visible consequences in everyday life. These are: competing demands of different emotional styles, the power of emotion names, and judging emotional "appropriateness."

The emotion double bind

In this book I have focused on two emotional styles strongly linked to gender. The two styles, extravagant expressiveness evident in nurturing, and the telegraphed style that characterizes manly emotion, can be contrasted in terms of their form and in terms of when each is framed as "appropriate." Each of these two emotional modes is defined as and defines a gendered style. Both, however, are also "correct" standards for felt emotion and emotional display in certain contexts (correct, that is, as defined by contemporary dominant culture). Extravagant emotion is a legitimate way to "do" nurturance; "manly emotion" is called for in just about every other situation. Manly emotion is strongly felt emotion under control, and the stronger the felt emotion, the more clearly visible is the control of that intense experience. It is evident in a telegraphed style that conveys the felt emotion through economy of gesture, vocalization, and facial expression. It is an understated style, and one, I believe, that has been overlooked as a type of emotional expression, because it lacks the "size" and openness of expressiveness that is immediately coded as "emotional." I believe it is also a style that derives and defines its value by its connection to a particular version of white, heterosexual, masculinity.

Manly emotion is not only a manner of showing one's own capacity to feel strongly while controlling or managing those feelings, but also a way to control others. Economical expressiveness provides an image of self-control and self-management that demands others' attentiveness to grasp its import and meaning. This minimalist style requires the attention of the observer, and requires the focused interpretive skill of those surrounding the expressor. Manly emotion cannot just be asserted, it also has to be acknowledged in order to have its full effect.

It is important here to reiterate that manly emotion is not simply men's emotion. Susan Bordo (1997) observes that "studying masculinity is not equivalent to studying men," and I would add that describing manly emotion is not identical to studying men's emotion. Masculinity, as Bordo notes, is actually about "ideologies and representations of gender, idealizations that affect (and that may also be resisted by) actual men in varying ways, that may be aspired to and embodied by women as well, and that may even come to be incorporated in dominant notions of femininity" (p. 149). Manly emotion is not male emotion, but a standard that both sexes are expected to aspire to and are measured against, and that is, as an ideal, unattainable in any full or sustained way by real people. As a standard of the dominant culture, it is a standard that marks other styles as styles of the outsider – the distinction between "them" and "us" can be made on emotional grounds as well as on appearance or language or other features.

The double bind for men; the double bind for women

Manly emotion, in aiming to show controlled, yet strongly felt, emotion, says "I am an independent actor. I can control my emotion (i.e., my *self*), and I can harness my emotion to control the situation." The subtext of extravagant expressiveness is "my emotion (i.e., my *self*) is at your service." Each of these two emotional modes defines a dominant culture gendered style, and spells out the "correct" criteria for felt emotion and emotional display. The emotional double bind for women, then, is the expectation that they will be appropriately nurturant (as shown in part through extravagant expressiveness), yet also conform to the overarching standard of manly emotion. For men the bind is how to approximate the elusive ideal of manly emotion. The pushes and pulls ensure that resolution is not simple. Contemporary dominant culture in the US encourages men to be good friends, good lovers, and good fathers, which means "be sensitive" and risk being feminine. Contemporary dominant culture also requires manly emotional self-control, which is often interpreted as "be inexpressive," a strategy which is not only incompatible with the emotional extravagance standard, but more threateningly, is potentially incompatible with genuineness as a person. The challenge of gendered emotion for both women and men is to become capable of reconciling competing emotional standards in a way that can be experienced as consistent with, or at least not undermining, a coherent sense of authentic identity. And one must be able to achieve this reconciliation while meeting the expectations and demands of others in one's various social roles. Keep in mind, however, that the double bind is not equal in its consequences for women and men. In Chapter 6 the discussion of the New Fatherhood illustrated the way in which appropriation and recharacterization of features of feminine-identified emotion can actually reinforce the gender divide between the manly and the merely feminine.

For women, the double bind is a no-win situation. No small reason for this is the impossibility of doing manly emotion in an uncompromising way, and the many and hurried transitions between emotion modes as one moves between personal and family responsibilities and those of work. More important, however, is the ever-present identification of female/feminine with the "merely emotional." In the workplace – a site in which metaphors of competitive sports and other indicators of masculinity abound – the economical expressiveness of manly emotion is the standard. However, in close personal relationships, nurturance and closeness require extravagant expressiveness. At 3 a.m. Mommy is expected to muster the energy for effusive and supportive emotion to care for a sick or frightened child. By 9 a.m., lack of sleep notwithstanding, she is expected to comport herself according to the workplace standard of manly emotion when she walks through the office door, and then she must move back to the extravagant style of nurturance when she goes back home – all the while watching out for the feminine emotionality that we are warned to be on guard against. Her experience of the double bind will be a function of her age and other social identities. Middle-class notions of mothering are especially heavy in emphasizing maternal expression of nurturance; African American women report that co-workers often turn to them as nurturing mother figures; and, younger women may be especially subject to tests of their emotional control in the workplace.[2]

Costs of the double bind

To what extent do the conflicting emotional expression demands of these different roles cause confusion, self-doubt, or social inadequacy in their execution? Is the cost of emotion management to the individual exacerbated when the management must occur rapidly or the boundaries between radically different emotion standards are not clearly marked? Simply adopting the manly emotion style does not guarantee that a woman will be taken seriously. The double bind is not just a conflict between different styles of appearance, or competition among display rules, but, rather, it involves the whole emotion package – felt emotion, readiness to experience emotion, depth of feeling, bedrock beliefs. In other words, competing demands of emotion "style" are inevitably about how one performs – through emotion – who one is *as a genuine person*.

While I have worked on these questions, I have had more than one female friend declare to me that, now realizing what a handicap expressive emotion can be in the workplace because of its equation with mere feminine emotionality, she was going to develop a stoic, inexpressive style. Should women try to stop acting emotional? Does this strategy work better (or worse) for some groups of women than others? And how is the accusation that one is "acting emotional" often used to mean being *too* emotional and to prevent us from getting what we want? How are the consequences different for some women than others, for men whose racial ethnicity is other than white European American?

Impassivity might work for some men, but the woman who tries it will be trading one problem for another. If she tries to adopt a style of manly emotion, she is "inexpressive" and quickly and disapprovingly labeled "cold."[3]

The organization of the workplace is undergoing massive change, and one change that would seem to level the playing field for women is the increasing emphasis on horizontality, team-based structures, and interpersonal skills. These newly valued skills should in theory make the competing demands of home and work emotion standards less of a strain on women. Not so far. Joyce Fletcher (1999) offers another way to look at the double bind. She maps how the collision of gender and power "disappears" the very advantages that women might bring to the workplace. She shows that enacting a relational style (and attendant extravagant expressiveness) within the workplace context sets women up for being misunderstood, exploited, or seen as inadequate. The alternative, to adopt a "masculinist" style (and aim for manly emotion), sets women up to be viewed by others as inappropriately "unfeminine" and themselves to experience the alien style as jarring and inauthentic.

Naming emotion

To name an emotion is to make a statement of value. A huge proportion of interpersonal interaction is taken up with comprehending and responding to emotion, or discussing emotion-laden situations and issues. And strong emotion is not a rarity. Oatley and Duncan (1994) conducted a diary study of emotion experiences among nonstudent adults. On average, their research participants recorded one episode of emotion each day that was described as strong enough to consume thoughts, to be accompanied by a perceptible bodily response, and to stimulate some urge to action. The importance and salience of emotional experience, as a feature both of subjective consciousness and of interpersonal relationships, contrasts dramatically with the comparative rarity of emotion words in conversation. Even though emotion, even strong emotion, occurs frequently and we give priority to reading others and managing our own emotion, emotion language is a very small proportion of natural speech. People do not use emotion labels with much frequency in regular conversation.[4]

Talking around emotion

The infrequency with which emotions are actually named could lead one to think that emotions might not be very important after all. In some respects, that is what happened to anthropologist Jean Briggs in her field research among an Inuit group in the Canadian Northwest Territories. Her classic ethnography, *Never in Anger* (1970), was taken by some as evidence of the absence of some emotions, particularly anger, in that culture. Briggs' original work among the Utku was not intended as a study of emotion, but developed serendipitously after she discovered that the topic she had planned to study – shamanism – appeared no longer relevant to Utku everyday life. She turned her attention to emotion when she observed that Utku adults did not express anger interpersonally or use anger or threats in childrearing. In contrast, it was clear that the Utku were troubled by Briggs' propensity to irritation and anger as she coped with the many frustrations of living as a stranger in a harsh climate and unpredictable circumstances.

Her ethnography of the Utku focused on the apparent indifference of the Utku to anger because anger was not explicitly labeled in their conversation. Briggs has more recently observed that her original assessment that anger was not a part of Utku life was an oversimplification. She remarks that in subsequent work she began a systematic study of Utku emotion concepts, discovering that "when I wrote *Never in Anger*, I had had the emotional vocabulary of a four-year-old; [and] that the Utkuhikhalingmiut had many emotion concepts; and that they talked about emotions all the time" (Briggs, 1995, p. 204).

Emotion euphemisms

Like the Utku, we talk about emotion all the time. Yet surprisingly, in natural conversation reference to emotion is often made in rather oblique terms, and not often with specific labels for emotion. Few researchers have undertaken the daunting task of collecting information about emotion talk in everyday conversation – it can take hours of tape recording to yield a handful of emotion labels.[5] Anderson and Leaper (1998) did one of the very few studies of actual conversation of people about emotion. They found that undergraduate women and men talked about the same kinds of emotions and referred to specific emotions equally frequently. The quantity of emotion talk was, however, quite sensitive to context. When participants were not given a specific conversational topic, the rate of emotion talk was much lower than when friends were asked to talk about "how family relations had changed since they entered college." Emotion labels, by virtue of their rarity, are a powerful statement of value, and, it would seem, are seldom applied in a value-neutral way. The act of labeling emotion is an act of evaluating the content of experience or behavior on several dimensions: its authenticity, rationality, legitimacy, and hedonic tone, to name the most obvious. Naming an emotion conveys something about controllability, intensity, appropriateness, whether in the term that is itself used or the context it is couched in. While people do not label emotion, they do refer to it in what my students and I call "emotional euphemisms." As highly socialized individuals we vigilantly monitor our own and others' face, voice, and style for information, including information relevant to emotional state. But naming emotion occurs far less frequently than one might think, given the significance of emotion information in our daily interactions. For example, in one early project concerned with emotion labels, my students and I looked at televised political commentary and found that speakers often used words and phrases that have emotional connotations but that do not strictly refer to emotion (Shields and MacDowell, 1987). Most often these emotional euphemisms referred to actions that may be totally or partially emotion motivated, for example "he took some shots at her" and "she jumped back at him." They also refer to the absence of emotion, as in "she was too low key" or "he didn't come unraveled."[6]

Emotion labels and emotional euphemisms can have a certain flexibility in their meaning. Briggs (1995, p. 207) points out that what the emotion term means, in part, depends on what the emotion is about:

> (like the concept of love in English, whose meaning changes fundamentally, depending on whether the object of that emotion is Mother, one's Neighbour, or ice cream). Meanings might also change according to the purposes of the user ... 'Love' will mean something quite different to me, depending on whether I have just fallen *in* or *out*.

Who controls meaning?

Emotion language is also heavily gendered in whom it describes and to whom it is directed. Parents, for example, use emotion language differently with their preschool daughters than with their sons.[7] And in earlier chapters I described vignette-type studies that tend to find that emotion language, in and of itself, conjures a quite different image, depending on whether research participants believe a female or male is being described. Comparative differences in status, too, invoke different assessments of emotion. Given its comparative rarity, explicit emotion labeling potently renders a gendered judgment of emotion quality and appropriateness.

Multiplicity of meaning and contextual dependence is true for even the most loaded word: *emotional*. When country Western star Terri Clark sings "[I'm an] Emotional Girl," she tries to recuperate the word from its connection with stereotypic feminine emotionality. Her song is an anthem to passion and a challenge to potential lovers:

Some folks say I'm too extreme
'Cause I can't stop once I start
But I never could do anything
With half my heart.

But the flexibility of emotion language has its limits, and the way *you* use it is not necessarily the way *others* will understand it. Terri Clark's stand for emotional engagement may feel to her like self-affirmation, but the connotative baggage that goes with "being emotional" cannot be avoided.

During the mid-1990s "trial of the century" of O. J. Simpson, the language of emotion was used to create pictures of who was reasonable, who was out of control, and whose judgment could be trusted. For example, defending attorney Johnnie Cochran, in one sidebar altercation, characterized lead prosecutor Marcia Clark as "hysterical" and assured Judge Lance Ito that he would not "yell at your Honor," thereby implying that Clark had.[8] Appropriating emotion language enables one to co-opt authority to speak from the heart. It is a ploy that nearly anyone can use in order to assert or reassert privilege. How successful that ploy is depends on the position the person starts from and what kind of authority she or he wishes to assert. American conversations about race, sexual orientation, disability rights – in fact, just about any issue that addresses the concerns of a "minority group" – almost inevitably asks "Why are 'they' always so angry?" Who is loud, pushy, and overemotional? Who is cold, unfeeling, and shallow? It depends on who gets to write the emotion rules.

Who decides when emotion is "appropriate"?

> The candidate that gets too emotional at the wrong times or for no apparent reason, *loses* points. If you get emotional for the right reason, meaning you are responding very fervently to an attack or you feel very deeply, you *get* points. (Sam Donaldson)

We all know that Sam is basically correct. Observations like Sam's are made routinely in every election cycle, but they are common in our own lives, too.[9] Essentially what we see played out in bids for political success is a reaffirmation of the general consensus that "appropriate" emotion is good and healthy; "inappropriate" emotion is bad. But on what basis do we differentiate between "correct" and "incorrect," "good" and "bad," "too much" and "too little" emotion? The ownership of appropriate emotion is a third area in which gendered emotion is at stake.

There are, within broad limits, agreements within a society as to what the limits of good and bad emotion are and the situations where they are expected: One should be happy when given a gift; angry when one's rights have been violated; refrain from humor at funerals; be proud of one's children's successes.[10] Within that broad range people do vary in their assessment of what emotion means, what it is, and how appropriate it is to the context. Most of everyday life is not lived at the extremes of emotional experience or expressivity, however, but somewhere in the indeterminate middle. In those very ordinary contexts, what guides us to judge how much happiness is the *right* amount of happiness? How do we recognize the *correct* anger? And who decides what those criteria are? Do some people have a greater entitlement to emotion?

Some years ago one of my senior colleagues was interviewed for the position of dean. She had always seemed to me, at the time a lowly assistant professor, a model of self-control and sophistication. As it turned out, one of the questions that came up in her interview was about her style of anger management. There was some concern among the interviewing committee that she was rumored to have come close to tears at a departmental faculty meeting a few years before, and the issue was whether she had the thick skin needed for a dean. The meeting in question was one that had been especially contentious in a fractious department. The meeting was marked by shouting, threats, and stormy exits. The lone woman in the group, my colleague, however, was the only one later recalled by others as having been "too emotional." (By the way, when she didn't get the position she was recruited by another university where her deanly skills were appreciated. She soon became a college president.) Given the very same situation, different observers can have divergent opinions on whether emotion was present, which emotions were present, and how much emotion was present. While we may watch others' expressions and listen to tone of voice carefully for emotion cues, much of the interpretation of that emotional display or inference about felt emotion may be in the eye of the beholder, a function of the *observer's* beliefs, values, and prejudices.

Policing the boundaries of appropriate emotion

The desirability of "appropriate" emotion and the disparagement of "inappropriate" emotion is woven into everyday life. The "wrong" kind of emotion might sometimes be an emotion that the observer thinks is incorrect for the situation – "He shouldn't be nervous, he should be happy!" But if we take a look at the ordinary emotional situation, rarely do we expect ourselves or anyone else to experience or show one single "pure" emotional state. More often we report and expect to see evidence of some emotional complexity in others. It may not be that the observer thinks there is a wrong emotion or a right emotion, but that *too much* or *too little* emotion is the problem. In thinking about the idea of appropriate emotion we need to recognize that inappropriate emotion isn't just a case of intense or frequent emotion, but some perceived deviation from what is correct or desirable. So what defines the limits?

Peggy Thoits (2000) examined the definition of various psychopathology definitions in the most recent edition of the *Diagnostic and Statistical Manual (DSM-IV)*, the American Psychiatric Association's official reference work that provides diagnostic criteria for personality and behavior disorders. She points out that the boundaries around pathologies are in flux and negotiated differently across time. Most important to our discussion is her observation that what emotion looks like is very important, especially at the borders of diagnostic criteria. She notes that violation of emotion norms is a critical dimension on which pathologies are identified. The *DSM-IV* lists 359 separately coded disorders. Thoits counted the proportion of symptoms that involved emotional deviations from hypothetical norm and found that 29 per cent of the disorders were defined by emotional deviance, and another eight implied some emotional problem. So a full 31 per cent of disorders involve emotional deviance as a defining feature. Emotion by itself does not define the psychopathological, but it becomes especially important in policing the borders between normal and problematic. Where exactly does normative leave off and the pathological begin? Thoits argues that the main changes over time in what is or is not identified as an incapacitating problem or a problem is worth serious note occur at the borders defined by emotion symptomatology.

The study of emotional expression in psychology has largely been concerned with identifying the parameters that enhance or interfere with people's accuracy in communicating ("encoding") or reading ("decoding") the expression of specific emotions. Thus empirical research considers what the perceiver brings to the perception in a very limited fashion in terms of what may interfere with or enhance the skill of decoding others' expressions of emotion. When researchers consider what it is about the actor that is perceived by others as emotion, they tend to limit their search to things that might influence how well or how poorly the person shows emotion clearly, or aspects of the situation that make it more difficult or easier for observers to identify the person's emotion accurately. In everyday life, however, evaluating others' emotional behavior is not limited to deciphering the other person's expressive behavior, but also making inferences about the genuineness, the self-control, the intensity, and the social "reasonableness" (*appropriateness* by another name) of the emotion. Successful negotiation of interpersonal relationships depends in large part on our multi-layered reading of the emotions of others. The police officer on the street, the counselor of troubled children, and the wife of an abusive husband, to name but a few particularly potent situations, all need to judge accurately not only which emotion or emotions are expressed, but what that expression stands for. They must be able to assess how controllable, intense, and "rational" the felt emotion is.

Appropriating emotion: The case of "emotional intelligence"

The appropriation of emotion is especially evident in the boom relating to "emotional intelligence."[11] The construct has become enormously popular in the business world since the first trade book on the subject was published in the mid-1990s. Emotional intelligence is touted as the key to excellent business and professional leadership, and the first successful popularizer of the construct, Daniel Goleman, declares that emotional intelligence accounts for "almost 90 percent of what sets stars apart from the mediocre."[12] Today it is easy to find books that apply the idea of emotional intelligence to childrearing, marriage, and self-help.

Although some version of the concept of emotional intelligence could be found in psychology for many decades, its popularization, I believe, goes hand in hand with the celebration of manly emotion. In popular literature, definitions of emotional intelligence are sufficiently vague to serve as a kind of catch-all description of competence in understanding, controlling, and responding appropriately to one's own and others' emotions. Goleman (1998) identifies five areas of emotional intelligence: self-awareness, self-regulation, motivation, empathy, and social skills. To be sure, people do vary in how well they are able to understand and manage their emotions, and these skills arguably contribute to success in all aspects of life that have a social component or that require self-management.

Critical reading of the various books and tests of emotional intelligence, what some popularizers have referred to as EQ, however, shows that emotional intelligence tends to be measured by the extent to which one has assimilated the culturally dominant views of appropriateness. Items on emotional tests constitute a catalog of what is valued. In one such test under development, the test-taker evaluates the efficacy of responses to particular emotion-evoking situations, to name the emotion that results when other emotions are "combined," and to identify the situations that can cause particular emotions.[13] Even though the test's developers acknowledge that there is no single factually verifiable and universally-accepted true answer for most items, one's score is still based on the sum of one's "correct" choices. The same sorts of criticisms that for years have been leveled against intelligence testing – that tests are tests of acculturation; of what is already learned, not of one's capacity for learning; that tests are biased in favor of those who are in the position to define what preferred knowledge is – can be leveled against EQ. Advice that improving one's emotional intelligence can contribute to success in life seems harmless enough. In fact, it seems rather banal. But the message is that if you are successful you already have this skill. So those who have the position of power are the ones, in effect, defined as already having emotional intelligence.

It would seem that an emphasis on the importance of emotional skills might actually be an advantage for women, that expectations and training for nurturance, cooperation, and other emotion-related features that are prized in girls and women, would have the EQ mavens look toward women for emotional intelligence exemplars. Not so. Rather, emotion intelligence experts emphasize that there are few or no gender differences in emotional intelligence, and in any event, emotional intelligence is an eminently teachable skill. The proof of emotional intelligence's validity is circular: the most successful, the ones at the top of the organization or who make the most money, are purportedly the ones more likely to have high EQ; therefore, high EQ is a major contributor to success. Emotional intelligence is a way to appropriate emotion standards to the people who already have the power. In other words, the "right way" to do emotion (and think about it and understand it) becomes by definition the property of those with high "EQ." Since EQ measures tend to focus on dominant culture emotion expression norms, "emotion outlaws," as I described them in the previous chapter, remain outlaws.

Speaking from the heart

Returning to the question of what is at stake in the contestation of emotion, we see that there are clearly both personal and political points to be made here. I am going to resist the academic's urge to end on a note that "further research is needed" because I do not want to lose sight of the practical dimensions of this project. Instead, I want to think about the people who inspired this project in the first place: students, friends and neighbors, and the occasional interested person on the plane, in the park, or at a party. It was the discrepancy, after all, between the "nonissue" of gender in conventional emotions research and the Big Issue of gender in everyday emotion that encouraged me to look for answers in the disparity between what everyone "knows" to be true about emotion and the way that beliefs about emotion actually seem to work.

I finished writing this book before the events of September 11, 2001 fundamentally changed the fabric of our everyday lives. Throughout the immediate days following, and in the tense and demanding months since then, emotion as a defining feature of humanity has been a recurring and central theme. If anything, conversations about emotion as a defining human quality have become freighted with even greater meaning than they had been before. In the days following September 11 we did not need *Who Wants to Be a Millionaire* to give us "real emotion on a television set." The raw emotion that we saw in print, on television, and in others' faces, we experienced through our own palpable depression, anger, and feeling of loss. Those chaotic emotions may now be muted by time, but they are not finished. Instead, what has been added to our understanding of this "after" world is concern with the legitimacy and genuineness of emotion.

Speaking from the heart, thereby "owning" emotional authenticity, has been significant at each point in this enormously complex shift in the conduct of everyday life. George W. Bush shed his President-Lite image as many were relieved to see him speak more consistently with emotional force. New York mayor Rudolph Giuliani, who withdrew from a run for the Republican senatorial candidacy because of health problems and a personal life in apparent disarray, became the patriarch who kept New York City on course in the deeply sad and confused days and weeks following the terror attack. Previously seen as more callous than compassionate, the genuineness of his concern for victims, their friends and families, and the city itself won over his harshest critics and even caused brief public discussion of whether there might be some way he could continue in office after his mayoral term expired. Attorney General John Ashcroft and Vice-President Dick Cheney, in contrast, have not seemed to be able to get emotion right and have been criticized for emotional detachment. Meanwhile, genuine emotion was claimed as the property of the US and its allies, and language used to described bin Laden and his cohorts and sympathizers emphasized the falseness and lack of legitimacy of their emotion claims.[14] That the world has changed since September 11 adds urgency to our questions about what difference the discourse of emotion makes in everyday life.

Because I wanted to explore the practical, real consequences of gendered emotion, I have advocated a particular approach that it seems to me can be especially productive. That is, if we want to understand the intricate interconnections that link gender (the psychological and social representation of sex) and the social meaning of emotion, we should approach emotion with the question "When does gender matter?" (Of course, we might also ask "When does gender *not* matter?" As we have seen throughout this book, where emotion's social meaning is concerned, the short answer is – not often.) In the course of this work, I have shown how asking the gender question opens the study of emotion to an array of issues that have not figured much in this field of research. For example, as researchers become more sophisticated in dealing with the intersections of gender and other social categories, we can begin to think more systematically about how patterns of social identity are linked to how one's emotion is defined and the privileges and liabilities that attend that definition. In other words, given our multiple social identities, which ones make a difference in emotion and when? Who has the authority to "speak from the heart"? When and how is that authority contested? These questions grow especially compelling as American society becomes more multicultural itself and less isolated from other national cultures. How will the exaggerated polarity of gendered emotion that characterizes American dominant culture be reconfigured as the composition of society continues to change? What happens when current dominant styles of emotion collide with other emotion communities' definitions of legitimate or appropriate emotion?

The idea for this book began as an alternative to the then-prevalent (and, I am sorry to say, still prevalent) tendency among psychologists to think of gender and emotion primarily in terms of enumerating similarities and differences. The work quickly moved to focus more on the ways in which emotion bedrock beliefs are gendered. Exposing the historically shifting and tacit assumptions on which those beliefs rest shows that the discourse of emotion is fundamentally concerned with judgments about the authenticity and legitimacy of experience, which are themselves gendering acts that create and maintain gender boundaries. In this book I have tried to show how judgments about the presence and meaning of emotion in oneself and others are not made casually or lightly. Who gets called "emotional" depends on who is doing the naming, who is named, and the circumstances in which emotion occurs. The relationship between gender and emotion is not just a subject of academic inquiry, but one that profoundly affects every aspect of our lives in ways that we often do not even suspect.

Notes

1 David Briggs, originator of "Who Wants to Be a Millionaire?" interviewed by Terry Gross on "Fresh Air" (National Public Radio, February 6, 2001).
2 See Stoppard (2000) for a discussion of class-related notions of good mothering. A number of under-35-year-old members of the Penn State Professional Women's Network of New York have given me many examples of situations in which the multiple-powerlessness of youth, job title, femaleness, and newness to the occupation places them at substantial disadvantage in responding to the emotion rules of the workplace.
3 Mary Crawford (1995) provides a telling critique of the assertiveness training movement of the 1970s and its misguided advice to solve communication decision-making problems with formulaic patterns.
4 Shimanoff (1983), Anderson and Leaper (1998), and Valenti *et al.* (1999) all studied natural conversation in adults. Fabes, Eisenberg, Hanish, and

Spinrad (in press) used unobtrusive observation to record preschoolers' and adults' emotion-related utterances in natural conversation. Emotion references were more complex in the older group (e.g., adults more often talked about others' emotions and talked about past emotion events), but females and males in both age groups tended to name emotions with the same frequency. Haviland and Goldston (1992) found that specific emotion labels were not often used in adolescents' writing about intense emotional experiences.

5 Judy Dunn's work on mother-child talk (e.g., 1988) includes reference to all internal states and is not limited to emotions, so the proportion of "internal state talk" is higher than one finds in studies of "emotion talk." The low incidence of explicit emotion references in natural talk parallels what we found in our advice literature research (Shields and Koster, 1989; Shields, Steinke, and Koster, 1995). Our research showed that themes of emotion are woven throughout the books' text, but only a comparatively small proportion of actual, direct emotion naming occurs.

6 A statement about another's emotions is an evaluation of that person's behavior, thoughts, or personality. At this point I cannot explain why emotional euphemisms are chosen or whether they are a preferred alternative to using specific emotion labels. It may be that using an emotional euphemism is just a lazy strategy, indicating the rarity with which observers make reasoned inferences about another's internal state. Or, of course, it may just be another signal of the long-lamented decline in the precision of American English. The most compelling explanation, though, is that given the power of emotion naming, such naming is not done lightly. Anderson and Leaper (1998) also reported that most references to emotion in conversation are indirect.

7 This conclusion is largely, though not exclusively, built on research with middle-class white families. See Eisenberg's (1999) study of Mexican American and Anglo American mothers and children from two social classes for an overview.

8 The Marcia Clark and Johnnie Cochran exchange is taken from "Defense Jumps on Witness's 'Airtight Alibi' Comment," *The Sacramento Bee* (May 25, 1995, p. A24). The Simpson trial was rife with gendered and racialized assertions and counter-assertions with some emotional flavor. At least one potential juror was excused when he asserted that Nicole Brown Simpson was in part responsible for her own murder because she provoked Simpson's anger. Susan Bordo (1997, p. 70) cites an interview with the jury forewoman who, after the trial, declared that the domestic abuse evidence was *irrelevant* to the case. The issue of emotional legitimacy is particularly volatile in cases of alleged sexual assault or rape. In Vermont, the conviction of a man who had sexually assaulted a 12-year-old friend of his daughter's was nearly overturned because, in the opinion of the appeals judge, the female prosecutor was too emotional, showing "a fury seldom seen this side of hell." Defense attorneys based their case for reversal on the fact that the defendant's daughter wept while being questioned on the witness stand, two jurors wept at different times during the trial, and the court reporter quit the trial for fear of breaking down in front of the jurors. (The defendant was found guilty. The conviction was overturned on appeal, but later upheld by the Vermont Supreme Court.)

9 Donaldson of *ABC News* made the comment during the course of television commentary following the October 11, 1984 vice-presidential candidates'

debate between Representative Geraldine Ferraro (D) and Vice-President George Bush (R).

10 See for example Heise and Calhan, 1995.

11 See Salovey and Mayer (1990) and Bar-On and Parker (2000).

12 From the cover of Goleman (1998).

13 Most of the indices of emotional intelligence rely heavily on verbal skill as well as knowledge of prevailing cultural emotion standards.

14 These are but a very few of the many newspaper, online, and magazine reports that addressed the significance of genuine emotion in the aftermath of September 11. Martha Brant, "President Softly: George W. Bush Knows When to Show Emotion and When Not To," October 17, 2001, *www.msnbc.com*. Frank Rich, "The Way We Live Now: 9-30-01: Close Reading: Elements of War; The Father Figure," September 30, 2001, *New York Times Magazine*. Patricia Leigh Brown, "Heavy Lifting Required: the Return of Manly Men." October 28, 2001, *New York Times Week in Review*, p. 5. Ken Kurson, "Inside Rudy's Command Post," November 2001, *Talk*, pp. 89–91.

References

Abreu, J. M. (1999). Conscious and nonconscious African American stereotypes: Impact on first impression and diagnostic ratings by therapists. *Journal of Consulting and Clinical Psychology, 67*, 387–393.

Abu Loghoud, L. (1986). *Veiled sentiments: Honor and poetry in a Bedouin society.* Berkeley, CA: University of California Press.

Abu Loghoud, L., and Lutz, C. (Eds.). (1990). *Language and the politics of emotion.* Cambridge, England. Cambridge University Press.

Aldous, J., Mulligan, G., and Biarnason, T. (1998). Fathering over time: What makes the difference? *Journal of Marriage and the Family, 60*, 809–820.

Algoe, S. B., Buswell, B. N., and DeLamater, J. D. (2000). Gender and job status as contextual cues for the interpretation of facial expression of emotion. *Sex Roles, 42*, 183–208.

Anderson, K. J., and Leaper, C. (1998). Emotion talk between same- and mixed-sex gender friends: Form and function. *Journal of Language and Social Psychology, 17*, 421–450.

Aquinas. (1964). *Commentary on Aristotle's Nichomachean ethics* (trans. C. I. Litzinger). Chicago: Henry Regnery.

Armstrong, N. (1987). *The ideology of conduct.* New York: Metheun.

Ashmore, R., and Del Boca, F. (Eds.) (1986). *The social psychology of female-male relations: A critical analysis of central concepts.* Orlando, FL: Academic Press.

Auerbach, N. (1982). *Woman and the demon.* Cambridge, MA: Harvard University Press.

Averill, J. R. (1982). *Anger and aggression.* New York: Springer-Verlag.

Averill, J. R. (1983). Studies on anger and aggression: Implications for theories of emotion. *American Psychologist, 38*, 1145–1160.

Averill, J. R. (1991). Emotions as episodic dispositions, cognitive schemas, and transitory social roles: Steps toward an integrated theory of emotion. In D. Ozer, J. M. Healy, and A. J. Stewart (Eds.), *Perspectives in personality, Vol. 3a* (pp. 137–165). London: Jessica Kingsley.

Bacchi, C. L. (1990). *Same difference: Feminism and sexual difference.* Boston, MA: Allen and Unwin.

Bacon, M. K., and Ashmore, R. D. (1985). How mothers and fathers categorize descriptions of social behavior attributed to daughters and sons. *Social Cognition, 3*, 193–217.

Bain, A. (1859). *The emotions and the will.* London: Longmans, Green.

Balswick, J. (1988). *The inexpressive male.* Lexington, MA: D.C. Heath.

Balswick, J., and Peek, C. (1971). The inexpressive male: A tragedy of American society. *The Family Coordinator, 20*, 363–368.

Bar-On, R., and Parker, J. D. A. (Eds.) (2000). *The handbook of emotional intelligence.* San Francisco: Jossey-Bass.

Barr, C. L., and Kleck, R. E. (1995). Self-other perception of the intensity of facial expressions of emotion: Do we know what we show? *Journal of Personality and Social Psychology, 68,* 608–618.

Baumeister, R. F., Stillwell, A., and Wotman, S. R. (1990). Victim and perpetrator accounts of interpersonal conflict: Autobiographical narratives about anger. *Journal of Personality and Social Psychology, 59,* 994–1005.

Bederman, G. (1995). *Manliness and civilization.* Chicago: University of Chicago Press.

Bem, S. L. (1981). Gender schema theory: A cognitive account of sex typing. *Psychological Review, 88,* 354–364.

Bem, S. L. (1993). *The lenses of gender.* New Haven, CT: Yale University Press.

Berkowitz, L. (2000). *Causes and consequences of feelings.* Cambridge, England: Cambridge University Press.

Berry, G. L., and Asamen, J. K. (Eds.) (1993). *Children and television: Images in a changing sociocultural world.* Newbury Park, CA: Sage.

Biaggio, M. (1991). *Gender differences in anger: Provocation, experience, and expression.* Unpublished manuscript.

Biernat, M. (1991). Gender stereotypes and the relationship between masculinity and femininity: A developmental analysis. *Journal of Personality and Social Psychology, 61,* 351–365.

Birnbaum, D. W., and Chemelski, B. E. (1984). Preschoolers' inferences about gender and emotion: The mediation of emotionality stereotypes. *Sex Roles, 10,* 505–511.

Birnbaum, D. W., and Croll, W. L. (1984). The etiology of children's stereotypes about sex differences in emotionality. *Sex Roles, 10,* 677–691.

Birnbaum, D. W., Nosanchuk, T. A., and Croll, W. L. (1980). Children's stereotypes about sex differences in emotionality. *Sex Roles, 6,* 435–443.

Bly, R. (1990). *Iron John: A book about men.* Reading, MA: Addison-Wesley.

Bohan, J. S. (1993). Regarding gender: Essentialism, constructionism, and feminist psychology. *Psychology of Women Quarterly, 17,* 5–21.

Bordo, S. (1993). *Unbearable weight: Feminism, Western culture, and the body.* Berkeley, CA: University of California Press.

Bordo, S. (1997). *Twilight zones: The hidden life of cultural images from Plato to O. J.* Berkeley, CA: University of California Press.

Bradley, B. S., and Gobbart, S. K. (1989). Determinants of gender-typed play in toddlers. *Journal of Genetic Psychology, 150,* 453–455.

Briggs, J. (1970). *Never in anger.* Cambridge, MA: Harvard University Press.

Briggs, J. (1995). The study of Inuit emotions: Lessons from a personal retrospective. In J. A. Russell, J. M. Fernández-Dols, A. S. R. Manstead, and J. Wellencamp (Eds.), *Everyday conceptions of emotion* (pp. 203–220). Dordrecht, Netherlands: Kluwer Academic Publishers.

Brody, L. (1985). Gender differences in emotional development: A review of theories and research. *Journal of Personality, 53,* 102–149.

Brody, L. (1993). On understanding gender difference in the expression of emotion: Gender roles, socialization and language. In S. Ablon, D. Brown, E. Khantzican and J. Mack (Eds.), *Human feelings: Explorations in affect, development and meaning* (pp. 89–121). Hillsdale, NJ: Analytic Press.

Brody, L. (1999). *Gender, emotion, and the family*. Cambridge, MA: Harvard University Press.

Brody, L. R., and Hall, J. A. (1993). Gender and emotion. In M. Lewis and J. Haviland (Eds.), *Handbook of emotions* (pp. 447–461). New York: Guilford.

Brody, L. R., Hay, D. H., and Vandewater, E. (1990). Gender, gender role identity, and children's reported feelings toward the same and opposite sex. *Sex Roles, 7/8*, 363–387.

Brody, L. R., Lovas, G. S., and Hay, D. H. (1995). Sex differences in anger and fear as a function of situational context. *Sex Roles, 32*, 47–78.

Bruns, B., and Tutko, T. (1986). Dealing with the emotions of childhood sports. In R. E. Lapchick (Ed.), *Fractured focus* (pp. 207–218). Lexington, MA: D.C. Heath.

Buck, R. (1983). Emotional development and emotional education. In R. Plutchik and H. Kellerman (Eds.), *Emotions in early development*. New York: Academic Press.

Buck, R. (1988). *Human motivation and emotion*. New York: John Wiley and Sons.

Buck, R., Baron, R., Goodman, N., and Shapiro, B. (1980). Unitization of spontaneous nonverbal behavior in the study of emotion communication. *Journal of Personality and Social Psychology, 30*, 587–529.

Bugental, D. E., Love, L. R., and Gianetto, R. M. (1971). Perfidious feminine faces. *Journal of Personality and Social Psychology, 17*, 314–318.

Buss, D. M. (1991). Conflict in married couples: Personality predictors of anger and upset. *Journal of Personality, 59*, 735–747.

Bylsma, W. H., and Major, B. (1992). Two routes to eliminating gender differences in personal entitlement: Social comparisons and performance evaluations. *Psychology of Women Quarterly, 16*, 193–200.

Campbell, A., and Muncer, S. (1987). Models of anger and aggression in the social talk of women and men. *Journal for the Theory of Social Behavior, 17*, 489–509.

Cancian, F. (1987). *Love in America: Gender and self-development*. New York: Cambridge University Press.

Cantor, N. L., and Gelfand, D. M. (1977). Effects of responsiveness and sex of children on children and adults' behavior. *Child Development, 48*, 232–238.

Caplan, P. J., and Hall-McCorquodale, I. (1985). Mother-blaming in major clinical journals. *American Journal of Orthopsychiatry, 55*, 345–353.

Carpenter, W. B. (1894). *The principles of human physiology*. New York: D. Appleton.

Cervantes, C. A., and Callanan, M. A. (1998). Labels and explanations in mother–child emotion talk: Age and gender differentiation. *Developmental Psychology, 34*, 88–98.

Chess, S. (1982). The "blame the mother" ideology. *International Journal of Mental Health, 2*, 95–107.

Chodorow, N. (1978). *The reproduction of mothering: Psychoanalysis and the reproduction of gender*. Berkeley, CA: University of California Press.

Chodorow, N. J. (1995). Gender as a personal and cultural construction. *Signs: Journal of Women in Culture and Society, 20*, 516–544.

Christensen, A., and Heavey, C. L. (1990). Gender and social structure in the demand/withdrawal pattern of marital conflict. *Journal of Personality and Social Psychology, 59*, 73–81.

Clark, M. S. (1996, August). What role might gender play in strategic self-presentation of emotion? In A. H. Fischer (Chair), *Gender and emotion*.

Symposium conducted at the meeting of the International Society for Research on Emotions, Toronto, Canada.

Clark, M. S., and Taraban, C. (1991). Reactions to and willingness to express emotion in communal and exchange relationships. *Journal of Experimental Social Psychology, 27*, 324–336.

Clark, M. S., Pataki, S. P., and Carver, V. H. (1996). Some thoughts and findings on self-presentation of emotions in relationships. In G. J. O. Fletcher and J. Fitness (Eds.), *Knowledge structures in close relationships: A social psychological approach* (pp. 247–274). Mahwah, NJ: Lawrence Erlbaum.

Coltrane, S. (1998). Gender, power, and emotional expression: Social and historical contexts for a process model of men in marriages and families. In A. Booth and A. C. Crouter (Eds.), *Men in families : When do they get involved? What difference does it make?* (pp. 193–212). Englewood Cliffs, NJ: Lawrence Erlbaum.

Coltrane, S. and Adams, M. (1997). Work-family imagery and gender stereotypes: Television and the reproduction of difference. *Journal of Vocational Behavior, 50*, 323–347.

Coltrane, S. and Adams, M. (2001). Men, women, and housework. In D. Vannoy (Ed.), *Gender mosaics: Social perspectives* (pp. 145–154). Los Angeles: Roxbury.

Coltrane, S., and Allan, K. (1994). "New" fathers and old stereotypes: Representations of masculinity in 1980s television advertising. *Masculinities, 2*, 43–66.

Constantinople, A. (1973). Masculinity-femininity: An exception to a famous dictum. *Psychological Bulletin, 80*, 389–407.

Conway, M., Giannopoulos, C., and Stiefenhofer, K. (1990). Response styles to sadness are related to sex and sex-role orientation. *Sex Roles, 9/10*, 579–587.

Cornelius, R. (1986, April). *Prescience in the pre-scientific study of weeping? A history of weeping in the popular press from the mid-1800s to the present.* Paper presented at the meeting of the Eastern Psychological Association, New York.

Cornelius, R. R. (1996). *The science of emotion: Research and tradition in the psychology of emotion.* Upper Saddle River, NJ: Prentice Hall.

Crawford, J., Kippax, S., Onyx, J., Gault, U., and Benton, P. (1990). Women theorising their experiences of anger: A study using memory-work. *Australian Psychologist, 25*, 333–350.

Crawford, J., Kippax, S., Onyx, J., Gault, U., and Benton, P. (1992). *Emotion and gender: Constructing meaning form memory.* London: Sage.

Crawford, M. (1995). *Talking difference: On gender and language.* Thousand Oaks, CA: Sage.

Crawford, M. (2000, March). *Mars and Venus collide: Discourse analysis and the representation of difference.* Paper presented at the City University of New York Conference on Qualitative Methods, New York.

Crosby, F. J., Pufall, A., Snyder, R. C., O'Connell, M., and Whalen, P. (1989). The denial of personal disadvantage among you, me, and all the other ostriches. In M. Crawford and M. Gentry (Eds.), *Gender and thought* (pp. 79–99). New York: Springer-Verlag.

Cupach, W. R., and Canary, D. J. (1995). Managing conflict and anger: Investigating the sex stereotype hypothesis. In P. J. Kalbfleisch and M. J. Cody (Eds.), *Gender, power and communication in human relationships* (pp. 233–252). Englewood Cliffs, NJ: Lawrence Erlbaum.

Dahlstrom, W. G., Welsh, G. S., and Dahlstrom, L. E. (1972). *An MMPI handbook. Volume 1. Clinical interpretation* (rev. ed.). Minneapolis, MN: University of Minnesota Press.

Daly, K. (1995). Reshaping fatherhood: Finding the models. In W. Marsiglio (Ed.), *Fatherhood: contemporary theory, research, and social policy* (pp. 21–40). Thousand Oaks, CA: Sage Publications.

Darwin, C. (1872). *The expression of the emotions in man and animals*. London: J. Murray.

Darwin, C. (1897). *The descent of man* (2nd ed.). New York: D. Appleton. (First edition published 1871).

de Lorimier, S., Doyle, A., and Tessier, O. (1995). Social coordination during pretend play: Comparisons with nonpretend play and effects on expressive content. *Merrill-Palmer Quarterly, 41*, 497–516.

De Sousa, R. (1987). *The rationality of emotion*. Cambridge, MA: MIT Press.

Deaux, K. (1993). Reconstructing social identity. *Personality and Social Psychology Bulletin, 19*, 4–12.

Deaux, K. (1996). Social identification. In E. T. Higgins and A. W. Kruglanski (Eds.), *Social psychology: Handbook of basic principles* (pp. 777–798). New York: Guilford.

Deaux, K. and Lewis, L. (1984). The structure of gender stereotypes: Interrelationships among components and gender label. *Journal of Personality and Social Psychology, 46*, 991–1004.

Deaux, K., and Kite, M. (1993). Gender stereotypes. In F. L. Denmark and M. A. Paludi (Eds.) *Psychology of women: A handbook of issues and theories* (pp. 107–139). Westport, CT: Greenwood Press.

Deaux, K., and Major, B. (1987). Putting gender into context: An interactive model of gender-related behavior. *Psychological Review, 94*, 369–389.

Delp, M. J., and Sackheim, H. A. (1987). Effects of mood on lacrimal flow: Sex differences and asymmetry. *Psychophysiology, 24*, 550–556.

Denham, G., and Bultemeier, K. (1993). Anger: Targets and triggers. In S. P. Thomas (Ed.), *Women and anger* (pp. 68–90). New York: Springer.

Denham, S. A. (1998). *Emotional development in young children*. New York: Guilford.

Diehl, L. A. (1986). The paradox of G. Stanley Hall: Foe of coeducation and educator of women. *American Psychologist, 41*, 868–878.

Doyle, J. (1983). *The male experience*. Dubuque, IA: W. C. Brown.

Draznin, Y. C. (2001). *Victorian London's middle-class housewife: What she did all day*. Westport, CN: Greenwood Press.

Duffy, E. (1941). An explanation of "emotional" phenomena without the use of the concept "emotion." *Journal of General Psychology, 25*, 283–293.

Dunn, J. (1988). *The beginnings of social understanding*. Oxford, UK: Basil Blackwell.

Dunn, J., Bretherton, I., and Munn, P. (1987). Conversations about feeling states between mothers and their young children. *Developmental Psychology, 23*, 132–139.

Dye, N. S. (1980). History of childbirth in America. *Signs: Journal of Women in Culture and Society, 6*, 97–108.

Eagly, A. H. (1987). *Sex differences in social behavior: A social-role interpretation*. Hillsdale, NJ: Lawrence Erlbaum Associates.

Egerton, M. (1988). Passionate women and passionate men: Sex differences in accounting for angry and weeping episodes. *British Journal of Social Psychology, 27*, 51–66.

Eisenberg, A. R. (1999). Emotion talk among Mexican American and Anglo American mothers and children from two social classes. *Merrill-Palmer Quarterly, 45*, 267–284.

Eisenberg, N., Cumberland, A., and Spinrad, T. L. (1998). Parental socialization of emotion. *Psychological Inquiry, 9*, 241–273.

Eisenberg, N., Fabes, R., Nyman, M., Bernzweig, J., and Pinulelas, A. (1994). The relations of emotionality and regulation to children's anger-related reactions. *Child Development, 65*, 109–128.

Ekman, P. (1993). Facial expression and emotion. *American Psychologist, 48*, 384–392.

Ekman, P., and Friesen, W. V. (1975). *Unmasking the face: A guide to recognizing emotions from facial cues*. Englewood Cliffs, NJ: Prentice-Hall.

Elias, N., and Dunning, E. (1986). *Quest for excitement: Sport and leisure in the civilizing process*. New York: Basil Blackwell.

Ellison, J. (1999). *Cato's tears and the making of Anglo-American emotion*. University of Chicago Press.

English, O. S., and Finch, S. M. (1951). *Emotional problems of growing up*. Chicago, IL: Science Research Association.

Erskine, F. (1995). The origin of the species and the science of female inferiority. In D. Amigoni and J. Wallace (Eds.), *Charles Darwin's "The origin of species": New interdisciplinary essays* (pp. 95–121). New York: Manchester University Press.

Fabes, R. A., Eisenberg, N., Hanish, L., and Spinrad, T. L. (in press). Preschoolers' spontaneous use of emotion language: Relations to social status. *Journal of Early Education and Development*.

Fagot, B. (1995). Psychosocial and cognitive determinants of early gender-role development. *Annual review of sex research, 6*, 1–31.

Fagot, B. I., and Hagan, R. (1991). Observations of parent reactions to sex-stereotyped behaviors: Age and sex effects. *Child Development, 62*, 617–628.

Fagot, B. I., and Leinbach, M. D. (1993). Gender-role development in young children: From discrimination to labeling. *Developmental Review, 13*, 205–224.

Fagot, B. I., Hagan, R., Leinbach, M. D., and Kronsberg, S. (1985). Differential reactions to assertive and communicative acts of toddler boys and girls. *Child Development, 56*, 1499–1505.

Fein, G. (1991). Bloodsuckers, blisters, cooked babies, and other curiosities: Affective themes in pretense. In Kessel, F. S., Bornstein, M. H., and Sameroff, A. J. (Eds.), *Contemporary constructions of the child: Essays in honor of William Kessen* (pp. 143–157). Hillsdale, NJ: Lawrence Erlbaum Associates.

Fein, G., and Kinney, P. (1994). He's a nice alligator: Observations on the affective organization of pretense. In A. Slade and D. P. Wolf (Eds.). *Children at play: Clinical and developmental approaches to meaning and representation* (pp. 188–205). New York: Oxford University Press.

Feirstein, B., and Lorenz, L. (1982). *Real Men Don't Eat Quiche*. New York: Pocket Books.

Feldman Barrett, L. and Morganstein, M. (1995, August). *Sex differences in the experience of emotion: Retrospective versus momentary ratings of emotion*. Paper presented at the meeting of the American Psychological Association, New York.

Feldman Barrett, L., Robin, L., Pietromonaco, P. R., and Eyssell, K. M. (1998). Are women the "more emotional" sex? Evidence from emotional experiences in social context. *Cognition and Emotion, 12*, 555–579.

Fernández-Dols, J. M., and Ruiz-Belda, M. A. (1995). Expression of emotion versus expressions of emotions: Everyday conceptions about spontaneous facial behavior. In J. A. Russell, J. M. Fernández-Dols, A. S. R. Manstead, and J. C. Wellenkamp (Eds.), *Everyday conceptions of emotion* (pp. 505–522). Dordrecht, Netherlands: Kluwer Academic Press.

Fine, G. A. (1987). *With the boys: Little League baseball and preadolescent culture.* Chicago: University of Chicago Press.

Fine, M. (1992). *Disruptive voices: The possibilities of feminist research.* Ann Arbor, MI: University of Michigan Press.

First, E. (1994). The leaving game, or I'll play you and you play me: The emergence of dramatic role play in 2-year-olds. In A. Slade, and D. P. Wolf, (Eds.), *Children at play: Clinical and developmental approaches to meaning and representation* (pp. 111–132). New York: Oxford University Press.

Fischer, A. H. (1993). Sex differences in emotionality: Fact or stereotype. *Feminism and Psychology, 3,* 303–318.

Fischer, A. H. (1995). Emotion concepts as a function of gender. In J. A. Russell and J. Fernández-Dols (Eds.), *Everyday conceptions of emotion* (pp. 457–474). Dordrecht, Netherlands: Kluwer.

Fischer, A. R., and Good, G. E. (1997). Men and psychotherapy: An investigation of alexithymia, intimacy, and masculine gender roles. *Psychotherapy, 34,* 160–170.

Fiske, S. T., and Taylor, S. E. (1991). *Social cognition* (2nd ed.). New York: McGraw-Hill.

Fivush, R., and Buckner, J. P. (2000). Gender, sadness, and depression: The development of emotional focus through gendered discourse. In A. H. Fischer (Ed), *Gender and emotion: Social psychological perspectives* (pp. 232–253). Cambridge, England: Cambridge University Press.

Fivush, R., and Kuebli, J. (1997). Making everyday events emotional: The construal of emotion in parent-child conversations about the past. In N. Stein, P. A. Ornstein, C. A. Brainerd, and B. Tversky (Eds.), *Memory for everyday and emotional events* (pp. 239–266). Hillsdale, NJ: Erlbaum.

Fivush, R., Brotman, M. A., Buckner, J. P., and Goodman, S. H. (2000). Gender differences in parent-child emotion narratives. *Sex Roles, 42,* 233–253.

Fletcher, J. K. (1999). *Disappearing acts: Gender, power, and relational practice at work.* Cambridge, MA: MIT Press.

Freedman, Paul (1998). Peasant anger in the late middle ages. In B. H. Rosenwein (Ed.), *Anger's past: The social uses of an emotion in the Middle Ages* (pp. 171–188). Ithaca, NY: Cornell University Press.

Frey, W. H., Hoffman-Ahern, C., Johnson, R. A., Lykken, D. T., and Tuason, V. B. (1983). Crying behavior in the human adult. *Integrative Psychiatry,* 94–98.

Fridland, A. J. (1994). *Human facial expression: An evolutionary view.* San Diego, CA: Academic Press.

Frijda, N. H. (1986). *The emotions.* Cambridge, England: Cambridge University Press.

Frodi, A. (1978). Experiential and physiological responses associated with anger and aggression in women and men. *Journal of Research in Personality, 12,* 335–349.

Frye, M. (1983). *The politics of reality: Essays in feminist theory.* Freedom, CA: The Crossing Press.

Fuqua, D. R., Leonard, E., Masters, M. A., Smith, R. J., Campbell, J. L., and Fischer, P. C. (1991). A structural analysis of the State-Trait Anger Expression Inventory. *Educational and Psychological Measurement, 51,* 439–446.

Gallagher, P. E. (1992). Individual differences in nonverbal behavior: Dimensions of style. *Journal of Personality and Social Psychology, 63,* 133–145.

Gamble, E. B. (1893/1894). *The evolution of woman: An inquiry into the dogma of her inferiority to man.* New York: G. P. Putnam's Sons.

Gaming, L. H., and Coleman, M. (1985). Sex, sex roles, and emotional expressiveness. *Journal of Genetic Psychology, 146,* 405–411.

Gardiner, H. N., Metcalf, R., and Beebe-Center, J. G. (1937). *Feeling and emotion: A history of theories.* New York: American.

Garner, P., Robertson, S., and Smith, G. (1997). Preschool children's emotional expressions with peers: The roles of gender and emotion socialization. *Sex Roles, 36,* 675–691.

Geddes, P., and Thomson, J. A. (1890). *The evolution of sex.* New York: Scribner and Wellford.

Gilligan, C. (1982). *In a different voice.* Cambridge, MA: Harvard University Press.

Gillis, J. R. (1995). Bringing up father: British paternal identities, 1700 to present. *Masculinities, 3,* 1–27.

Gladstone, W. E. (1888, May). 'Robert Elsmere' and the battle of belief. *The Nineteenth Century,* 766–788.

Glenn, E. N. (1999). The social construction and institutionalization of gender and race. In M. M. Ferree, J. Lorber, and B. B. Hess (Eds.). *Revisioning gender* (pp. 3–43). Thousand Oaks, CA: Sage.

Goldberg, H. (1976). *The hazards of being male: Surviving the myth of masculine privilege.* New York: Nash Publications.

Goldfried, M. R., and Friedman, J. M. (1982). Clinical behavior therapy and the male sex role. In K. Solomon and N. B. Levy (Eds.), *Men in transition: Theory and therapy* (pp. 309–341). New York: Plenum.

Goldstein, J. H. (1994). Sex differences in toy play and use of video games. In Goldstein, J. H. (Ed.), *Toys, play, and child development* (pp. 110–129). New York: Cambridge University Press.

Goleman, D. (1998). *Working with emotional intelligence.* New York: Bantam Books.

Goncu, A. (1993). Development of intersubjectivity in social pretend play. *Human Development, 36,* 185–198.

Gordon, S. (1989). The socialization of children's emotions: Emotional culture, competence, and exposure. In C. Saarni and P. L. Harris (Eds.), *Children's understanding of emotion* (pp. 319–349). Cambridge, England: Cambridge University Press.

Gottman, J. M., and Levenson, R. W. (1988). The social psychophysiology of marriage. In P. Noller and M. A. Fitzpatrick (Eds.). *Perspectives on marital interaction* (pp. 182–200). San Diego, CA: College Hill Press.

Gottman, J. M., and Levenson, R. W. (1992). Marital processes predictive of later dissolution: Behavior, physiology and health. *Journal of Personality and Social Psychology, 63,* 221–233.

Gottman, J. M., and Levenson, R. W. (1999). Dysfunctional marital conflict: Women are being unfairly blamed. *Journal of Divorce and Remarriage, 31,* 1–17.

Gough, H. G. (1952). Identifying psychological femininity. *Educational and Psychological Measurement, 12,* 427–439.

Gould, S. J. (1981). *The mismeasure of man.* New York: W. W. Norton.

Gray, John. (1992). *Men are from Mars, women are from Venus.* New York: HarperCollins.

Greenberg, L. S., and Pavio, S. C. (1997). *Working with emotions in psychotherapy.* New York: Guilford.

Greenspan, P. (1987). Unfreedom and responsibility. In F. Schoeman (Ed.), *Responsibility, character, and the emotions* (pp. 63–80). Cambridge, England: Cambridge University Press.

Griffiths, P. E. (1997). *What emotions really are.* Chicago: University of Chicago Press.

Griswold, R. L. (1993). *Fatherhood in America: A history.* New York: Basic Books.

Grossman, M., and Wood, W. (1993). Sex differences in intensity of emotional experience: A social role interpretation. *Journal of Personality and Social Psychology, 65,* 1010–1022.

Guilford, J. P., and Zimmerman, W. S. (1956). Fourteen dimensions of temperament. *Psychological Monographs, 70,* 11–24.

Haley, B. (1978). *The healthy body and Victorian culture.* Cambridge, MA: Harvard University Press.

Hall, G. S. (1918). *Youth, its education, regimen and hygiene.* New York: Appleton.

Hall, J. A. (1987). On explaining gender differences: The case of nonverbal communication. In P. Shaver and C. Hendrick (Eds.), *Review of personality and social psychology: Volume 7* (pp. 177–200). Beverly Hills, CA: Sage.

Hall, R. (1986). What nursery school teachers ask us about: Psychoanalytic consultations in preschools: Living with Spiderman *et al.*: Mastering aggression and excitement. *Emotions and Behavior Monographs, Monograph no. 5,* 89–99.

Hall, W. H. (1994). New Fatherhood: Myths and realities. *Public Health Nursing, 11,* 219–228.

Hare-Mustin, R. T and Marecek, J. (1988). The meaning of difference: Gender theory, postmodernism, and psychology. *American Psychologist, 43,* 455–464.

Harper, C. (1963). Can contact sports be justified as a part of the educational program? In *Administration of high school athletics* (pp. 86–90). (Report of the First National Conference on Secondary School Athletic Administration, 1962). Washington, DC: American Association for Health, Physical Education, and Recreation.

Harris, A. C. (1994). Ethnicity as a determinant of sex role identity: A replication study of item selection for the Bem Sex Role Inventory. *Sex Roles, 31,* 241–273.

Harris, P. L. (1989). *Children and emotion.* New York: Basil Blackwell.

Hartsock, N. (1983). *Money, sex and power: Toward a feminist historical materialism.* Boston: Northeastern University Press.

Haviland, J. M., and Goldston, R. B. (1992). Emotion and narrative: The agony and the ecstasy. In K. T. Strongman (Ed.), *International review of studies on emotion, Vol. 2.* (pp. 219–247). Chichester, UK: John Wiley and Sons.

Heesacker, M., and Prichard, S. (1992). In a different voice, revisited: Men, women, and emotion. *Journal of Mental Health Counseling, 14,* 274–290.

Heise, D. R., and Calhan, C. (1995). Emotion norms in interpersonal events. *Social Psychology Quarterly, 58,* 223–240.

Henley, N. M., Miller, M., and Beazley, J. A. (1995). Syntax, semantics, and sexual violence: Agency and the passive voice, *Journal of Language and Social Psychology, 14,* 60–84.

Hess, U., Banse, R., and Kappas, A. (1995). The intensity of facial expression is determined by underlying affective state and social situation. *Journal of Personality and Social Psychology, 69,* 280–288.

Hochschild, A. R. (1983). *The managed heart.* Berkeley, CA: University of California Press.

Homans, M. (1998). *Royal representations: Queen Victoria and British Culture, 1837–1876.* Chicago: University of Chicago Press.

Hughes, L. A. (1988). "But that's not really mean": Competing in a cooperative mode. *Sex Roles, 19,* 669–687.

Ishii-Kuntz, M. (1995). Paternal involvement and perception toward father's roles: A comparison between Japan and the United States. In W. Marsiglio (Ed.), *Fatherhood: Contemporary theory, research, and social policy* (pp. 102–118). Thousand Oaks, CA: Sage Publications.

Jacklin, C. N., and Reynolds, C. (1993) Gender and childhood socialization. In A. Beall and R. J. Sternberg (Eds.), *The psychology of gender* (pp. 197–214). New York: Guilford.

Jacobsen, M. B., Antonelli, J., Winning, P. U., and Opeil, D. (1977). Women as authority figures: The use and nonuse of authority. *Sex Roles, 3,* 365–375.

Jaggar, A. M. (1992). Love and knowledge: Emotion in feminist epistemology. In E. D. Harvey and K. O'Kruhlik (Eds.), *Women and reason* (pp. 115–142). Ann Arbor, MI: University of Michigan Press.

James, W. (1884). What is an emotion? *Mind, 9,* 188–205.

Jansz, J. (2000). Masculine identity and restrictive emotionality. In A. H. Fischer (Ed.), *Gender and emotion: Social psychological perspectives* (pp. 166–186). Cambridge, England: Cambridge University Press.

Jeffords, S. (1994). *Hard bodies: Hollywood masculinity in the Reagan era.* New Brunswick, NJ: Rutgers University Press.

Johnson, J. T., and Shulman, G. A. (1988). More alike than meets the eye: Perceived gender differences in subjective experience and its display. *Sex Roles, 19,* 67–79.

Johnson, M. M. (1988). *Strong mothers, weak wives: The search for gender equality.* Berkeley, CA: University of California Press.

Jourard, S. M. (1971). *The transparent self.* New York: Van Nostrand.

Kane, S. R., and Furth, H. G. (1993). Children constructing social reality: A frame analysis of social pretend play. *Human Development, 36,* 199–214.

Karbon, M., Fabes, R. A., Carlo, G., and Martin, C. L. (1992). Preschoolers' beliefs about sex and age differences in emotionality. *Sex Roles, 27,* 377–390.

Kaschak, E. (1992). *Engendered lives: A new psychology of women's experience.* New York: Basic Books.

Katz, J. (1999). *How emotions work.* Chicago: University of Chicago Press.

Kelly, J. R., and Hutson-Comeaux, S. L. (1999). Gender-emotion stereotypes are context specific. *Sex Roles, 40,* 107–120.

Kemp, S., and Strongman, K. T. (1995). Anger theory and management: A historical analysis. *American Journal of Psychology, 108,* 397–417.

Kernis, M. H., Grannemann, B. D., and Barclay, L. C. (1989). Stability and level of self-esteem as predictors of anger arousal and hostility. *Journal of Personality and Social Psychology, 56,* 1013–1022.

Kimmel, M. S. (1987). The contemporary "crisis" of masculinity in historical perspective. In H. Brod (Ed.), *The making of masculinities: The new men's studies* (pp. 121–153). Boston, MA: Allen and Unwin.

Kleck, R. E., Hess, U., Adams, R., and Walbott, H. (2000, August). The influence of perceived gender on the perception of emotional facial expressions. In U. Hess and R. Kleck (Chairs), *The influence of beliefs regarding men's and women's emotions on the perception and self-perception of emotions.* Symposium conducted at the meeting of the International Society for Research on Emotions, Quebec City, Canada.

Kline, S. (1989). Limits to the imagination: Marketing and children's culture. In I. Angus and S. Jhally (Eds.), *Cultural politics in contemporary America* (pp. 299–316). New York: Routledge.

Koestner, R., and Aube, J. (1995). A multifactorial approach to the study of gender characteristics. *Journal of Personality, 63,* 681–710.

Kopper, B. A., and Epperson, D. L. (1991). Women and anger: Sex and sex-role comparisons in the expression of anger. *Psychology of Women Quarterly, 15,* 7–14.

Kopper, B. A., and Epperson, D. L. (1996). The experience and expression of anger: Relationships with gender, gender role socialization, depression, and mental health functioning. *Journal of Counseling Psychology, 43*, 158–165.

Kraemer, D. L., and Hastrup, J. L. (1988). Crying in adults: Self-control and autonomic correlates, *Journal of Social and Clinical Psychology, 6*, 53–68.

Kring, A. (2000). Gender and anger. In A. H. Fischer (Ed.), *Gender and emotion: Social psychological perspectives* (pp. 211–231). Cambridge, England: Cambridge University Press.

Kring, A. M., Smith, D. A., and Neale, J. M. (1994). Individual differences in dispositional expressiveness: Development and validation of the Emotional Expressivity Scale. *Journal of Personality and Social Psychology, 66*, 934–949.

Kunin, M. (1995). *Living a political life: One of America's first woman governors tells her story.* New York: Vintage Books.

L'Abate, L. (1980). Inexpressive males or overexpressive females? A reply to Balswick. *Family Relations, 29*, 229–230.

Labott, S. M., Martin, R. B., Eason, P. S., and Berkey, E. Y. (1991). Social reactions to the expression of emotion. Cognition and Emotion, 5, 397–417.

LaFrance, M., Brownell, H., and Hahn, E. (1997). Interpersonal verbs, gender, and implicit causality. *Social Psychology Quarterly, 60*, 138–152.

LaFrance, M. (1993, June). Towards a reconsideration of the gender-emotion relationship. In S. A. Shields (Chair), *New views on gender and emotion.* Symposium conducted at the meeting of the American Psychological Society, Chicago IL.

LaFrance, M. (1998). Pressure to be pleasant: Effects of sex and power on reactions to not smiling. *International Review of Social Psychology, 2*, 95–108.

LaFrance, M., and Banaji, M. (1992). Towards a reconsideration of the gender-emotion relationship. In M. Clark (Ed.), *Review of personality and social psychology: Volume 14.* Beverly Hills, CA: Sage.

LaFrance, M., and Hecht, M. A. (2000). Gender and smiling: A meta-analysis. In A. H. Fischer (Ed.), *Gender and emotion: Social psychological perspectives* (pp. 118–142). Cambridge, England: Cambridge University Press.

Lakoff, G. (1987). *Women, fire, and dangerous things.* University of Chicago Press.

Lamb, M. E. (1986). The changing role of fathers. In M. E. Lamb (Ed.), *The father's role: Applied perspectives* (pp. 3–27). New York: Wiley.

Landrine, H. (1985). Race x class stereotypes of women. *Sex Roles, 13*, 65–75.

LaRossa, R. (1988). Fatherhood and social change. *Family Relations, 37*, 451–457.

LaRossa, R. (1997). *The modernization of fatherhood.* Chicago: University of Chicago Press.

Leaper, C., Leve, L., Strasser, T., and Schwartz, R. (1995). Mother-child communication sequences: Play activity, child gender, and marital status effects. *Merrill-Palmer Quarterly, 41*, 307–327.

Lederer, W. (1982). Counter epilogue. In K. Solomon and N. B. Levy (Eds.), *Men in transition: Theory and therapy* (pp. 475–492). New York: Plenum.

LeDoux, J. (1996). *The emotional brain.* New York: Simon and Shuster.

Lemerise, E. A., and Dodge, K. A. (1993). The development of anger and hostile interactions. In M. Lewis and J. M. Haviland (Eds.), *Handbook of emotions* (pp. 537–546). New York: Guilford.

Lerner, G. (1979). *The majority finds its past.* New York: Oxford University Press.

Lerner, H. (1985). *The dance of anger: A woman's guide to changing the patterns of intimate relationships.* New York: Harper Perennial.

Levant, R. F. (1995). Toward the reconstruction of masculinity. In R. F. Levant and W. S. Pollack (Eds.), *A new psychology of men* (pp. 229–251). New York: Basic Books.

Lewin, M. (1984a). "Rather worse than folly?" Psychology measures femininity and masculinity, 1: From Terman and Miles to the Guilfords. In M. Lewin (Ed.), *In the shadow of the past: Psychology portrays the sexes* (pp. 155–178). New York: Columbia University Press.

Lewin, M. (1984b). Psychology measures femininity and masculinity, 2: From "13 gay men" to the instrumental-expressive distinction. In M. Lewin (Ed.), *In the shadow of the past: Psychology portrays the sexes* (pp. 179–204). New York: Columbia University Press.

Ley, K. (1963). Interscholastic athletics for girls. In *Administration of high school athletics* (pp. 20–29). (Report of the First National Conference on Secondary School Athletic Administration, 1962). Washington, DC: American Association for Health, Physical Education, and Recreation.

Lloyd, G. (1984). *The man of reason: "Male" and "female" in Western philosophy.* Minneapolis, MN: University of Minnesota Press.

Lombardo, W. K., Cretser, G. A., Lombardo, B., and Mathis, S. L. (1983). Fer cryin' out loud – There is a sex difference. *Sex Roles, 9,* 987–995.

Lombroso C., and Ferrero W. (1899). *The female offender.* New York: Appleton.

Lott, B., and Saxon, S. (1998, August). *Beliefs about women related to their ethnicity and social class.* Paper presented at the meeting of the American Psychological Association, San Francisco.

Lutz, C. (1988). *Unnatural emotions: Everyday sentiments on a Micronesian atoll and their challenge to Western theory.* Chicago: University of Chicago Press.

Lutz, T. (1999). *Crying: The natural and cultural history of tears.* New York: W. W. Norton.

Maccoby, E. E. (1988). Gender as a social category. *Developmental Psychology, 24,* 755–765.

Maccoby, E. E. (1990). Gender and relationships: A developmental account. *American Psychologist, 45,* 513–520.

Maccoby, E. E. (1998). *The two sexes: Growing up apart, coming together.* Cambridge, MA: Harvard University Press.

Major, B. (1989). Gender differences in comparisons and entitlement: Implications for comparable worth. *Journal of Social Issues, 45,* 99–115.

Malatesta, C. Z., and Kalnok, M. (1984). Emotional experience in younger and older adults. *Journal of Gerontology, 39,* 301–308.

Manstead, A. S. R. (1992). Gender differences in emotion. In M. A. Gale and M. W. Eysenck (Eds.), *Handbook of individual differences: Biological perspectives* (pp. 355–387). Chichester, England: Wiley.

Marsiglio, W. (1995a). Fatherhood scholarship: An overview and agenda for the future. In W. Marsiglio (Ed.), *Fatherhood: contemporary theory, research, and social policy* (pp. 1–20). Thousand Oaks, CA: Sage Publications.

Marsiglio, W. (1995b). Fathers' diverse life course patterns and roles: Theory and social interventions. In W. Marsiglio (Ed.), *Fatherhood: contemporary theory, research, and social policy* (pp. 78–101). Thousand Oaks, CA: Sage Publications.

Martin, C. L., Fabes, R. A., Eisenbud, L., Karbon, M. M., and Rose, H. A. (1990, March). *Boys don't cry: Children's distortions of others' emotions.* Paper presented at the Southwestern Society for Research in Human Development, Tempe, AZ.

Martineau, J. (1898). *Types of ethical theory, Vol. II* (3rd ed., revised). Oxford, England: Clarendon Press.

Matlin, M. W. (2000). *The psychology of women* (4th ed.). New York: Harcourt College Publishers.

Maybury, K. K. (1997). *The influence of status and sex on observer judgements of anger displays.* Unpublished doctoral dissertation, University of California, Davis.

Mayo, C. and Henley, N. M. (Eds.) (1981). Gender and nonverbal behavior. New York: Springer-Verlag.

McAdams, D. P. (1995). What do we know when we know a person? *Journal of Personality, 63,* 365–396.

McConnell, R. W. (1987). *Gender and power.* Stanford, CA: Stanford University Press.

McDougall, W. (1923). *Outline of psychology.* New York: Scribner's.

McFarlane, J., and Williams, T. M. (1990). The enigma of premenstrual syndrome. *Canadian Psychology, 31,* 95–108.

McFarlane, J., and Williams, T. M. (1994). Placing premenstrual syndrome in perspective. *Psychology of Women Quarterly, 18,* 339–373.

McGarty, C., Yzerbyt, V., and Spears, R. (Eds.) (2002). *Stereotypes as explanations.* Cambridge University Press.

McGuire, W. J., and McGuire, C. V. (1986). Differences in conceptualizing self versus conceptualizing other people as manifested in contrasting verb types used in natural speech. *Journal of Personality and Social Psychology, 51,* 1135–1143.

McLoyd, V. C., Warren, D., and Thomas, E. A. (1984). Anticipatory and fantastic role enactment in preschool triads. *Developmental Psychology, 20,* 807–814.

Mesquita, B., and Frijda, N. (1992). Cultural variations in emotions: A review. *Psychological Bulletin, 112,* 179–204.

Messner, M. (1992). *Power at play: Sports and the problem of masculinity.* Boston, MA: Beacon Press.

Messner, M., Dunbar, M., and Hunt, D. (2000). The televised sports manhood formula. *Journal of Sport and Social Issues, 24,* 380–394.

Miller, J. B. (1991). Women's and men's scripts for interpersonal conflict. *Psychology of Women Quarterly, 15,* 15–29.

Mintz, S. (1998). From patriarch to androgyny and other myths: Placing men's family roles in historical perspective. In A. Booth and A. Crouter (Eds.), *Men in families: When do they get involved: What difference does it make?* (pp. 3–30). Mahwah, NJ: Lawrence Erlbaum Associates, Inc.

Morawski, J. G. (1987). The troubled quest for masculinity, femininity, and androgyny. In P. Shaver and C. Hendrick (Eds.), *Review of personality and social psychology: Volume 7* (pp. 44–69). Beverly Hills, CA: Sage.

Moskowitz, D. S. (1986). Comparison of self-reports, reports by knowledgeable informants, and behavioral observation data. *Journal of Personality, 54,* 294–317.

Nemiah, J. C. (1996). Alexithymia: Present, past – and future? *Psychosomatic Medicine, 58,* 217–218.

Neumann, R. (2000). The causal influences of attributions on emotions: A procedural priming approach. *Psychological Science, 11,* 179–182.

Noller, P. (1993). Gender and emotional communication in marriage: Different cultures or differential social power? *Journal of Language and Social Psychology, 12,* 132–152.

O'Farrell, M. A. (1997). *Telling complexions: The nineteenth-century English novel and the blush.* Durham, NC: Duke University Press.

O'Neil, J. M. (1981). Male sex role conflicts, sexism, and masculinity: Psychological implications for men, women, and the counseling psychologist. *The Counseling Psychologist 9,* 61–80.

Oatley, K. and Duncan, E. (1994). The experience of emotions in everyday life. *Cognition and Emotion, 8,* 369–381.

Oatley, K., and Jenkins, J. (1996). *Understanding emotions*. Cambridge, MA: Blackwell.

Orbuch, T. L., and Timmer, S. G. (2001). Differences in his marriage and her marriage. In D. Vannoy (Ed.), *Gender mosaics: Social perspectives* (pp. 155–164). Los Angeles: Roxbury.

Panksepp, J. (1998). *Affective neuroscience: The foundations of human and animal emotions*. New York: Oxford University Press.

Parker, J. G., and Gottman, J. M. (1989). Social and emotional development in a relational context: Friendship interaction from early childhood to adolescence. In T. J. Berndt, and G. W. Ladd (Eds.), *Peer relationships in child development* (pp. 95–131). New York: John Wiley and Sons.

Parlee, M. B. (1995). [book review]. *Feminism and Psychology, 5*, 375–381.

Parsons, T. (1942). Age and sex in the social structure of the U.S. *American Sociological Review, 7*, 604–616.

Parsons, T., and Bales, R. (1955). *Family, socialization, and interaction process*. Glencoe, IL: Free Press.

Paxton, N. L. (1991). *George Eliot and Herbert Spencer: Feminism, evolutionism, and the reconstruction of gender*. Princeton, NJ: Princeton University Press.

Pennebaker, J. W., Colder, M., and Sharp, L. K. (1990). Accelerating the coping process. *Journal of Personality and Social Psychology, 58*, 528–537.

Plant, E. A., Hyde, J. S., Keltner, D., Devine, P. G. (2000). The gender stereotyping of emotions. *Psychology of Women Quarterly, 24*, 81–92.

Pleck, J. H. (1984). The theory of male sex role identity: Its rise and fall, 1936 to the present. (pp. 205–225). In M. Lewin (Ed.), *In the shadow of the past: Psychology portrays the sexes*. New York: Columbia University Press.

Pleck, J. H. (1984). The theory of male sex role identity: Its rise and fall, 1936 to the present. In M. Lewin (Ed.), *In the shadow of the past: Psychology portrays the sexes* (pp. 205–225). New York: Columbia University Press.

Pratto, F., and Bargh, J. A. (1991). Stereotyping based on apparently individuating information: Trait and global components of sex stereotypes under attention overload. *Journal of Experimental Social Psychology, 27*, 26–47.

Radke-Yarrow, M., and Kochanska, G. (1990). Anger in young children. In N. Stein, B. Leventhal, and T. Trabasso (Eds.), *Psychological and biological approaches to emotion* (pp. 297–310). Hillsdale, NJ: Erlbaum.

Ramsden, S. R. (1999, April). *The role of sociometric status and gender in children's knowledge of display rules for anger*. Poster session presented at the biannual meeting for the Society for Research in Child Development, Albuquerque, NM.

Ribot, T. (1898). *The psychology of the emotions*. London: Walter Scott.

Richards, E. (1997). Redrawing the boundaries: Darwinian science and Victorian women intellectuals. In B. Lightman (Ed.), *Victorian science in context* (pp. 119–142). Chicago: University of Chicago Press.

Riggio, R. E., and Friedman, H. (1986). Impression formation: The role of expressive behavior. *Journal of Personality and Social Psychology, 50*, 421–427.

Rimé, B., Finkenauer, C., Luminet, O., Zech, E., and Philippot, P. (1998). Social sharing of emotion: New evidence and new questions. In W. Stroebe and M. Hewstone (Eds.), *European Review of Social Psychology, Volume 9* (pp. 145–189).

Risman, B. J. (1998). *Gender vertigo*. New Haven, CT: Yale University Press.

Robinson, M. D., Johnson, J. T., and Shields, S. A. (1998). The gender heuristic and the data base: Factors affecting the perception of gender-related differences in the experience and display of emotions. *Basic and Applied Social Psychology, 20,* 206–219.

Robinson, R. J., and Pennebaker, J. W. (1991). In K. T. Strongman (Ed.), *International review of studies on emotion: Vol. 1* (pp. 247–268). New York: John Wiley.

Roeder, G. (1993). *The censored war.* New Haven, CT: Yale University Press.

Rosaldo, M. Z. (1984). Toward an anthropology of self and feeling. In R. Shweder and R. Levine (Eds.), *Culture theory: Essays on mind, self, and emotion.* New York: Cambridge University Press.

Rosch, L. (October 1988). The professional image report. *Working Woman Magazine,* pp. 109–113.

Ross, C. E., and Mirowsky, J. (1984). Men who cry. *Social Psychology Quarterly, 47,* 138–146.

Ruddick, S. (1980). *Maternal thinking: Toward a politics of peace.* Boston, MA: Beacon Press.

Rusbult, C. E. (1993). Understanding responses to dissatisfaction in close relationships. The exit-voice-loyalty-neglect model. In S. Worchel and J. A. Simpson (Eds.), *Conflict between people and groups: Causes, processes, and resolutions* (pp. 30–59). Chicago: Nelson-Hall.

Russell, J. A. (1997). Reading emotions from and into faces: Resurrecting a dimensional-contextual perspective (pp. 295–320). In J. A. Russell and J. M. Fernández-Dols (Eds.). *The psychology of facial expression.* Cambridge, England: Cambridge University Press.

Russett, C. (1989). *Sexual science: The Victorian construction of womanhood.* Cambridge, MA: Harvard University Press.

Saarni, C. (1988). Children's understanding of the interpersonal consequences of dissemblance of nonverbal emotional-expressive behavior. *Journal of Nonverbal Behavior, 12,* 275–294.

Saarni, C. (1989). Children's understanding of strategic control of emotional expression in social transactions. In C. Saarni and P. L. Harris (Eds.), *Children's understanding of emotion* (pp. 181–208). Cambridge, England: Cambridge University Press.

Saarni, C. (1993). Socialization of emotion. In M. Lewis and J. M. Haviland (Eds.), *Handbook of emotions* (pp. 435–446). New York: Guilford.

Saarni, C. (1998). Issues of cultural meaningfulness in emotional development. *Developmental Psychology, 34,* 647–652.

Saarni, C. (1999). *The development of emotional competence.* New York: Guilford.

Saarni, C., and Harris, P. L. (Eds.). (1989). *Children's understanding of emotion.* Cambridge, England: Cambridge University Press.

Saarni, C., and Weber, H. (1999). Emotional displays and dissemblance in childhood: Implications for self-presentation. In P. Philippot, and R. S. Feldman (Eds.), *The social context of nonverbal behavior.* (pp. 71–105). New York: Cambridge University Press.

Salovey, P., and Mayer, J. D. (1990). Emotional intelligence. *Imagination, Cognition, and Personality, 9,* 185–211.

Sattel, J. W. (1976). The inexpressive male: Tragedy or sexual politics? *Social Problems, 23,* 469–477.

Scarborough, E., and Furumoto, L. (1987). *Untold lives: The first generation of American women psychologists.* New York: Columbia University Press.

Seidler, V. J. (1997). *Man enough: Embodying masculinities.* Thousand Oaks, CA: Sage.

Sharkin, B. S. (1993). Anger and gender: Theory, research, and implications. *Journal of Counseling and Development, 71*, 386–389.

Sheldon, A. (1992). Conflict talk: Sociolinguistic challenges to self-assertion and how young girls meet them. *Merrill-Palmer Quarterly, 38*, 95–117.

Sheldon, A. (1993). Pickle fights: Gendered talk in preschool disputes. In D. Tannen (Ed.), *Gender and conversational interaction* (pp. 83–109). New York: Oxford University Press.

Sherif, C. W. (1982). Needed concepts in the study of gender identity. *Psychology of Women Quarterly, 6*, 375–398.

Shields, S. A. (1975a). Functionalism, Darwinism, and the psychology of women: A study in social myth. *American Psychologist, 30*, 739–754.

Shields, S. A. (1975b). Ms. Pilgrim's progress: The contributions of Leta Stetter Hollingworth to the psychology of women. *American Psychologist, 30*, 852–857.

Shields, S. A. (1980). Nineteenth-century evolutionary theory and male scientific bias. In G. W. Barlow and J. Silverberg (Eds.), *Sociobiology: Beyond nature/nurture? AAAS Selected Symposium #35.* Boulder, CO: Westview Press.

Shields, S. A. (1982). The variability hypothesis: History of a biological model of sex differences in intelligence. *Signs: Journal of Women in Culture and Society, 7*, 769–797.

Shields, S. A. (1984). "To pet, coddle, and 'do for'": Caretaking and the concept of maternal instinct. In M. Lewin (Ed.), *In the shadow of the past: Psychology examines the sexes* (pp. 256–273). New York: Columbia University Press.

Shields, S. A. (1987). Women, men, and the dilemma of emotion. In P. Shaver and C. Hendrick (Eds.), *Review of personality and social psychology: Volume 7* (pp. 229–250). Beverly Hills, CA: Sage.

Shields, S. A. (1991a). Gender in the psychology of emotion. In K. T. Strongman (Ed.), *International review of studies on emotion: Vol. 1* (pp. 227–245). New York: John Wiley.

Shields, S. A. (1991b, August). Doing emotion/doing gender. In Carol Tavris (Chair), *A world apart: Emotion experience in women and men.* Symposium conducted at the meeting of the American Psychological Association, San Francisco.

Shields, S. A. (1994). Blindsight: Overcoming mainstream psychology's resistance to feminist theory and research. *Psychological Inquiry, 5*, 92–94.

Shields, S. A. (1994, August). Practicing social constructionism: Confessions of a feminist empiricist. In. R. Hare-Mustin (Chair), *Taking social constructionism seriously: Feminist theory and feminist psychology.* Symposium conducted at the meeting of the American Psychological Association, Los Angeles.

Shields, S. A. (1995). The role of emotion beliefs and values in gender development. In N. Eisenberg (Ed.), *Review of personality and social psychology, Vol. 15* (pp. 212–232). Thousand Oaks, CA: Sage.

Shields, S. A. (2001). It takes a real man to cry: What *Jerry Maguire* reveals about masculinity and emotion. Unpublished manuscript.

Shields, S. A., and Crowley, J. C. (1996). Appropriating questionnaires and rating scales for a feminist psychology: A multi-method approach to gender and emotion. In S. Wilkinson (Ed.), *Feminist social psychologies* (pp. 218–232). Buckingham, Great Britain: Open University Press.

Shields, S. A., and Crowley, J. C. (2000, August). Stereotypes of "emotionality": The role of the target's racial ethnicity, status, and gender. In U. Hess and R. Kleck (Chairs), *The influence of beliefs regarding men's and women's emotions on the perception and self-perception of emotions.* Symposium conducted at the meeting of the International Society for Research on Emotions, Quebec City, Canada.

Shields, S. A., and Koster, B. A. (1989). Emotional stereotyping of parents in child rearing manuals, 1915-1980. *Social Psychology Quarterly, 52,* 44–55.

Shields, S. A., and MacDowell, K. A. (1987). "Appropriate" emotion in politicians: Judgments of a televised debate. *Journal of Communication, 37,* 78–89.

Shields, S. A., and Mallory, M. E. (1987). Leta Stetter Hollingworth speaks on "Columbia's Legacy." *Psychology of Women Quarterly, 11,* 285–300.

Shields, S. A., and Simon, A. (2001). *Concurrent versus retrospective reports of emotional states: The case of romantic love.* Unpublished manuscript.

Shields, S. A., Steinke, P., and Koster, B. A. (1995). The double bind of caregiving: Representation of emotion in American advice literature. *Sex Roles, 33,* 417–438.

Shimanoff, S. B. (1983). The role of gender in linguistic references to emotive states. *Communication Quarterly, 30,* 174–179.

Signorielli, N. (1993). Television, the portrayal of women, and children's attitudes. In G. L. Berry and J. K. Asamen (Eds.), *Children and television* (pp. 229–242). Newberry Park, CA: Sage.

Singer, J. L. (1994). Imaginative play and adaptive development. In Goldstein, J. H. (Ed.), *Toys, play, and child development* (pp. 6–26). New York: Cambridge University Press.

Smith, M., and Walden, T. (1998). Developmental trends in emotion understanding among a diverse sample of African-American preschool children. *Journal of Applied Developmental Psychology, 19,* 177–198.

Smith, W. L. (1994). *Self-styled gender: Its relationship to gender stereotyping in person perception.* Unpublished doctoral dissertation, The Wright Institute, Berkeley.

Snell, W. E., Belk, S. S., and Hawkins, R. C. (1986). The masculine role as a moderator of stress-distress relationships. *Sex Roles, 15,* 359–366.

Snyder, E. (1990). Emotion and sport: A case study of collegiate women gymnasts. *Psychology of Sport Journal, 7,* 254–270.

Solomon, K. and N. B. Levy (1982). (Eds.), *Men in transition: Theory and therapy.* New York: Plenum.

Solomon, R. C. (1993). *The passions.* Indianapolis, IN: Hackett.

Sonnemans, J., and Frijda, N. H. (1994). The structure of subjective emotional intensity. *Cognition and Emotion, 8,* 329–350.

Spence, J. T. (1984). Masculinity, femininity, and gender-related traits: A conceptual analysis and critique of current research. In B. A. Maher and W. Maher (Eds.), *Progress in experimental research in personality. Vol. 13.* (pp. 2–97). San Diego, CA: Academic Press.

Spence, J. T. (1993). Gender-related traits and gender ideology: Evidence for a multifactorial theory. *Journal of Personality and Social Psychology, 64,* 624–635.

Spence, J. T. (1999). Thirty years of gender research: A personal chronicle. In W. B. Swann, Jr., J. H. Langlois, and L. A. Gilbert (Eds.), *Sexism and stereotypes in modern society* (pp. 255–289). Washington, DC: American Psychological Association.

Spencer, H. (1897). *The principles of psychology (Vol. I).* New York: D. Appleton and Company.

Spencer, H. (1902). *The study of sociology.* New York: D. Appleton and Company.

Spielberger, C. D. (1988). *Manual for the State-Trait Anger Expression Scale (STAX).* Odessa, FL: Psychological Assessment Resources, Inc.

Stearns, C. Z., and Stearns, P. N. (1986). *Anger: The struggle for emotional control in America's history*. University of Chicago Press.

Stearns, P. (1979). *Be a man! Males in modern society*. New York: Holmes and Meier.

Stearns, P. N. (1992). Gender and emotion: A twentieth-century transition. In V. Gecas and D. D. Franks (Eds.), *Social perspectives on emotion, Volume 1* (pp. 127–160). New York: JAI Press.

Steil, J. M. (1997). *Marital equality: Its relationship to the well-being of husbands and wives*. London: Sage.

Stein, N. L., and Levine, L. J. (1990). Making sense out of emotion: The representation and use of goal-structured knowledge. In N. L. Stein and B. Leventhal (Eds.), *Psychological and biological approaches to emotion* (pp. 45–73). Hillsdale, NJ: Lawrence Erlbaum.

Steinke, P., and Shields, S. A. (1992). *Self-report as a research method: Innovation from "limitations."* Unpublished manuscript.

Stern, D. N. (1985). *The interpersonal world of the infant*. New York: Basic Books.

Sternberg, C. R., and Campos, J. J. (1990). The development of anger expressions in infancy. In N. L. Stein and B. Leventhal (Eds.), *Psychological and biological approaches to emotion* (pp. 247–282). Hillsdale, NJ: Lawrence Erlbaum.

Stoppard, J. M. (1993, June). Beyond gender stereotypes: Putting the gender-emotion relationship into context. In S. Shields (Chair), *New views on gender and emotion*. Symposium conducted at the annual meeting of the American Psychological Society, Chicago, IL.

Stoppard, J. M. (2000). *Understanding depression: Feminist social constructionist approaches*. New York: Routledge.

Stoppard, J. M., and Gunn Gruchy, C. D. (1993). Gender, context, and expression of positive emotion. *Personality and Social Psychology Bulletin, 19,* 143–150.

Strayer, J. (1989). What children know and feel in response to witnessing affective events. In C. Saarni and P. L. Harris (Eds.), *Children's understanding of emotion* (pp. 259–289). Cambridge University Press.

Strongman, K. T. (1987). *The psychology of emotion*. Chichester, England: Wiley.

Sutherland, A. (1898). *The origin and growth of the moral instinct. Vol. 1*. London: Longmans, Green.

Tavris, C. (1989). *Anger: The misunderstood emotion* (revised edition). New York: Touchstone Books.

Tavris, C. (1992). *The mismeasure of woman*. New York: Simon and Schuster.

Templeton, L. M. (1999, April). *Children's gender-schematic processing of ambiguous situations*. Paper presented at the meeting of the Society for Research in Child Development, Albuquerque, NM.

Terman, L. M., and Miles, C. C. (1936). *Sex and personality*. New York: Russell and Russell.

Thomas, S. P. (1989). Gender differences in anger expression: Health implications. *Research in Nursing and Health, 12,* 389–398.

Thomas, S. P. (1996). Women's anger: Causes, manifestations, and correlates. In C. D. Spielberger and I. G. Sarason (Ed.), *Stress and emotion: Anxiety, anger, and curiosity, 15* (pp. 53–74). San Francisco: Taylor and Francis.

Thorndike, E. L. (1914). *Educational psychology (Vol. 3)*. New York: Teachers College, Columbia University.

Thorne, B. (1993). Gender play: *Girls and boys in school*. New Brunswick, NJ: Rutgers University Press.

Tiedens, L. Z., Ellsworth, P. C., and Mesquita, B. (2000). Stereotypes about sentiments and status: Emotional expectations for high- and low-status group members. *Personality and Social Psychology Bulletin, 26*, 560–574.

Timmers, M., Fischer, A. H., and Manstead, A. S. R. (1998). Gender differences in motives for regulating emotions. *Personality and Social Psychology Bulletin, 24*, 974–985.

Tredennick, H. (1969). *The last days of Socrates*. New York: Penguin Classics.

Unger, R. (1979). Toward a redefinition of sex and gender. *American Psychologist, 34*, 1085–1094.

Unger, R. K. (1996). Using the master's tools: Epistemology and empiricism. In S. Wilkinson (Ed.), *Feminist social psychologies: International perspectives* (pp. 165–181). Philadelphia, PA: Open University Press.

Unger, R. K. (1998). *Resisting gender: Twenty-five years of feminist psychology*. Thousand Oaks, CA: Sage.

Valenti, S. S., Bhagavathula, S., Goldstein, J., Follari, G., Mitchell, C., and Wagner, K. (1999, April). *Modeling adolescent conversations: Males reciprocate verbalized affect more than do females*. Paper presented at the meeting of the Society for Research in Child Development, Albuquerque, NM.

Vannoy, D. (2001). Collapsing the walls of patriarchy and masculine hegemony. In D. Vannoy (Ed.), *Gender mosaics* (pp. 508–513). Los Angeles: Roxbury.

Verba, M. (1993). Construction and sharing of meanings in pretend play among young children. In M. Stambak and H. Sinclair (Eds.), *Pretend play among 3-year-olds* (pp. 1–29). Hillsdale, NJ: Lawrence Erlbaum Associates.

Vingerhoets, A. J. J. M., Cornelius, R. R., Van Heck, G. L., and Becht, M. C. (2000). Adult crying: A model and review of the literature. *Review of General Psychology, 4*, 354–377.

von Salisch, M. (1997). Emotional processes in children's relationships with siblings and friends. (pp. 61–80). In S. Duck (Ed.). *Handbook of personal relationships* (2nd ed.). Chichester, England: John Wiley.

Walker, A. (1850). *Woman physiologically considered*. New York: J and H. G. Langley.

Ward, M. H. (1888). *Robert Elsmere*. London: Smith, Elder, and Co.

Weber, H. (1998, August). *The social construction of the regulation of anger*. Paper presented at the meeting of The International Society for Research on Emotions, Würzburg, Germany.

Weiner, D. E. B. (1994). *Architecture and social reform in late-Victorian London*. Manchester, England: Manchester University Press.

West, C., and Fenstermaker, S. (1995). Doing difference. *Gender & Society, 9*, 8–37.

West, C., and Zimmerman, D. H. (1987). Doing gender. *Gender & Society, 1*, 125–151.

Whalen, M. (1995). Working toward play: Complexity in children's fantasy activities. *Language in Society, 24*, 315–348.

Wilcox, E. W. (1894). *Men, women, and emotions*. Chicago: W. B. Conkey.

Williams, D. G. (1982). Weeping by adults: Personality correlates and sex differences. *Journal of Psychology, 110*, 217–226.

Williams, J. E., and and Bennett, S. M. (1975). The definition of sex stereotypes via the adjective check list. *Sex Roles, 1*, 327–337.

Wintre, M. G., Polivy, J., and Murray, M. A. (1990). Self-predictions of emotional response patterns: Age, sex, and of situational determinants. *Child Development, 61*, 1124–1133.

Woolley, H. T. (1910). Psychological literature: A review of the recent literature on the psychology of sex. *Psychological Bulletin, 7,* 335–342.

Worcel, S. D., Smith, W. L., and Shields, S. A. (under review). The development and validation of the Self-Styled Gender Scale.

Wyche, K F. (1998). On reading "Bias in Psychology": The more things change, the more they stay the same. *Feminism and Psychology, 8,* 90–93.

Wyer, N. A., Sherman, J. W, and Stroessner, S. J. (1998). The spontaneous suppression of racial stereotypes. *Social Cognition, 16,* 340–352.

Yoder, J. D., and Kahn, A. S. (1993). Working toward an inclusive psychology of women. *American Psychologist, 48,* 844–850.

Zammuner, V. L. (2000). Men's and women's lay theory of emotion. In A. H. Fischer (Ed.), *Gender and emotion: Social psychological perspectives* (pp. 48–70). London: Cambridge University Press.

Zurcher, L. A. (1982). The staging of emotion: A dramaturgical analysis. *Symbolic Interaction, 5,* 1–22.

Index

Note: Page numbers followed by 'n' refer to notes.

Abreu, J.M., 148
Abu-Loghoud, L., 15
accountability *see* responsibility
advertising, 133–4, 96–7
advice literature, 64n.3, 77, 92
age-related differences, 31, 34–5, 62–3
aggression, and anger, 145–6
Allan, K., 133–4
Allen, Tim, 133
Anderson, K.J., 177
androcentrism, 171
androgyny, 52, 66–7n.15–16
anger
  concepts and meanings of, 141–6, 165
  entitlement to, 141
    costs and consequences, 152–7
    gender differences, 149–50
    in marital interaction, 154–7
    power, status and, 146–9
    trait or situational, 151–2
  functions of, 139, 165
  gender and experiences of, 30
  gender and social context of, 27
  internalizing or externalizing, 157–61
  link with masculinity, 140, 146
  not recognized as emotion, 139
  parental responses to, 115n.6
  research on, 140
  and weeping, 162, 164–5
appropriateness *see* emotional
    appropriateness
Aquinas, 70
Armstrong, N., 77
Ashmore, R., 53, 95–6
authenticity *see* emotional authenticity
authority *see* social status
Averill, J.R., 30, 142, 143

Bacon, M., 95–6
Balswick, J., 120–1
Barr, C.L., 37

beliefs, 10–11, 19n.15, 31–2, 83–4
  about emotion, 49–54
  gender-coded beliefs, 45–9, 60, 64n.3
Bem, S.L., 52, 171
Bem Sex Role Inventory (BSRI), 66n.16
Benton, P., 61–2, 153
Biernat, M., 62
biological essentialism, 171
biology
  in nineteenth century theory, 73–4
  and sex-gender distinction, 11–12
Birnbaum, D.W., 28
Bly, R., 84
Bordo, S., 173
Briggs, J., 177, 178
Brody, L., 35, 106, 156
Buck, R., 91
Bugental, D.E., 39
Burt, Jim, 117
Bush, George, 48
Bush, George W., 1–2, 125

Campbell, A., 160
Campos, J.J., 139, 142, 165
Cancian, F., 15
caregivers
  stereotypes of children, 59
  see also parents
Carpenter, W.B., 69
Cathy, 21
childrearing advice, 64n.3, 92
children
  caregivers' gendered stereotypes of, 59
  experiences of emotion, 31, 62
  expression of emotion, 34–5, 56–7,
    159–60
  gender-coded gifts for, 55
  parents' emotional education of, 95–6,
    115–16n.4–7
  parents' emotional expression with, 39
  practicing emotion in play, 99–108

practicing gendered emotion, 57–9
use of gendered emotion stereotypes,
47, 58–9
Chodorow, N., 67–8n.23
Christensen, A., 154
Clark, M.S., 153, 154
Clark, Terri, 178–9
cognitive shortcut, stereotypes as, 60–1
cognitive-appraisal theories, 6–7
cognitive-developmental perspective, 100
Coltrane, S., 133–4
competitive play, 107
competitive sports, 89–90, 108–11, 117–18
complementarity of sexes, 69, 70–7
constructionism, 7, 100, 142
control of emotion, 46, 53, 77–80, 85, 100–1
    anger, 144–5
    emotion double bind, 173–6
    weeping, 162, 163–4
cooperative play, 107
core gender identity, 12
Crawford, J., 61–2, 153, 162
Crawford, M., 84–5
Crosby, F.J., 150
Crowley, J., 45–7
crying *see* weeping
culture, and beliefs, 10–11, 19n.15

Darwin, C., 72–3, 81
Deaux, K., 54, 56, 98, 113
Del Boca, F., 53
Delp, M.J., 163
demand strategy, 154–5
Diagnostic and Statistical Manual (DSM-IV),
    181
difference model, 21, 22, 40
    problems of, 44, 113
    see also complementarity of sexes
display rules, 56–7, 112
doing emotion
    and being human, 170–1, 183–4
    and doing gender, 54–9, 170
doing gender, 43–4
    and doing emotion, 54–9, 170
Donaldson, Sam, 179
double bind, of emotional styles, 173–6
Duffy, E., 4
Duncan, E., 176
education *see* emotional education
Egerton, M., 27
Eisenberg, N., 159–60
Ekman, P., 38
emotion
    anger not recognized as, 139
    approaches to studying, 5–9
        emotion experiences, 29–33, 41–2n.7–9

emotional expression, 33–9
    in feminist theory, 14–16
    gender in, 12–13, 25–6, 39–41, 80–3
    in nineteenth century, 80–3
    understandings of emotion, 26–8
    control of *see* control of emotion
    defining, 2, 4, 5–6
    "doing," 54–9, 170–1
    gender-coded beliefs about, 45–9
    as gendered, 2–4
    and humanity, 170–1, 183–4
    language related to *see* language
    link with sport, 89–90, 118
    natural, typical and ideal, 84, 85
    paradoxical beliefs about, 11
    and reason, 72, 171
    social meaning of, 9–11, 94, 165–6
emotion beliefs, 57, 58
    about gender, 49–54
emotion display rules, 56–7, 112
emotion management
    and competing emotional styles,
        173–6
    see also control of emotion
emotion master stereotype, 2–3, 11, 45, 50,
    83–4, 119
emotion narratives as identity narratives,
    61–3
emotion work, 113
emotional appropriateness, 46, 90, 91–3,
    179–83
emotional authenticity, 94, 97–9,
    169–70
    and emotional education, 112, 114
    in *Jerry Maguire*, 126–30
    and September 11 attacks, 184
    weeping, 163, 164
    in *Who Wants to Be a Millionaire?*, 169
emotional competence, 94
emotional education, 91–4
    competitive sports, 108–11
    and gender improvization, 97–9
    practicing emotion in play, 99–108
    role of parents and television, 94–7,
        115n.4–7
    and social identity, 111–14
emotional euphemisms, 178, 186n.6
emotional experience
    age differences, 31, 62–3
    shaped by stereotypes, 60–1
    studies of, 29–33, 41–2n.7–9
emotional expression
    of anger
        externalizing anger, 157–61
        gender differences, 152–7
    children's, 34–5, 56–7, 159–60

emotional (cont.)
  studies of, 33–9
  see also display rules; extravagant
    emotion; masculine inexpressivity
emotional intelligence, 182–3
emotional lability, 74–5
emotional maturity, 93–4
emotional stereotypes *see* gendered
    emotion stereotypes
emotional styles, competition between,
    173–6
emotionality *see* female emotionality
entitlement
  gender differences, 150–1
  to anger, 141
    costs and consequences, 152–7
    gender differences, 149–50
    in marital interaction, 154–7
    power, status and, 146–9
    trait or situational, 151–2
Eperson, D.L., 159
EQ, 182–3
ethnicity *see* racial ethnicity
evolutionary theory, 71, 72–3, 75, 78, 79–80
experience *see* emotional experience
expression *see* emotional expression
expressiveness, 38, 53, 67n.17
Expressivity Demand Theory, 34
externalizing anger, 157–61
extravagant emotion, 113–14, 130–1, 173,
    174, 175
  see also female emotionality

Fabes, R.A., 58
facial expression, 33–5, 38
Fagot, B.I., 59
fallacy of misplaced concreteness, 143
fatherhood, 76, 117–18, 125, 130–5, 136
Fawlty Towers, 151
feeling, emotion as, 4
feeling rules, 112
Fein, G., 99–100, 101, 102
Feldman Barrett, L., 61
female emotionality, 70, 82–3
  and complementarity of sexes, 69, 70–7
  control of, 77–8
femininity, emotion in coding of, 49–54,
    64n.7, 65–6n.11
feminist theory, 14–16, 19–20n.20
Fernández-Dols, J.M., 36
Ferraro, Geraldine, 48
film *see* television and film
Fine, G.A., 110
First Wives Club, The, 158
Fischer, A.H., 10, 148–9
Fletcher, J.K., 176
football, 117, 136–7n.2

Foursquare, 107
Freedman, P., 147
Friedman, H., 37
Frodi, A., 30, 152
Frye, M., 139, 142
fundamental emotions theories, 6

Gallagher, P.E., 37
Gault, U., 61–2, 153
Geddes, P., 71
gender
  and anger
    differences in expression, 152–7
    entitlement to, 147–9
    internalizing or externalizing, 157–61
  approaches to studying emotion and,
    12–13, 25–6, 39–41, 80–3
    emotional experience, 29–33,
      41–2n. 7–9
    emotional expression, 33–9
    understandings of emotion, 26–8
  differences in entitlement, 150–1
  "doing," 43–4, 54–9, 170
  emotion as gendered, 2–4
  and beliefs about emotion, 49–54
  lenses of, 171
  link with sport, 108–11
  nature of, 11–12, 19n.17, 54
  and play, 103–8
  and social identity, 111
  and social meaning of emotion, 9–10, 11
  and weeping, 125, 129, 161–5, 167n.20
  see also difference model
gender identity, 12, 51–2
gender improvization, emotional practice
    as, 97–9
gender performance, 43–4, 54–5, 98
gender polarization, 171
gender schemas, 58, 59, 62, 63, 68n.29
gender stereotypes
  in advertising, 133–4
  research on, 53
  used by caregivers, 59
  see also gendered emotion stereotypes
gender-coded behavior, 41
gender-coded beliefs
  about emotion, 45–9, 60, 64n.3
  see also gendered emotion stereotypes
gendered emotion
  consequences
    competition between emotional styles,
      173–6
    emotional appropriateness, 179–83
    naming emotion, 176–9, 185–6n.4–6
  learning and practicing, 57–9, 93, 103–8
gendered emotion stereotypes, 45–9, 64n.3
  children's use of, 47, 58–9

emotion master stereotype, 2–3, 11, 45,
  50, 83–4, 119
female emotionality, 69, 70–8, 82–3
feminist theory, 14–15
historical contexts, 69–70
masculine inexpressivity, 118,
  119–24
of nineteenth century, 69
  complementarity of sexes, 69, 70–7
  control of emotion, 77–80
  in parenting, 95–6
  perpetuation of, 171–2
  reliance on, 27–8, 60–1
  in self-reports, 30–1, 32–3
  on television, 96–7
gentility, 74
gestures, 37–8
Gillis, J.R., 131–2
girls emotional socialization, 93
  participation in sport, 90, 110
Giuliani, Rudoloph, 184
Glenn, E.N., 147–8
Goleman, D., 182
Goncu, A., 101
Gore, Al, 1, 2
Gottman, J.M., 102, 107, 154
Greenspan, P., 145–6
Gunn Gruchy, C.D., 153–4

Hall, G.S., 73, 75–6
Hall, J.A., 34
Hall, R., 100–1
Hastrup, J.L., 163
Hay, D.H., 156
Heavey, C.L., 154
Hochschild, A.R., 15, 112
Home Improvement, 133
homosexuality, 51, 65n.10
Hughes, L.A., 107
humanity, and emotion, 170–1,
  183–4
Hutson-Comeaux, S.L., 28

ideal emotion, 84, 85, 126, 130
identity
  core gender identity, 12
  and emotional education, 111–14
  and gender performance, 54–5
  role of emotion, 55–6
  sex role identity, 51–2
  see also emotional authenticity
identity narratives, emotion narratives as,
  61–3
income, gender differences, 150–1
inexpressivity *see* masculine inexpressivity
information processing models, 7
instrumentality, 53, 67n.17

internalizing anger, 157–61
International Society for Research on
  Emotions (ISRE), 23
interpersonal context, 27, 98

Jacklin, C.N., 105
Jacobsen, M.B., 156
Jaggar, A.M., 158
James, W., 80–1, 87n.18, 87–8n.21
Jenkins, J., 5–6
Jerry Maguire, 126–30, 133, 137–8n.10–13
Johnson, J.T., 60–1
Johnson, M.M., 14–15
justice, anger as restoration, 144

Kalnok, M., 29
Katz, J., 98–9, 162
Kelly, J.R., 28
Kimmel, M.S., 136
Kippax, S., 61–2, 153
Kleck, R.E., 37
Kline, S., 97
Knight, Bob, 109
Kopper, B.A., 159
Kraemer, D.L., 163
Kring, A.M., 37
Kunin, Madeline, 161

L'Abate, L., 123
LaFrance, M., 34, 60
Lakoff, G., 144–5
Lamb, M.E., 131
Landrine, H., 49
language
  emotion name-calling, 108
  naming emotion, 176–9, 185–6n.4–6
  plasticity of, 47–8
  and self-control, 100–1
LaRossa, R., 134–5
Leaper, C., 177
Lederer, W., 120
legitimacy *see* emotional authenticity;
  entitlement
Lerner, H., 157
Levenson, R.W., 154
Levine, L.J., 144
Lewin, M., 67n.17
Lloyd, G., 70–1
Lovas, G.S., 156
Lutz, C., 9, 15
Lutz, T., 163

McAdams, D.P., 67n.22
Maccoby, E.E., 104–5
McConnell, R.W., 172
McDougall, W., 74
MacDowell, K.A., 48

Major, B., 54, 98, 150–1
Malatesta, C.Z., 29
manly emotion, 173
    changing nature of, 135–6
    and competing emotional styles, 113–14,
        119, 130–5, 174–5
    in competitive sport, 90, 110–11
    as ideal, 84, 85, 126, 130
    in *Jerry Maguire*, 126–30, 137–8n.10–13
    and weeping, 162, 164
Manstead, A.S.R., 35
marital interaction, 154–7
Marsiglio, W., 131, 132
Martin, C.L., 47, 58
Martineau, J., 75
masculine emotion
    celebration of, 124–30
    as ideal emotion, 84
    New Fatherhood, 130–5, 136
    passion, 72, 78–9, 80, 171
    see also manly emotion
masculine inexpressivity, 118, 119–24
masculinity
    defining, 173
    emotion in coding of, 49–54, 64n.7,
        65–6n.11
    link with anger, 140, 146
    link with sport, 90
    negotiation of, 136
Masculinity/Femininity (M/F) scales, 50,
    51, 52–3, 64n.7, 65–6n.11, 66n.14
maternal instinct, 75–6, 135
maturity (emotional), 93–4
Maybury, K.K., 156–7
memory, and self-reports, 31
memory-work, 61–2, 153
men
    reason and emotion of, 72, 171
    weeping, 125, 129, 161, 162–3, 164–5,
        167n.20–1
Messner, M., 110
metabolic theory of sex differences, 71
Miles, C.C., 50
Miller, J.B., 152
"Miss Manners," 145, 158
Morawski, J.G., 66n.15
Moskowitz, D.S., 60
Muncer, S., 160
Muskie, Edmund, 161, 164–5,
    167n.21

name-calling, 108
naming emotion, 176–9, 185–6n.4–6
natural emotion, 84, 85
Neale, J.M., 37
neurobiology, 7
New Fatherhood, 17, 130–5, 136

newspapers and magazines, fatherhood
    in, 132
nurturance
    and extravagant emotion, 173, 174, 175
    and New Fatherhood, 130–5

Oatley, K., 5–6, 176
occupational segregation, 150–1
O'Neill, J.M., 119–20
Onyx, J., 61–2, 153
outlaw emotions, 158

parents
    advice for, 64n.3, 92
    emotional education by, 95–6,
        115–16n.4–7
    emotional expression of, 39
    instincts of, 75–6, 135
    see also fatherhood
Parker, J.G., 102, 107
Parsons, T., 67n.17
participants, in research, 26
passion, 72, 78–9, 80, 171
paternal instinct, 76
pay, gender differences, 150–1
peer groups, practicing emotion in, 57–8,
    104–8
perceptiveness, 74
performance *see* doing emotion; doing
    gender; gender performance
Personal Attributes Questionnaire (PAQ),
    66–7n.16
personality factors in emotional
    responses, 46–7
personality tests *see*
    Masculinity/Femininity scales
personality traits, and anger, 151–2
phenomenology, 7
physiological psychology, 69, 73–4
Plato, 3, 18n.4
play
    practicing emotion in, 99–101
    peer group play, 104–8
    pretend play, 100, 101–4
politics
    US presidential campaign, 1–2, 48
    use of emotion language in, 48
    and weeping, 125, 161, 164–5, 167n.20–1
power, anger and status, 144, 146–7
Power Puff Girls, 96–7
pretend play, 100, 101–4
priming, 148
Priscilla, Queen of the Desert, 43–4
protection of women by men, 76
psychology
    neglect of social context, 24–5
    physiological, 69, 73–4

psychology of emotion, gender in, 12–13
psychopathology, 181

racial ethnicity, 24–5
  and entitlement to anger, 147–8
  and gender stereotypes, 49
  and images of fatherhood, 131
Reagan, Maureen, 48
reason, and emotion, 72, 171
Replacements, The, 130
responsibility
  for anger, 145–6
  for masculine inexpressivity, 122–4
Reynolds, C., 105
Riggio, R.E., 37
rights *see* entitlement
Risman, B.J., 172
Robert Elsmere, 79
Robinson, M.D., 60–1
Ruiz-Belda, M.A., 36
rules, 56–7, 112
Rusbult, C.E., 155–6

Saarni, C., 56–7, 93–4, 159
Sackheim, H.A., 163
Schemas, 58, 59, 62, 63, 68n.29
Schroeder, Patricia, 125, 161, 164
self-control *see* control of emotion
self-presentation, practicing, 107–8
self-report, 29–33, 41–2n.7–9
  on emotional expression, 37
  on masculine inexpressivity, 120–1, 122
  shaped by stereotypes, 60, 61
  on women's anger, 159
  see also M/F scales
sentimentality, 75
September 11, 2001, 2, 125, 162, 183–4
sex, and gender, 11, 19n.17
sex differences
  metabolic theory of, 71
  see also difference model
sex role identity, 51–2
sex-segregated play, 104–7
"sexual inversion," 51, 65n.10
Sharkin, B.S., 159
Sheldon, A., 57–8
Sherman, J.W., 148
Shields, S.A., 45–7, 48, 60–1
Simpson, O.J., trial of, 179, 186n.8
situational factors
  in emotional responses, 47
  in entitlement to anger, 151
  see also social context
smiling, 38–9
Smith, D.A., 37

social class
  and concepts of women, 74, 75, 76–7, 79
  and emotional qualities, 149
  and stereotypes of fatherhood, 131
social constructionism, 7, 100, 142
social context
  of emotional expression, 34, 36–7
  importance of, 27–8, 44–5
  of masculine inexpressivity, 123
  neglected in psychology, 24–5
  see also situational factors
social identity, 25, 54, 55, 56, 175, 185
  and emotional education, 111–14
social meaning of emotion, 9–11, 94, 165–6
social status
  and anger, 146–9, 156–7
  and emotional language, 179
socialization, 92–3, 97–8, 115n.2, 135–6
  problems of masculine, 119, 122–3
  see also emotional education
Socrates, 3, 16, 170
Solomon, R.C., 143, 166n.3
Spence, J.T., 12, 53, 54, 67n.20
Spencer, H., 75, 78, 82–3, 87n.21
Spielberger, C.D., 151
sport, 89–90, 108–11, 117–18
standards of emotion, 91
  see also emotional appropriateness; rules
State-Trait Anger Expression Inventory (STAXI), 151
Stearns, C.Z., 145, 166n.6
Stearns, P.N., 145, 166n.6
Steil, J.M., 155
Stein, N.L., 144
Steinem, Gloria, 48
stereotypes, 3
  as cognitive shortcut, 60–1
  priming in study of, 148
  see also gender stereotypes; gendered emotion stereotypes
Sternberg, C.R., 139, 142, 165
Stoppard, J.M., 122, 153–4
Stroessner, S.J., 148
Super Bowl, 117, 136–7n.2
Sutherland, A., 76

Tavris, C., 166n.2
tears *see* weeping
telegraphed emotion *see* manly emotion
television and film
  anger in, 151, 158
  emotional authenticity in, 169
  fatherhood in, 133–4
  gender performance in, 43–4
  gender stereotypes in, 96–7
  manly emotion in, 126–30, 137–8n.10–13

Terman, L.M., 49–51, 65n.9–10
Thoits, P., 181
Thomas, S.P., 152, 154–5, 159
Thomson, J.A., 71
Thorne, B., 106–7
Tiedens, L.Z., 147
toys, 55, 103–4
traits, and entitlement to anger, 151–2
typical emotion, 84

uncontrollability of anger, 144–5
universality of anger, 143–4
Utku culture, 177

Vannoy, D., 171–2
variability hypothesis, 71

Walker, A., 71
Walster, E., 166n.1
Weber, H., 152
weeping, 125, 129, 161–5, 167n.20,
    168n.25

West, C., 43
Who Wants to Be a Millionaire?, 169
Wilcox, E.W., 77
Winfrey, Oprah, 2, 17–18n.2
withdrawal strategy, 154, 155
women
    emotional double bind for, 174–6
    female emotionality, 69, 70–8, 82–3
    participation in sport, 90, 110
    self-reports on anger, 159
    weeping, 125, 161–2, 163
women's conduct manuals, 77
Woolley, H.T., 39
work
    emotion management at, 175–6
    pay differences, 150–1
Wundt, W., 80
Wyer, N.A., 148

Yaeger, M., 43

Zimmerman, D.H., 43